Spectrum of Lifelong Education

About the Editor

Dr. Rameshwari Pandya received her B.Sc., B.Ed. from Lady Irwin College, New Delhi and her M.Sc., M.Ed. and Ph.D. in Home Science from The Maharaja Sayaji Rao University, Baroda in 1994 and received the Shrimati Leelaben Shah Gold Medal. She is a senior faculty member in the Department of Extension and Communication, Faculty of Family and Community Sciences, The M.S. University, Baroda, Gujarat.

Dr. Pandya has worked with WHO/ICDS project and in the Population Research Centre as Research Officer. She has published more than 100 research papers, peer- reviewed papers and several technical reports. Her work have been published in different professional journals of repute and she has to her credit 12 books.

She is the coordinator of the Urban Extension Programme of the Department. She is the In-Charge of "PRAGATI" the Urban Extension Centre. She has successfully conducted many training programmes and participated in many Seminars, Conferences, Workshops at National and International level.

A member of the Board of Studies, Senate and Faculty Board, is as the only lady member in the Syndicate (the highest decision making body) of the University.

She has successfully completed several projects and has recently completed a major project funded by Indian Council of Social Science Research (ICSSR) on "Promotion of Communal Harmony". She has been involved in Teaching, Research and Extension. She is an active member of several professional organizations.

Spectrum of Lifelong Education

Edited by

Rameshwari Pandya

CONCEPT PUBLISHING COMPANY PVT. LTD.
NEW DELHI-110059

ISBN: 13-978-81-8069-744-9

First Published 2011

Published and Printed by

Concept
Since 1974

Concept Publishing Company Pvt. Ltd.
Regd. Office:
A/15-16, Commercial Block, Mohan Garden
New Delhi-110059 (India)
Phones : 25351460, 25351794, *Fax* : 091-11-25357109
Email : publishing@conceptpub.com
Website: www.conceptpub.com

Editorial Office:
H-13, Bali Nagar, New Delhi-110 015, India.

Cataloging in Publication Data--Courtesy: D.K. Agencies (P) Ltd. <docinfo@dkagencies.com>

Spectrum of lifelong education / edited by Rameshwari Pandya.
p. cm.
Contributed articles.
Includes bibliographical references and index.
ISBN 9788180697449

1. Continuing education--India. 2. Adult education--India. I. Pandya, Rameshwari.

DDC 374.954 22

Dedicated to the Professionals
Interested in
Adult and Lifelong Education

Preface

This book contains 21 contributions dealing with various dimensions of lifelong education and different issues related to Adult and Lifelong Education like the Government efforts, Pedagogy have been addressed and examined in this book. Adult Education and Role of Universities in promotion of education as a core concept and the different problems which are the road blocks in the Highway of Development has also been discussed.

Lifelong Education

1. The work of **H.C. Jain** concentrates on education and llifelong learning. The three major stages of life which are youth, adulthood and old age. In each stage of life everybody needs some new knowledge, skills and practice. Formal education is foundation of lifelong learning. It is initially important to develop knowledge, values, skills and sustainable livelihoods. Learning for self-growth, learning for caring, individual development, and for personality development. Need of life long learning is to keep pace with the development of new knowledge, to empower, enhancing capacity building and to reconstruct new set of values. The time has come that the education system should be treated with tight norms and have good human relations. It is important to know that learning has various forms such as prelearning, reinforcement of learning. Learning itself is ultimately an individualized and

lifelong process, where by transformation occurs within the individual but the final outcome of the learning is the application of knowledge and skill for the benefit of the society, nation and world.

2. **Rajesh Paliwal and Deepak Paliwal** addresses the impact of continuing education programme. Literacy and education has always been an area of importance and concern for the policy-makers, social scientists and the academicians. The scheme of CE was launched in 1995 as fully funded centrally sponsored scheme. The scheme of CE for neo-literates as visualized by NLM is an attempt to provide systematic organized and well coordinated mechanisms to mobilize all resources in support of CE in the perspective of life long education. A study was conducted in Uttarakhand to evaluate the functioning of Adult Education centres. It was found during the study that the level of activities on culture and sports were comparatively less. Majority of the centres do not organize Charcha Mandals. The topic of health, hygiene, concept of small family and its significance, advantage of reading are least discussed in the centres. Preraks are the vital elements in the CES system at the grassroots level, their performance influences the performance of the centres to a large extent. The study has clearly shown that the performance and working of Preraks have been quite good despite the fact that they have not been paid the honorarium for the last fourteen months. Preraks which play an important role in the implementation pattern of CEP and their performance influences the performance of the centres to a large extent. The honorarium amount which is Rs. 700 per month must be suitably rationalized and must be paid in time.
3. Social constructivist approach for education for all is explained well by **Tupe Navnath**. We know that present situation of education is not up to the mark as it is unable to satisfy the needs of the learner

because it is not relevant to the real life setting. Social constructivist approach is a way of making education effective, interesting and relevant to real life setting as in this approach the individual actively construct knowledge. This theory proposes learning through analysis, critically reviewing, sharing, discussing their own as well as other's ideas and interaction. This approach is often used alongside with task based approach or problem based learning approach in classroom practices. Students are the co-builders of knowledge and have to respond to challenges and review their own and other's work critically. The major role of teachers is to design classroom activities in which students can participate in knowledge co-construction and exploration. If we want effective results of education in sustainable development we should transform the total education system such as Teaching methods turn into Teaching models. One way instruction design turns into anchored instruction, lazy environment of learning turn into enthusiastic learning environment, passive learner turns into active learner, teacher turns into facilitator, competitive exam turns into collaborative learning summative evaluation and formal education turns into non-formal lifelong education. The students are capable to construct the knowledge, skills and attitude for solving their day-to-day problems without the help of others. People can become self-reliant by education.

4. **G.C. Bhattacharya** in his paper explains how life long learning is important. After acquisition of reading and writing skills along with some arithmetical and numerical abilities, it is felt needed that Neo-literates may not give up learning because formal mode is not inevitable for acquisition of knowledge and skills now-a-days on account of expansion of print and electronic media and technology concerned. If they do not aspire to learn continuously and throughout

the life span, formation of a 'learning society' is not possible which is an essential aspect for maintenance of democratic way of life and social setup. Here, an attempt has been made to justify the need of Life-long Learning and to rationalize the process requirements, not only for the neo-learners but also for the well educated persons as well as professionals too to remain up-to-date in terms of new developments, inventions, innovations and technological advancements.

5. **Asha Patil** in her paper 'Functional Literacy' gives the details of non-formal education in India. However, this study focuses mainly on the different five year plans and policies of education and the importance given by the government for promotion of education. In spite of the different efforts by government from time to time we are unable to achieve the target. There is a shift in emphasis from the traditional 3Rs concept of literacy to new 3Fs programme, i.e. functional literacy, food production, family welfare. Government changed the implementation strategy and a joint venture organized by the Department of Education and Social Welfare. The concept of functional literacy widened elaborately in the Declaration of Persepolis. It included all dimensions of human development—political, economic, social and cultural. It states that "Just as development is not only economic growth, so literacy must aim above all to arouse in the individual a critical awareness of social reality and to enable him or her to understand, master his or her destiny."

Adult Literacy in India has come a long way. From the above discussion it is clear that functional literacy has still a long way to go. Unfortunately, the literacy programme is still stuck with the teaching of 3Rs. We have to see that the 3R's are directly linked with real life situation. It is high time that efforts should be made to achieve the functional literacy. Otherwise, we would not be able to bring the marginalized strata of society that is adult illiterates (both men and women) into the mainstream of national development. For this we have to create the need for literacy among the psyche of people. Otherwise, the dream would not come true.

Role of Media in Adult Education

6. **Anjali Pattanaik** and **Gunum Pattanaik** have explained the role of media in Social change in the rural setting. A total of 150 samples were collected randomly from two villages of Ganjam district of Orissa State. From the study it was observed that, media had played praiseworthy roles in extending information to the rural people regarding various welfare oriented schemes of the government and non-government organizations through which people became aware about child welfare, better health and sanitation and socio-political affairs.
7. **Manoj Dayal** in his paper 'Media as a Partner in Adult and Non-Formal Education' has highlighted the concept of Education and Sustainable development. Education is the cornerstone of socio-economic development of a country. Value-based education is a holistic approach to develop the social, cultural and moral personality of a student. It keeps in developing sensitivity of human values and ideals. When these ideas are internalized and habitually practiced, they give right directions to desire, emotions and outward behaviour of individuals and are reflected in the total personality. Only such person can lead a good life and create a good society. The cost ineffectiveness of High Education is a cause of concern. Another finding of interest is that cost of educating one student of higher education is equal to the cost of education of six students of primary level. In boosting Adult and Non-Formal Education

media can turn out to be a big partner. Media should often play a creative, constructive and positive role and emerge as a partner in a sensitive matter like Adult and Non-Formal Education. It is recommended that more knowledge based Radio programmes, T.V. Programmes and films should be produced and telecast which would help the students of Adult and Non-Formal students to enhance their knowledge in relevant subject area.

8. **Vanisha S. Nambiar** addresses the problems of Food and Nutrition Security of India as it is influenced by several factors ranging from income, poverty, education, employment, availability of resources, gender bias, beliefs and attitudes, available accessible and affordable health care. Advocacy is generally a necessary first step for any nutrition intervention. Decision-makers must be convinced of the epidemiological need, the feasibility and the cost effectiveness of new directions. Nutrition health education imparted as a part of non-formal education or as adult education, if imparted appropriately leads to an increase in knowledge, change in attitude and initiation of a practice which is good for the improvement of their health and nutritional status. The study highlights on human capital and involved the development of human skills capacity and the effective use of managerial, professional and technical staff and beneficiaries. At the present time, there is a need for a comprehensive approach for nutrition communication intervention to be fully effective as an action oriented strategy for nutritional development especially in India, where large segments of the populations are still uneducated deprived of their basic needs and are the target of the political corruption. Thus it is imperative that the researches conducted in the laboratories and stored in the libraries be disseminated to the field. There is an urgent need to transfer the technology from

laboratory to the field. India needs good educators and it is time that academicians move out of their classrooms towards community development.

9. **Sarjoo Patel** and **Maneesha Shukul** have highlighted the need of proper communication in the family. Communication among family members is very closely interwoven with daily living. It is the foundation stone for all types of human relations whether it is between husband and wife, adults and children or within family members. Stability of the home depends upon the good interpersonal communication among youths and adults; otherwise it cannot be called a home. Since interpersonal communication is basic to all types of human relations, it was studied in detail that how interpersonal communication takes place among adults and youth in families. The families where the extent of communication was found to be low case-studies were done to get deep insight into the dynamics of such families. Also a booklet was developed and counselling sessions carried out which included the guidelines for effective interpersonal communication in Indian families. The paper throws light on how adults should be made aware of barriers, facilitators, guidelines for improving interpersonal communication in Indian families. The paper also suggests what is the role of NGOs, government and educational institutions in improving the interpersonal communication in families and how adults should be educated about the importance of communication and its use to overcome barriers and practice good relationship among family members.

Adult and Non-Formal Education

10. **Anjali Dewan** has explained how diet is related to nutritional deficiencies. Diet and nutrition are important factors in the promotion and maintenance

of good health. Income, prices, individual preferences, cultural traditions, social and economic factors all interact in a complex manner to shape dietary consumption patterns. Health and nutritional status of an individual depends on the food they eat. The components of the diet must be chosen judiciously to provide all the nutrients needed in adequate amounts and proportions. A normal balanced diet must include daily foods from the various food groups in sufficient amounts to meet the needs of an individual. Selection of foods from the different food groups also results in variety in the diet, which not only ensures nutritional adequacy but also increases food acceptability. Food habits are an important part of our diet which affects the amount and type of food consumed and thus the nutritional status of the women. The diets of the women were mainly based on cereals and deficient in vegetables and fruits. The low intake of these protective foods resulted in nutritional disorders. The clinical signs of malnutrition, anaemia and vitamin B complex deficiencies were observed. Promoting healthy diets and lifestyles to reduce the burden of malnutrition and non-communicable diseases require a multi-sectorial approach.

11. Education being a process of teaching and learning plays crucial role in all aspects of life of a person as it opens the windows of several life supporting opportunities by enhancing knowledge, skills and awareness. **Sheetal Helaiya** has pin-pointed the significance of Consumer Education and has considered it as very important aspect in Lifelong Education. It is important to know the Consumer Rights and Responsibilities in this age of globalization. With implementation of Consumer Protection Act (1986), right to safety, informed, choose, heard, redressal, right to consumer education is also very important aspect in today's world.

Today's market is a complex system because it is flooded with products. The new developments and innovations in science and technology have brought about changes in the life style and standards of consumers and they are becoming confused as to what they should buy? Consumer Education helps in understanding process of economy functions, redressal mechanism and skill to safeguard. Consumer Education in Non-formal Education can be incorporated using innovative teaching methods. Action research projects can be conducted at community level. This will help in building a more responsive and human world.

12. **M.C. Reddeppa Reddy** addresses the problem of livelihood of rural population and the importance of education. Development index is usually based on the income generated by a country and is measured with the food security and health status of the community. The United Nations Millennium Development Goals, formulated in 2002 are world's time-bound and quantified targets for addressing extreme poverty in its many dimensions. They are the basic human rights to health, education, shelter, and security (www.un.org/millenniumgoals). This paper provides only a brief overview of the need to advocate for nutrition; the challenge of integrating nutrition in clinic- and community-based programmes; and an outline of behavioural issues related to some intervention areas. The term 'livelihood' means to make a living. For a livelihood to be sustainable it must be adaptive and able to withstand stress and it should safeguard the natural environment. To make the living sustainable, literacy/education for the people is very important. The paper entitled 'Education for Sustainable Livelihoods in Rural Areas' is presented under three sections. In Section I, the definitions of livelihoods, livelihood interventions and sustainable livelihoods and the livelihood principles are discussed. In Section 2, the

Status of livelihood opportunities, the problems in unorganized sector and the determinants of sustainable livelihoods are discussed. The strategies to address the livelihood problems and the need of educational programmes for sustainable livelihoods, and the reforms needed in educational for sustainable livelihoods are also discussed in Section 3.

13. **Prof. Rekha Talmaki** explains the important issue of Sustainable Development. It is explained well how the sustainable development ties together concern for the carrying capacity of natural systems with social challenges which humanity is facing. The field of Sustainable Development can be conceptually broken into three constituent parts: Environmental Sustainability, Economic Sustainability and Socio-Political Sustainability. It is important that we become sensitive towards environment and have sustainable accounting. Environmentalists have coined the term "sustainability" to classify the desired balance between economic growth on the one hand and environmental preservation on the other. To achieve this end an increasing number of countries are seeking to establish programmes for sustainable development that is a pattern of development that does not reduce production but changes its quality so as to satisfy the needs of the present generation without compromising the ability of future generations to meet their own needs. Sustainable Development has to be a long term process, and one may say it to be a continuing process. Similarly, equity and justice are equally important for sustainable development, which can be looked at from a variety of perspectives, such as environmental, economic, social, political, cultural and technological. Despite all these laws, the environmental situation in India and globally is not better. Today it is late, but tomorrow it will be too late.

14. **Rameshwari Pandya** in her paper highlights the role of universities in imparting adult education. The adult education relates learning to living, to the environment, the work, the family, the community. A university is a closed academic community of scholars and helps in disseminating knowledge. In terms of manpower, infrastructure and finances they are in an advantageous position and can play a major role in dealing with some of the problems of the society and in contributing to social development and change. In doing so, they would have to go outside the four walls of the campus and address themselves to the needs of local communities and evolve ways and means of redressing their problems. The universities have strong system which can be accountable for carry this work of Lifelong Education. They can organize programmes, prepare materials like posters, drama skits, newspaper, articles have role plays. They can train various functionaries for adult education programmes. The university can provide research support to the Adult Education Programmes. There is no end to the good which the universities can do to the community. It is, however, necessary that each university should measure its own opportunities and plan the best that it can do to be of service to the society which it serves.
15. **Rameshwari Pandya** has elaborated the problems of Adult Education in India. The main aim and objective of adult education is to transform the society. If we look at it from the individual point of view, it is of remedial, vocational, health, social skill, recreational and cultural. From the point of view of the society, it is for promoting social cohesion, conservation and improvement of natural resources and inculcating social ideology. There are many different reasons for people to dropout from adult education class such as the job pattern, family problems, migration of labour, economic needs, etc.

women and girls are overburdened with domestic work so they dropout. The instructors are not well trained and are not competent and cannot cater to the different groups. The instructors are less resourceful, less imaginative and less helpful because of lack of training. The instructor may be tempted to employ the teaching strategies of formal education which assume a captive audience and an authoritarian atmosphere in the class. Learners are less motivated. Universities should give the leadership in policy planning, development of appropriate materials and methodologies and evaluation.

Women and Non-Formal Education

16. Women Education is an important aspect and needs proper attention by the policy-makers and society at large. **K. Muralidaran** and **D. Preetha** have considered the importance of roots and fruits of women education. The paper gives details of history of education in India in general and the women education in specific. Need for Women Education for the nation's prosperity is well explained. For full development of our human resources, the improvement of homes and for moulding the character of children during the most impressionable years of infancy, the education of women is of even greater importance than that of men. Women education objectives are many like familial management, work life balance, equal opportunity, decision making, sense of worth, income generation legal rights, participation in public affair, gain in knowledge, achievement and motivation. In spite of these many benefits it is not gaining speed because of many reasons. The suggestive measures like social attitudes, fiscal backwardness, lack of proper facilities, faulty curriculum, lack of suitable incentives to girl students, acute shortage of women educator etc. An overview of women education and

women development across 1886 to 2009 has been given to show how women have become empowered. Education and egalitarianism are unified concepts, thus the ultimate righteousness demands that all citizens should have freedom from want, freedom from fear and freedom from ignorance. The social and economic life of the country has undergone a far-reaching change with the help of women education.

17. **Anjali Pattanaik** and **Snigdha Rani** have highlighted the important role of women teacher in development. The present study was conducted to assess the level of awareness pertaining to political, economic and social information of women school teachers both in the rural and urban area. The area of the study was confined to two districts of the state (Orissa) of India. A total of 600 samples with 300 from each area were selected randomly. The primary data were collected through a structured interview schedule that comprised areas like demographic background; awareness level of political, economic and social information; and media exposure. Statistical analysis was done by using percentage, mean, coefficient of correlation and students t-test. Results revealed that rural teachers were highly aware of economic information whereas urban teachers showed more interest in gathering social information. Print media was more familiar among the urban teachers and extension personnel were popular amongst the rural teachers. Moreover, almost all the demographic variables had shown positive relationships with the awareness level of information.

18. The work of **Avani Maniar** is on "Television and Health". She reveals that the world is experiencing an unprecedented demographic transformation and by 2050, the number of persons aged 60 and over will increase tremendously. Ageing population implies a greater increase in the number of elderly women as compared to elderly men, a phenomenon experienced

by most societies of the world. More older women than older men are facing health problems because of restricted access treatment, the cost of surgery or medicine, little family support for treatment and low self-esteem about herself becomes barriers in taking treatment. Woman, who has compromised her health all through her life, has to face various diseases of older years like diabetes, osteoporosis, heart diseases, arthritis, cancer, Alzheimer's etc. As the age increases so do the diseases in elderlies. The Television viewing and health of elderly women is interesting to know the relationship. The television has an important place in the lives of elderly women. They spend more time of their leisure time in watching T.V. It is important that Mass Media should be aware of this findings and make more health and Food and Nutrition programmes for the elderlies. Which will be particularly helpful to older persons who for various reasons suffer from restricted mobility or are completely homebound. It can bring to them all useful announcements and information right in their living rooms. It is high time that mass media realizes their role and duty towards development of the country as well as its people. Mass media and especially T.V. should consider issues related to ageing which can help aged live a happy and healthy life. Media must play an important role in achieving this goal of the society.

Extension Education

19. **Rameshwari Pandya** and **Babita Shukla** have explained how capacity building of extension personnel is important and needs to be strengthened. The extension education is the process of teaching rural people how to live better by learning ways that improve their farm, home and community institutions. The training is needed and instructor must know that learner is very important in the whole process. He/she should be clear about the

objective, knowledge, communication skills, set good examples of educational leadership. The instructor has to carry out multiple roles of the sculptor, entertainer, coach and the manager. If the instructor is well trained he/she will use cooperative extension approach and will work with people, use creative methods. Must use feedback to adjust actions to fit the task goal and reflect on the goal-action-feedback cycle. The institutional training should be supplemented with planned visit to villages for field extension work. A coordinated programme of work of various departments such as agriculture, cooperation, panchayats, animal husbandry etc. should be taken into consideration while formulating the teaching programmes so that the trainees have a clear understanding of the necessity of implementing a coordinated and integrated programme in the field of Agriculture, Health, Literacy, Social Education, Income Generation, Environment, etc.

20. **Sudha Rani, Srilatha Kishori** and **T. Ananda** have studied the knowledge, attitude and practice of reproductive health of continuing education centre (CEC) learners of Chittoor district of Andhra Pradesh. The major objective was to find out the influence of SES on the knowledge and practice of the CEC learners and to collect suggestions for better reproductive health care practices. A total of 1143 Zila Saksharta Samiti and 2 mandals (1 rural and 1 urban) was selected. Purposive sampling method was used. Questionnaire and attitude scale was used for data collection. It was found that learners had moderate knowledge and had moderate levels of practice level of reproductive health. 33 per cent of the respondents had unfavourable level and 30 per cent had indifferent attitude towards reproductive health. 40 per cent of the Muslim women had low knowledge and moderate practice of reproductive health. Majority of the Hindu fall in high level knowledge and practice of reproductive health. They suggested new

and simple ways of imparting reproductive health to adult learners have to be found out so that the learners can understand and put them into practice. This problem needs further research. Merely incorporating lessons in primers on population issues does not bring results but what is required is effective communication by the teachers (preraks) in the adult education centres.

21. The work of **Lalita** concentrates on life skills development among students, so that they can cope with life and living successfully. There is need to develop general skills like communication skill, decision making skill, stress coping skill, problem solving skill, social skill etc. related to a wide variety of areas such as health and social skill needs. It is through these skills that students can fight with social challenges, drug addiction, violence, health problems and AIDS. It will also help them to understand civic and legal issues related to personal and social problems. Teachers and parents may solve problems of their wards. Life skills education is closer to social science education, therefore, a teacher can solve students' social problems very effectively. Learning by doing, Learning by living, Learning without tears are the main characteristics of the modern concept of education. Education accordingly is seen in terms of 7Rs, i.e. Reading, Writing, Arithmetic, Rights, Responsibilities, Recreation and Relationship. The school is not merely a place of formal learning whose main concern is to communicate a certain prescribed quantum of knowledge but rather as a living and organic community which is primarily interested in training to its students in what we have called the gracious art of living. Knowledge and learning are undoubtedly of value but they must be acquired as a by-product of activity because it is only then that they can become a vital part of the student's mind and personality and influence his behaviour. Life Skill Education is actually Reengineering of the human capital.

Contents

Preface vii
List of Contributors xxv

LIFELONG EDUCATION

1. Education and Lifelong Learning 3
   H.C. Jain
2. Continuing Education Programme and its Impact 13
   Rajesh Paliwal and *Deepak Paliwal*
3. Social Constructivist Approach for Education for All 28
   Tupe Navnath
4. Need of Lifelong Learning for Neoliterates and Professionals 46
   G.C. Bhattacharya
5. Functional Literacy 58
   Asha Patil

ROLE OF MEDIA IN ADULT EDUCATION

6. Role of Media in Social Change 87
   Anjali Pattanaik and *Gunum Pattanayak*
7. Media as a Partner in Adult and Non-Formal Education 96
   Manoj Dayal
8. Communication for the Development and Food and Nutrition Security of India 104
   Vanisha S. Nambiar
9. Educating the Adults : Communication to Strengthen Interpersonal Relationship 111
   Sarjoo Patel and *Maneesha Shukul*

ADULT AND NON-FORMAL EDUCATION

10. Dietary Pattern and Nutritional Deficiencies in Rural Areas of Shimla District 125
Anjali Dewan

11. Need of Consumer Education in Non-formal Education 135
Sheetal Helaiya

12. Education for Sustainable Livelihoods in Rural Areas 154
M.C. Reddeppa Reddy

13. Sustainable Development 168
Rekha Talmaki

14. Role of Universities in Imparting Adult Education 181
Rameshwari Pandya

15. Problems in Adult Education 196
Rameshwari Pandya

WOMEN AND NON-FORMAL EDUCATION

16. The Roots and Fruits of Women Education 219
K. Muralidaran and *D. Preetha*

17. Participation of Women Teacher in Development 243
Anjali Pattanaik and *Snigdha Rani Swain*

18. Third Age Women, Their Health and Role of Television 254
Avani Maniar

EXTENSION EDUCATION

19. Capacity Building of Extension Personnel 267
Rameshwari Pandya and *Babita Shukla*

20. Knowledge Attitude and Practice of Reproductive Health among CEC Learners 282
K. Sudha Rani, K. Srilatha Kishori and *T. Ananda*

21. Life Skill Education : Re-engineering of the Human Capital 293
Lalita Sharma

Index 306

List of Contributors

Anjali Dewan, Head, Department of Home Science, St. Bede's College, Shimla, Himachal Pradesh-171002.

Anjali Pattanaik, Reader, P.G. Department of Home Science, Berhampur University, Orissa-760007.

Asha Patil, Associate Professor, Department of Continuing and Adult Education and Extension Work, S.N.D.T. Women's University, Mumbai-400020.

Avani Maniar, Senior Lecturer, Department of Extension and Communication, Faculty of Family and Community Sciences, The M.S.U. Baroda, Gujarat.

Babita Shukla, Lecturer, Department of Extension and Communication, Faculty of Family and Community Sciences, The M.S.U. Baroda, Gujarat.

D. Preetha, Research Scholar, Department of Social Work; PSG College of Arts & Science, Coimbatore-14.

Deepak Paliwal, Lecturer, Department of Sociology, Govt. Degree College, Kotabagh, Nainital, Uttarakhand.

G.C. Bhattacharya, Faculty of Education, Kamachha Campus, Banaras Hindu University, Varanasi-221010.

Gunum Pattanayak, Research Scholar, P.G. Department of Home Science, Berhampur University, Orissa-760007.

H.C. Jain, Reader, Department of Adult, Continuing Education & Extension, Dr. H.S. Gour University, Sagar, Madhya Pradesh.

K. Muralidaran, Head, Department of Social Work; PSG College of Arts & Science, Coimbatore-14.

K. Srilatha Kishori, Research Scholar, Department of Adult

Education, S.V. University, Tirupati.

K. Sudha Rani, Associate Professor, Department of Adult and Continuing Education, S.V. University, Tirupati.

Lalita Sharma, Lecturer, B.Ed. College, Hatundi, Ajmer, Rajasthan.

M.C. Reddeppa Reddy, Director, Department of Adult and Continuing Education, SVUCESS, S.V. University, Tirupati.

Maneesha Shukul, Head, Department of Home Management, Faculty of Family and Community Sciences, The M.S.U., Baroda, Gujarat.

Manoj Dayal, Dean, Faculty of Media Studies and Chairperson, Department of Communication Management and Technology, Guru Jambheshwar University of Science and Technology, Hisar, Haryana.

Rajesh Chandra Paliwal, Lecturer, Department of Political Science, BSM P.G. College, Roorkee, Hardwar, Uttarakhand.

Rameshwari Pandya, Senior Lecturer, Department of Extension and Communication, Faculty of Family and Community Sciences, The M.S.U. Baroda, Gujarat.

Rekha Talmaki, Department of Economics, S.N.D.T. Women's University, Churchgate, Mumbai.

Sarjoo Patel, Senior Lecturer, Department of Home Management, Faculty of Family and Community Sciences, The M.S.U., Baroda, Gujarat.

Sheetal Helaiya, Lecturer, Department of Education, CASE, Faculty of Education Psychology, The M.S.U., Baroda, Gujarat-390002.

Snigdha Rani Swain, Research Scholar, P.G. Department of Home Science, Berhampur University, Orissa-760007.

T. Ananda, Research Scholar, Department of Adult Education, S.V. University, Tirupati.

Tupe Navnath, Lecturer, Adult Continuing Education and Extension, University of Pune, Pune-7.

Vanisha S. Nambiar, Senior Lecturer, Department of Food and Nutrition, Faculty of Family and Community Sciences, The M.S.U., Baroda, Gujarat.

LIFELONG EDUCATION

1 Education and Lifelong Learning

H.C. Jain

In all human societies, education is a cornerstone. Therefore, the process of Education and Learning is as old as human society itself. Without education, a society cannot further enhance or function well. It has very important role in transformation of society. It is transmitted from one generation to another through language, work experience and search. Education implies in the change of behavioural pattern of human beings as well as the indicator of change in human society.

The word 'Education' is derived from the Greek word 'Educatum' which means "Bringing out the best" in an individual. Various potentialities of a person come out due to education and one becomes potent. Every individual has different kinds of capacities. Education does not help in bringing about the pernicious qualities of a person. Instruction and training are purposely related to the educational activities.

Late Prime Minister Mr. Rajiv Gandhi rightly expressed his views on the importance of education, "Education must make our people the master of technology and not its slaves. We must understand, modify and use knowledge for our benefit and for the country's benefit. Education must fight injustice, intolerance and superstition."

The importance and value of Learning and Education in the words of Mr. Varbe is cited here:

"Education is a companion, which has no misfortune

No crime destroy

No enemy alienate
No despotism enslave
At home a friend
Abroad an introduction
In Solitude a shoe
In society an ornament
Without it what is man?
A splendid slave and a reasoning savage."

In fact, a human being is not, in real sense, a human being till he is learned. Swami Vivekananda rightly expressed about the importance of education, "Death is better than a vegetating ignorant life, it is better to die on the battlefield than to live a life of defeat." Thus, the purpose of education is several folds. Jawaharlal Nehru, in his message to the Hindustani Talim Sangh (28.11.1957) expressed the importance of education, "No subject is of greater importance than that of education. It is the men and women in a country that make and build a nation and it is education that is supposed to build those men and women." Dr. APJ Abdul Kalam (2009) in his address at a function said that education is not just the ability to read and write but also process of human transformation. Hence, the synergy between education and learning has to be perceived and operationalised. Education is an aid to generate Learning.

Concept of Lifelong Learning

Learning and life are closely linked. The concept of Lifelong Learning has been embedded in almost all societies. But academically the concept of Lifelong learning first originated in France during the period of French Revolution in Paris when the philosopher and legislator Marquis de Condor put a proposal in April 1792 before the Legislative Assembly. It was adopted later on.

"Education should not leave the individuals after they have left school. It should embrace all ages, because learning is necessary for everybody. Education should be provided to everybody of all ages. It should provide facilities for retaining what they have learnt or to acquire new knowledge."

Thus, in this regard, France took a lead in the development of the concept, programme and action by adopting the 1959 Law of Social Progress. Then a series of action plans on the Lifelong Learning were formulated and adopted. Later on, UNESCO also initiated conceptual development of Lifelong Education by sponsoring the work of Paul Lengrand. UNESCO also initiated some projects on Lifelong Learning. Some important publications on Lifelong Education are given below which lead the way to institutionalise the concept.

- An Introduction to Lifelong Learning: Paul Lengrand, UNESCO Report, 1970.
- Learning to Be: Report of International Commission on the Development of Education, 1972.
- Recurrent Education: a strategy for lifelong learning—OECD, 1973.
- No Limits to Learning: Bridging the Human Gap, Report, Club of Rome, 1979.

The term of lifelong education was replaced by the term lifelong learning in the nineties which covers not only basic education but also humanistic and social aspects of life. It is a process of forming of whole beings—their knowledge and aptitude as well as the critical faculty and ability to act. Today, there is a movement to provide Learning opportunities for elderly persons also.

Learning for Third Age

There are three major stages of life which may be as follows: Youth, adulthood and old age. In each stage of life everybody needs some new knowledge, skills and practice. Formal education is foundation of lifelong learning. It is initially important to develop knowledge, values, skills and sustainable livelihoods.

It is possible to distinguish learning needs common to all forms the specific needs of particular groups of learners. Improvement of personal and professional needs of adults are different from a older person's needs. The ageing population of developed countries will continue to increase in next few decades and so their needs. To meet this challenge, the educational institutions have to develop new packages of learning.

Lifelong learning for "third age" will help to meet the following needs—for Individual health, to strengthen community and family, for productive employment, and for self-enrichment.

Today, there is an international movement to provide learning opportunities for elderly persons. Even several countries have established "Universities of the third age". Some of them are as follows :

- Lifelong Learning at Oxford University, Oxford, England
- University of the Third Age, Sydney, Australia
- University of the Third Age, Pine Rivers, Australia
- McGill Institute for Learning in Retirement, Canada
- University of the Third Age, Aylesbury, England
- University of the Third Age, Harrow, England
- University of the Third Age, Geneva, Switzerland
- University of the Third Age, Canberra, Australia
- University of the Third Age, Hampshire, England
- University of the Third Age, Hobart, Inc. Australia
- University of the Third Age, Hume, Melbourne, Victoria
- University of the Third Age, Taupe, New Zealand
- University Della Terza Eta, Italy

Most of the institutes and universities listed above are engaged in the activities related to the learning of elderly persons.

Learning for Self-Growth

Education not only imparts values and skills but also encourages cultivation of self or individuality. For what Lifelong Learning is? Learning is to make a world as dream by Nobel Laureate Rabindra Nath Tagore (1901) where the mind is without fear and the head is held high.

Where knowledge is free
Where the world has not been broken into the fragments
by narrow domestic walls
Where words come out from the depth of truth.
Where tireless striving stretches its arms towards perfection
Where the clear stream of reason has not lost its way
into the dreary desert sand of dead habit
Where the mind is let forwards by Thee
into ever widening thought and action
into that heaven of freedom, my father, let my country awake.

— Gitanjali

Thus, learning brings power, joy, fire, glory, enthusiasm, all the beautiful and positive things in life. With changing age everybody needs a different type of learning with new experience in life. The ultimate goal in life is happiness which needs to be defined by each individual. Happiness is linked to the extent to which man and his environment are in harmony.

Learning for Caring

The report of the International Symposium and Round Table, stressed upon the need to pay attention to many aspects of caring :

- Caring for oneself, including one's health,
- Caring for the social, economic and ecological welfare of one's society and nation,
- Caring for human rights,
- Caring for other species,
- Caring for the liveability of the Earth,
- Caring for truth, knowledge and learning.

Learning for Individual Development

Growth is the yardstick of success for an individual, regardless of one's position. It is possible only through lifelong learning for which structured and focused opportunities are essential. Though, very few think of creating a plan for individual development but the times have changed and now every organisation is taking the extra efforts to draw up a development plan for the employees. Also they are prepared jointly by the employees and their employers. But there must be commitment on both the sides to realise the plan.

Learning for Personality Development

The term 'personality' refers to the sum of qualities that shape a person's character. Relatively speaking, the term individual denotes a purely psychological unit, whereas personality is a unit of cultural pattern. Though, it is very difficult to define a perfect personality. Yet in general, it may be harmonious development of head, heart and hand. In this regard, Swami Vivekanand also emphasised the development of these three things.—"We need to have three things—the heart to feel, the brain to conceive and hand to work. Make yourself a dynamo." In every field of life, personality has an important place. In history, literature and religious doctrine, personality has dominant place, because in the words of G.W. Allport, "Personality is the dynamic organization within the individual of those psycho-physical systems that determine his/her unique adjustment to his environment."

In *Bhagawad Gita* a good personality is characterised in the following words :

"Be humble, be harmless, have no pretence
Be upright, forbearable
Serve your teachers in true obedience
Keep the mind and body clean
Tranquil apart from the things of senses
Free from self
Awareness of the weakness in mortal nature"

Need for lifelong learning in general may be summarised into the following points :

- To keep pace with the development of new knowledge.
- To empower people specially deprived sections of society.
- Enhancing capacity to solve problems.
- To provide skill and ethic needed in market economy.
- To reconstruct a new set of values.

Agencies of Lifelong Learning

Basically, there are three types of agencies which may provide Lifelong Learning :

(1) The Formal Agencies—Schools, Colleges, Universities
(2) The non-formal agencies—J.S.S., NLM, Open Schools and Open Universities
(3) The informal Agencies:
 (i) Structural—T.V., Radio, Cinema etc.
 (ii) Unstructured—Club, Sport Councils, libraries, religious institutions, mass media, family etc.

Career Advancement

In these times when growth of knowledge and social change

go on with such phenomenal speed that students of higher education continuously need modern and employment oriented education or more specialised education in all fields of life. This is the time of survival of the fittest. On the other hand, the system of higher education is producing the large number of educated unemployed youth in the country. The graduate and the post-graduate students are unable to find jobs in the market because they have no skill oriented education. In this situation they need second chance education to improve their skill and knowledge.

Guracharan Das rightly commented on the pathetic state of education: "For 50 years we promoted rote learning, incompetent faculty and mediocrity. We punish original thinking and failed to create an employable graduate. We pushed students into a parallel universe of coaching classes, which ironically took their obligation to students for more seriously. We deserve to die." This is the status of Indian Education system. To overcome from this situation, we need Lifelong Learning.

Here are 6 basic principles of business etiquette which have been given by Gary Yukl as the foundation for good human relations in corporations and in society:

1. Be on time—Be punctual by sensibly scheduling appointments. Show respect for other people's time and their own pre-occupations.
2. Be discreet—So that you are sensitive to the impact that information might have on those working with it, as well as what the competition might do if they find it.
3. Be courteous, pleasant and positive and this is irrespective of the pressures on you or your company.
4. Be concerned with others, not just yourself—People careers are ended stalled reversed because they lacked concern for others.
5. Dress appropriately—First impressions are first impressions, You only make one.
6. Use proper written and spoken language—Because

people who can express themselves clearly are always at a definite advantage.

Learning has various forms such as pre-learning, reinforcement of learning, classroom learning, individualized and independent learning of small groups or large masses, enrichment learning, self-learning, and self-directed or self-managed learning. Learning itself is ultimately an individualized and lifelong process, whereby transformation occurs within the individual but the final outcome of the learning is the application of knowledge and skill for the benefit of the society, nation and world.

References

1. Bhola, H.S. (2003) "Adult and Lifelong Education for Sustainable Development in India: Great Achievement, Greater Expectations", *International Journal of Adult and Lifelong Education,* Vol. 1 (2), September 2003, pp. 5-16.
2. Fordham, Paul (2004) "Lifelong Learning and Adult Education: Changing Terminology and Changing Ideas: A Complex Inter-relationship."
3. Jhansi, S.C. and Mishra, Santosh Kumar (2007), "Lifelong Learning for the Third Age—Significance and case studies from selected countries", *Indian Journal of Adult Education,* Vol. 68 (1-2).
4. Kalam, APJ Abdul (2009) Address at the function of Nehru and Tagore Literacy Awards, Indian Adult Education Association, New Delhi, July 31, 2009.
5. Kurrien, John (2007) "Say No to Rote Learning," *The Times of India,* New Delhi, December 17, 2007.
6. Jain, H.C. (2000) *Madhya Pradesh Men Proudh Shiksha,* Madhya Pradesh Hindi Granth Academy, Bhopal, M.P.
7. Sanyal, Bikas C. (2004) "Lifelong Learning in the Twenty-first Century", *International Journal of Adult and Lifelong Education,* Vol 2 (1), April 2004.
8. Rana, Yashwant Singh (2007) "Living and Learning together: The Role and Responsibilities of Educators and their Unions." *Indian Journal of Adult Education*: Vol. 68 (1-2).

9. Reddy, Reddeppa (2009) "Opportunities and Challenges to Lifelong Learning", *Indian Journal of Adult Education*. Vol, 70.
10. Singh, R.S.; Singh, Sajjan and Baghel, D.S. (2007) "Education for the Third Age: Rationale and Structure", *Indian Journal of Community Psychology*, Vol. 3 (2), September 2007.
11. *The Times of India*, New Delhi, June 17, 2009.
12. Venugopal, C.N. "Education and Society", in Oommen, T.K. & Venugopal, C.N. (ed. 1995), *Sociology for Law Students*, Eastern Book Co., Lucknow.
13. Verma, J.S. (2002-03) *Significance of Ethic in Education*, UGC Golden Jubilee Lecture Series UGC, New Delhi.

2 Continuing Education Programme and its Impact

Rajesh Paliwal
Deepak Paliwal

Literacy and education has always been an area of importance and concern for the planners, policy-makers, social scientists and the academicians The involvement of the whole community for social planning and development is one of the important factors in development of any nation. Illiteracy and poverty are intertwined. The Indian society is experiencing this truth even after six decades of its independence. In the complex society like India which is multi-racial, multi-lingual, multi-religious and beset with innumerable problems, the problem of illiteracy is a big challenge on the way of its development. Only the combined efforts of all the people with public participation can meet this challenge. The entire nation would have to take the pledge to wipe out the illiteracy problem referred as 'Sin and Shame' by Mahatma Gandhi at the time of India's independence. In fact, the mass literacy endeavour is a challenge which needs dedication and missionary zeal. It needs to inspire creativity and innovation to muster youth power, to secure voluntary effort and above all to ensure people's participation and their whole-hearted support. In order to remove the illiteracy on the one hand and to improve literacy ratio on the other, the Government of India has launched a number of literacy programmes. The formation of National Literacy Mission, New Delhi, in 1988 has also been one such endeavour that primarily aims at addressing the cause of adult illiteracy. It adopts campaign approach to achieve its objective by means of TLC, PLC and CEP. The Total

Literacy Campaign (TLC) emphasises on strengthening the basic literacy skills of the learners and Post Literacy Campaign (PLC) focuses on creating such opportunities for neo-literates so as to make them economically, socially, culturally, spiritually and morally competent so that they could make better in their socio-economic conditions. The continuing education programme places greater emphasis on skill development. It is a basic literacy and post-literacy continuum process. Continuing Education Programme provides an opportunity to the people at grassroots level to strengthen their literacy skills and take up other activities and motivate the people concerned to continue their education, increase their income and improve the quality of their lives. It promotes self-confidence amongst them to improve their personal and socio-economic conditions too. Continuing Education (CE) is a continuum of basic literacy and post-literacy phases. Continuing Education Programme (CEP) means to enable the neo-literates persist with their newly acquired literacy. CE includes post-literacy for neo-literates and school dropouts—for retention of literacy skills, continuing of learning beyond elementary literacy and application of this learning for improving their living conditions. CE includes all of the learning opportunities all people want or need outside of basic literacy education and primary education. CE provides an opportunity to the people at grassroots level to strengthen their literacy skills and take up other activities such as, to continue their education, increase their income and improve the quality of their lives. It promotes self-confidence amongst them to improve their personal, social and economic conditions. It is a process of life-long learning which includes all types of learning which they want according to their needs and interest (T. Sundaresan Nair, 2006).

The scheme of CE was launched in 1995 as fully-funded centrally sponsored scheme. The scheme of CE for neo-literates as visualized by National Literacy Mission (NLM) is an attempt to provide systematic organized and well-coordinated mechanisms to mobilize all resources in support of CE in the perspective of lifelong education. In a rapidly changing society which calls for a radical transformation of the content and methods of education, continuing education will play a vital innovation. As is understood by the term, education is a life-long process, and should not be confined to certain age-groups and to four walls of schools, colleges and universities, should be available not only to the selected few but to all throughout their lives both under organized, structured learning situations and non-formal set-up. CEP is taken up only in those districts which have completed both Total Literacy Programme (TLP) and Post-Literacy Programme (PLP) phases and the external evaluation of TLP has been conducted. The scheme of CEP aims at providing an institutionalized mechanism of CE through continuing education centres (CECs) with a view to enabling the neo-literates to retain, improve and apply their day-to-day needs and aspirations. CE is also an indispensable aspect of the strategy of human resources development and of the goal of creation of a learning society. CE provides a second chance to those who missed formal education and is responsive to learner's needs, directly addresses it to structural inequalities. CE is the opportunity to engage in lifelong learning, it is now emerging as the main component of the boarded view of education as a whole. In continuing education, human resources development becomes the focus of attention. Thus, CE is also an essential extension of literacy to promote human resources development. It encompasses opening of CECs giving employment oriented knowledge to beneficiaries through assistance of employees, government associates and institutions; develop libraries and provide special reading material for neo-literates.

The aim of CE is to devise and develop educational contents and provide opportunities responsive to the needs and wants, suitable to the images and voices of the designated sub-sectors of the population, and enable them to engage in lifelong learning. The UNESCO (1972) extended the scope of education as an intervention that could create a learning society in which all agencies of society are education providers and all citizens are engaged in learning. In India, the growth of this movement has been closely related to the degree of availability of literacy provisions to its vast majority of people. Total Literacy Campaign achievement provided the opportunity of creation of demand for the provision of post-literacy and continuing education (J.P. Dubey, 2006). A document of the British Open University (1976) describes CE "All learning opportunities which are taken up after full time compulsory schooling has ceased". The same document suggests that the CEP should meet personal, economic, vocational and social needs (Yashwant Singh Rana, 2006). CE is the penultimate stage of TLP and therefore is rightly regarded as the most crucial stage that tends to link the basic literacy skills with the human skills. Hence after the initial total literacy phase, greater emphasis is placed on acquisition and skill upgradation, in both post-literacy and continuing education phases. It is based on the premise that increasing use of economic opportunity could only be availed by those who have skills or have upgraded. CE visualizes individuals adjusting to a rapidly changing world and willing to take on anew job or play anew social role with eagerness and enthusiasm, not fear and reluctance. It presupposes an effective climate which foster in individuals confidence and assurance to acquire an adequate basic repertoire of skills in order to assimilate further knowledge and to incorporate new skills and roles into their personality without personal disequilibrium and disintegration.

- It is a multi-faceted scheme and enjoys extreme flexibility to allow the grassroots community participation and managerial initiatives. The CEP is directed to provide.
- Provide facilities for retention of literacy skills and continuing education to enable the learners to continue their learning beyond basic literacy.
- Create scope for application of functional literacy for improvement of living conditions and quality.
- Disseminate information on development programmes and widening and improving participation of traditionally deprived sections of the society.
- Create awareness about national concerns such as national integration, conservation and improvement of the environment, women's equality, observance of

small family norms etc. and sharing of common problems of the community.

- Improve economic conditions and general well-being as well as improvement of productivity by organizing short duration training programmes, orientation courses for providing vocational skills and by taking up linkage activities for establishing direct linkages between CE and development activities.
- Provide facilities for library and reading rooms for creating an environment conducive for literacy efforts and a learning society.
- Organize cultural and recreational activities with effective community participation.

The central aim of CE Programmes is to ensure that a range of appropriate and effective opportunities for lifelong learning are available to all adults everywhere. The premises on which foundations for CE are developed have been diverse and are based on success stories from within and outside the country. One of the significant changes assimilated in the theory of CE is to view the literacy, post-literacy and continuing education as a coherent learning continuum by the NLM. Secondly, CE envisions to establishing a responsive, alternative structure of learning striving to meet the variety of needs of all sections of society. It also aims at making it a process of capacity building of its people who work in a context that respects the technical and cultural ethos of the local people rather than attempting to impose skills and culture alien to them, because such effort could lead to their estrangement from the programme specially, if it has not come from themselves. The scheme of CE is taken up in a district only after it has completed the TLC and PLC phases, which makes the learner aware of the power and significance of education. Establishment of CECs and NCECs is the principal mode of implementing continuing education programme. The centres follow an area-specific, community-based approach. The scheme envisages one CEC for each village to serve a population of about 1,500-2,000 people. About 10 such centres form a cluster with one or more acting as the nodal CEC. The centres are run by full-time facilitators or Preraks, and Assistant Preraks who are drawn from the community itself.

The CE centres serve as providers of the following facilities :

- Library – A depository of learning materials
- Reading Room – A place which encourages people to read
- Learning Centre – A provider of CE programme
- Training Centre – For short duration training programmes to upgrade skills
- Information Centre – For securing information on various development programmes
- Charcha Mandal – Community meeting place for sharing ideas and solving problems
- Cultural Centre – A place for cultural activities
- Sports Centre – For recreation and healthy living.

Thus, CE besides imparting and sustaining the literacy skills to new literates also focuses on other critical aspects of literacy like the teaching of primers, identification of target groups, environments building activities and other allied activities that aim of eradication of illiteracy. The continuing education scheme is thus a multifaceted programme that enjoys supreme flexibility, to encourage and allow grassroots community to participate.

In Uttarakhand, State Literacy Mission Authority (SLMA) was formed with the aim of illiteracy eradication and imparting functional literacy to the people within the age-group of 15-35. From the year 1992, the responsibility of illiteracy eradication was entrusted to the district literacy committees. The Total Literacy Campaign was conducted by the district literacy committees from 1992 were completed in all the 13 districts of Uttarakhand in 2000-01. Under this campaign 53,238 illiterates of the identified 7,48,564 were turned into literates according to the norms of the National Literacy Mission. To make the people literate and to raise the skills of the neo-literates a Post Literacy Programme (PLP) was started as a subsidiary programme of TLC. PLP has now completed in the entire 13 districts. In this programme 5,63,995 participants have benefited. At present out of 13 districts of Uttarakhand CEP is running in 12 districts except that of Uttarkashi.

The detailed scenario is shown in Table 2.1.

Table 2.1

District	*CEC*	*NCEC*
Almora	440	44
Bageshwar	98	09
Pithoragarh	210	21
Nainital	278	27
Champawat	82	08
Udham Singh Nagar	450	44
Dehradun	466	46
Pauri	254	25
Tehri	220	22
Rudrayprayag	83	08
Chamoli	135	13
Haridwar	526	52
Total	3242	319

Various studies regarding CEP and its impact on the beneficiaries have been conducted by many social scientists in India. Today CEP has become an area of concern even for the social scientists. In this very context the studies conducted by Harsingh Chouhan (2007), J.P. Dubey (2006), Yashwant Singh Rana (2006), T. Sundaresan Nair (2006), M. Shanthi Priya (2006), Anuradha Sharma (2006), Rajan (2004), B.K. Sahoo (2004), Krishna (2004), Nagambika Devi (2004), Sachidanand (1995), Kholi (1995), Lakshmi Naryanan (1983), Trivedi (1984), Mishra (1986) are of great importance.

Therefore, the need of the hour is to make an intensive and extensive study of the CEP to evaluate its implementing pattern, success ratio, achievement, constraints and the relevance. It is yet to be seen as how far the CEP is successful in realizing its objectives. In this background, the researcher has made an attempt to undertake the study for finding the impact of the CEP on beneficiaries. The study has been focused on the following objectives.

Objectives

1. To present an overview of continuing education programme in particular reference of Uttarakhand State.
2. To study how far the continuing education programme has achieved its objectives implied with it.
3. To study the awareness, attitude and the behaviour pattern of the target group towards continuing education programme.
4. To study the impact of CEP on the social and economic life of the target group.
5. To make an evaluative study of the role of Preraks in the implementation of CEP.
6. To analyze the perspectives, problems and prospects of continuing education programme in the district of Nainital.

Research Methodology

In view of the objective of the present research work, exploratory research design is used for the study. All the Nodal Centres (NCs) and Continuing Education Centres (CECs) located in eight developmental blocks of Nainital district constitute the universe of the present work.

Out of the universe the sample units have been selected through stratified random sampling method. For this purpose at first one Developmental Block (Haldwani) has been selected for the study using purposive sampling method. At the second step two NCs, namely Kuwarpur and Nagarkshetra-Haldwani from sampled development block have been selected through random sampling method (lottery method). The sampled NCs consist of

23 CECs having total 2355 beneficiaries. At the third step 20 per cent beneficiaries out of the total 2355 have been selected through random sampling method (regular marking method) and one Prerak from each CEC have been selected purposively for the study. The sampled NCs and break up of total number of beneficiaries and CEC are shown in Table 2.2.

Table 2.2

NCs	*CECs*	*Total Nos. of Beneficiaries*	*Sampled Units*
Kuwarpur	a. Sultannagari	38	08
	b. Khera	168	33
	c. Nawarkhera	195	39
	d. Dewlamalla	161	32
	e. Dewlatalla	76	15
	f. Nayagaon	42	08
	g. Lakshampur	187	37
	h. Jagatpur	157	31
	i. Kishanpur Paudiyal	168	33
	j. Basantpur	153	30
	k. Bhawanipur	142	28
	l. Lakhanmandi	52	10
	m. NC Kuwarpur	129	25
Nagarkshetra-Haldwani	a. Pv Railway Bazar, Haldwani	55	11
	b. Pv Banphulpura	73	14
	c. Pv Gandhinagar	109	20
	d. Pv (male) Rajpura	61	12
	e. Pv (female) Rajpura	80	16
	f. Pv Indranagar	48	09
	g. Pv Vataganj	48	09
	h. Vajaran	95	17
	i. Indranagar	60	12
	j. Pv (male), Rampur NC	55	11

Thus total 460 beneficiaries and 23 Preraks altogether form the study group of the present study.

In the present study, interview schedule method has been used for collecting first hand information. The respondents were personally contacted and interviewed with the help of structured interviewed schedule. On the basis of personal interview by avoiding certain types of errors, various pieces of important information were collected and verified by using all senses, means and methods so that no false information could deviate the scientific conclusions. Prior to interview a good rapport was established by contacting frequently the informants and tried to get every possible co-operation from them. Besides this secondary sources like reference books, journals, public records, manuscripts, survey reports and many other related studies and their findings have also been used as the source of secondary information. The fact thus collected were subsequently tabulated and analyzed to draw some empirical conclusions.

Findings

The profile of the respondents which was selected for the study shows that, 37 respondents (8.04 per cent) were male and the rest 423 (91.96 per cent) were female respondents. The study shows that majority of the respondents (36.88 per cent) are in the age-group of 21-30 years and the minimum respondents were in the age-group of 31-40 year.

The professional background of the respondents shows that, 154 (33.48%) were working as a labourer, 117 (25.43%) were housewives, 61 (13.26%) were from agricultural background and the rest, 14 (3.04%) were doing their own small business.

Infrastructural and other facilities available in these continuing education centres show that majority of these centres were functioning in the public buildings such as schools, panchayat buildings while some are running in Preraks' houses.

The findings of the study shows that the awareness level of the majority of the respondents were not so high. They even were not aware of the conceptual meanings of CEP and its objectives. Their only concern is with the activities performed in the continuing education centres. The facts also reveal that the majority of the married female respondents were not aware of the CEP. They were having education up to pre-primary level only. No centre-wise variation was noticed in the views of the beneficiaries belonging to the same socio-economic background. This shows that socio-economic background plays an important role in shaping the attitude, awareness and behaviour pattern of the beneficiaries in comparison to their ecological background.

In order to assess the attitude and behavioural pattern of the beneficiaries towards CEP, a five-point scale was used by the researcher. The findings of the study show that majority of the beneficiaries were satisfied with the performance of the CEP, a positive attitude towards CEP were found among the beneficiaries. They were of the views that because of CEP they have gained self-confidence and better status in the society. They had learned to keep their budget account correctly, which they felt could help them to control the earnings of their families. According to them, the technical skill they developed from CEP can be utilized in earnings. One of the interesting findings found during the study was that cent-per-cent of the beneficiaries like to motivate others to join CEP. They were of the view that after attending CEP a new approach can be developed towards life. They were of the opinion that they are no looser they are in position to get something new which will be helpful for them and their family. Besides this the researcher also tried to assess the impact of CEP on the attitude and social-behaviour of the respondent. The study shows that a positive change was occurred among the beneficiaries. Majority of the respondents were of the view that socio-economic life has been changed due to CEP. A positive attitude towards reading and education has been developed among the learners. For example, the majority of the learners now prefer medical treatment instead of visiting religious healers like Ojhas and Moulvis in their neighbourhood. Almost all the learners now consult the private practitioners for medical treatment and medicine. Attitude of the respondents towards child education has changed. They believe in gender equality. In this respect some learners said that they consider and treat equally the male and the female children. For them both the children are the gifts of God. Though the female learner's attitude towards the girl child is reportedly changed, yet a study reveals that expansion of family caused by successive births of girls still took place in the society. In case of three or four daughters born one after another, the family still hankered for a son. Dowry for a daughter's marriage has long been a problem for the society and has been primarily responsible for the deep apathy towards the girl child. But with the impact of CEP more and more learners are beginning to feel that dowry considerations are becoming less and of less importance.

So far the infrastructure facilities of imparting CEP is concerned it was found during the study that the rooms did not have adequate space to accommodate additional influx of participants. The conditions of verandah and classrooms of some of the government schools where CEP is being run were not in functional conditions and required repairing or renovation on priority basis. The reading material was insufficient. Only few old magazines were available in CECs. Because their subscription has been banned hence new arrivals have not taken place and old magazine have been put on display. Books on moral education, culture, national unity, legal information, government schemes, and the story books had been found in insufficient number in the library. None of the centres subscribe Employment News which provides information regarding employment opportunities. Most of the centres did not have electric connections that affected their performance and the vocational training could not be properly conducted. Majority of the centres have only three or four sewing machines due to which all the participants were not able to get machines as there were no machines in their houses due to which their regular practice get interrupted. If the CECs are equipped with sewing machines the beneficiaries would have a place where they could practice. The machine would enable them to gain experience initially and then enter the market with more confidence. None of the centres have information window from where the beneficiaries get information regarding various government schemes.

It was found during the study that the level of activities on culture and sports were comparatively less as compared to other activities of the centres. It needs to be underlined that cultural and sports activities play an important role in personality development. The centres were generally seen to be organizing religious musical programme. However, under the sports the items provided were carom board and rackets only. Therefore, in order to make the cultural and sports activities more attractive and vibrant other sport items need to be made available in the centres. Majority of the centres do not organize Charcha Mandals. The target specific programmes like equivalency programmes, quality of life improvement programme, individual interest programmes were non-existent except in few cases. The topic of health, hygiene, concept of small family and its significance, advantage of reading are least discussed in the centres.

Preraks are the vital elements in the CEC system at the grassroots levels; their performance influences the performance of the centres to a large extent. The functions of the Preraks are entrusted with responsibilities of organizing 'charcha mandal' on socially relevant issues, organize their CEC as windows for information useful for surrounding community and organization cultural, adventure and sports activities to motivate their beneficiaries and community members. The study has clearly shown that the performance and working of Preraks have been quite good despite the fact that they have not been paid the honorarium for the last fourteen months. Though they were willing to work, however, the pain and anguish was want on their faces. The procrastination on part of the government is likely to demotivate them in the large term and may discourage the other prospective functionaries.

Suggestions

On the basis of the findings of the research study the following suggestions can be made :

- Proper monitoring and evaluation of the programme should be made for effective functioning of the centres.
- The Continuing Education Centres should be provided adequate physical facilities, books and sports material.
- The grants should be released regularly without any delay under any pretext.
- Besides teaching and learning education, the beneficiaries should be given information related to general knowledge, awareness etc.
- Information regarding employment and development should be provided to participants.
- Besides sewing machines, computer facility should also be provided to the participants and a certificate should be issued to them after successful completion of the course.
- Preraks which play an important role in the implementation pattern of CEP and their performance influences the performance of the centres to a large extent. The honorarium amount which is Rs. 700 per month must be suitably rationalized and must be paid in time.

References

1. Black, James A. and Dean J. Champion. (1976) *Methods and Issues in Social Research*. New York: John Willey and Sons.
2. Bajpai, S.R. (1997) *Methods of Social Survey and Research*. Kanpur: Kitab Ghar.
3. Chouhan, Harsingh and Ram Prakash Mishra (2007). 'Literacy level of Neo- Literates: A Research Study', *Indian Journal of Adult Education*.
4. Chouhan, Harsingh (2007). 'Impact of Literacy on Voluntary Adoption of Family Planning', *Indian Journal of Adult Education*.
5. Chouhan, Harsingh and Rajesh Mishra (2004.) 'A comprehensive critical evaluation of J.V.C.', *Indian Journal of Adult Education*.

6. Chopra, R. (1994). *Adult Education*. New Delhi: Himalaya Publishing House, New Delhi.
7. Dubey, J.P. (2006.) 'Continuing Education: Changing Perspectives', *Indian Journal of Adult Education*.
8. Dhoundiyal, Vijaya (2005). 'Role of Women Motivators of CEP in Empowerment of Rural Women: A Study', *Indian Journal of Adult Education*.
9. Grover, R. and Rita Chopra. (1998). *Adult Education*. The Indian Publication, Ambala.
10. Government of India (1988). *National Literacy Mission*, Ministry of Human Resource Development.
11. Government of India (1986). *National Policy on Education*, Ministry of Human Resource Development Literacy Mission.

3 Social Constructivist Approach for Education for All

Tupe Navnath

Education is an important agency of social control and social transformation. Mahatma Gandhi also supported this principle while he described education as, "an all-round drawing out of the best in the child and man—body, mind and spirit." John Dewey regards education as, "the development of all those capacities in the individual, which will enable him to control his environment and fulfil his possibilities." Therefore, opportunity of education must be given to everyone in the society. In this regard, the World Health Organisation declared in 1948, "Everyone has a right to education". Majority of countries around the world they have taken the lesson from this universal declaration of Human Rights; and enacted laws making schooling compulsory for at least up to the elementary level. India is also included in them. There is special provision of compulsory education in the Constitution of India under the Articles 21A and 45. According to the constitutional provision of education, Central and State governments have made serious efforts to expand the education. Recently Mahila Samakhya Schemes, D.P.E.P. Project, learning with pleasure, Sarva Shiksha Abhiyan have been launched to pursue universalization of elementary education and Total Literacy Campaign launched on a mission mode. However, the picture has not much changed, the ASER (Annual State Education Report) survey report released on 17th January, 2006 was undertaken between October and December 2005, it covered about 1,90,000 households and 3,30,000 children in 485 districts of 28 states. This survey concludes that 6.6 per cent of children between the ages of 6 and 14 (nearly 11 million) are out of school, however, processor inside the classroom are different issue altogether. A disturbing finding of ASER is that of the children surveyed in classes VI to VIII in government run schools 22 per cent could not read passages while 40 per cent could not do simple division (*The Times of India*, Pune, Monday February 6, 2006). According to Census of India 2001, 34.62 per cent of people are illiterate in India. According to this data, how Indian people will be capable to business in the global societies. I want to mention here Dr. Mashelkar's statement who is a great scientist. He says, "India's future is in IT but not in it as Information Technology but in IT as in Indian Talent. Giving every opportunity possible to Indian Talent to reach its real potential would truly empower India." What does happen with Indian Talent today? Table 3.1 shows us some hard facts.

Table 3.1: Dropout Rates of all Categories of Students 2005-06

Education Level	*Boys*	*Girls*	*Total*
Primary (I-V)	28.71	21.77	25.67
Elementary (I-VIII)	48.67	48.98	48.80
Secondary (I- X)	60.10	63.56	61.62

Table 3.1 shows that, the dropout rates of all categories of students at primary level were 25.67 per cent and 48.80 per cent at elementary level and 61.62 per cent rate of dropouts at secondary level in the year 2005 to 2006. It means that only 40 per cent talents of India go ahead from Matriculation. At higher education, our colleges and universities are standing for Welcome to only 10 per cent of Indian youth and 90 per cent are deprived from higher education. This is only a tip of the iceberg, of which only very small parts shine. Why a huge part of the iceberg remains submerged and dark even the World Bank gives loan to education for all. World Bank gives loan to the country for basic education and expects minimum learning level such as reading, writing, numeracy skills. We launch the

programmes for Education for All under the pressure of World Bank to fulfil its aims, which are very limited to literacy and numeracy, so called core components of basic education. Quality of our elementary education is very low due to low expectation from students, teachers, educational authority and planners. Some other factors of educational system are responsible for a huge part of the iceberg remains submerged and dark. Some of them can be described as follows :

1. Condensed curriculum (Our curriculum of basic education and higher education does not fulfil the student's needs).
2. Poor quality of textual/learning materials.
3. Inadequate physical facilities—overcrowded learning centres, more often than not, classes conducted in small rooms, backyards, deserted public buildings, farms and huts, etc.
4. Meagre education facilities.
5. Poorly paid instructors, with poor training.
6. No provision for proper evaluation of pupil achievement (P.N. Dave, 1992).

It is actual fact that all learning centres of Education for All are dearth environment of learning in India such as primary school, Adult Education Centre, Community Learning Centre, High School as well as colleges. Students never like such type of boring environment, therefore, they dropout from the schools and colleges. Dress, midday meal, other learning accessories are being given to the students up to the elementary education. People only send their children to school but poor children could not attend the school regularly even so many facilities are provided to them by government. Because poor people do not believe that education can eradicate poverty. If we consider education as an investment for future and as an enjoyment of life. Investment for future and enjoyment of life both are not aim of poor people. They are struggling to fulfil their basic needs of day-to-day life.

"One size does not fit all" but in India, similar education system is adopted which is very rigid; it is called formal education. Formally, there are two categories of educational system. One is formal which is applied for regular students and another one is Non-formal, which is used for irregular students or out of school students or adult learner in India. Some non-formal education programmes were being conducted in India such as Mahila Samakhya Schemes, Mahatma Phule Education Guaranty Schemes, community learning centres and Alternative classes in D.P.E.P. Open Schooling, Night Schooling and open universities are running in India as a Non-formal Education mode. In these entire non-formal and formal educational centres actually skills and education differ from real life situation. The role of the content, the role of the context, the role of assessment and role of teacher and the role of students are same in formal and non-formal education except time. It means that same chemical in different bottles. So both systems of education could not success to fulfil the objectives of education for all.

We should apply non-formal and formal education system for regular and irregular learner as per needs. For the purpose of education for all, we should develop the flexible educational system where anybody, anywhere, anytime, any speed can learn. We need to change the contemporary module of education for all and replace the suitable module for all where nobody is deprived from education and its quality should be maintained. In order to transform the module, a social constructivist approach to learning should be applied. This emphasises the individual student and his or her way of studying through self-governed work, while one-way lectures are considered less important. Schultz and Tonnesen (2006) argue that the traditional curriculum and the oral tradition of lectures within (higher) education are two central barriers to the implementation of distance learning and blended learning. However, we believe that the social constructivist emphasis on self-government work for students could remove these barriers. Social constructivist approach could be applied at higher education level as well as school education level.

Social Constructivist Approach

Vygotsky developed the social constructivist approach. He emphasised the critical importance of culture and the importance of the social context for cognitive development. Vygotsky's the Zone of Proximal Development is his best-known concept. Vygotsky's the Zone of Proximal Development emphasises his belief that learning is fundamentally, a socially mediated activity. Thinking and problem solving skills can according to Vygotsky, be placed in three categories. The child can perform some things independently. Others cannot be performed even with help. Between these two extremes are skills the child can perform with the help from others. Those skills are in the ZPD. If a child uses these cognitive processes with help of others, such as teachers, parents, and fellow students, they will develop skills that can be independently practiced. As Vygotsky (1987) puts it "what the child is able to do in collaboration today he will be able to do independently tomorrow". According to social constructivist approach, learning is considered an active, social process in which individuals actively construct knowledge (Vygotsky, 1978; Brown *et al.*, 1989) within the social environment and so knowledge cannot be transferred. This means that learning necessitates the active and self-governed work of students. Social constructivist theory proposes that learning occurs through students'—

- Sharing
- Discussing
- Critically reviewing
- Interaction

This approach is often used alongside with task-based approach/problem based learning approach in classroom practices. Students are the co-builders of knowledge and have to respond to challenges and review their own and others, work/ideas critically. The major role of teachers is to design classroom activities in which students can participate in knowledge co-construction and exploration. Vygotsky (1978), Leont'ev (1978), Dewey (1916) and Wertsch (1998) stress the goal-directed and mediated nature of self-governed activities. A problem represents a goal that cannot immediately be achieved. The mediated nature of activities means that a goal-directed person uses resources to solve a problem. Knowledge is constructed in this goal-directed activity. According to this approach, students should be directed at solving a problem and should direct the problem-solving process themselves. C. Dalsgaard and M. Godsk (2007) stated that problem-based and self-governed activities are opened and ill-structured processes, because students do not know how to solve the problem and so it is not possible to predetermine their activities.

If we want to apply the constructivist approach in non-formal education we should change the setting of educational system according to five aspects such as given below.

Five Settings for Constructivist approach

1. Instructional Design
2. Learning Environment
3. Content Development
4. Student's Role
5. Teacher's Role

I. Instructional Design

Lecturing is one of the most useful instructional tools in traditional module. Information and knowledge are predetermined and sequenced in this module. Teacher gives the information and knowledge to students while he does not think about real life situation. Students acquire knowledge but they do not know of when and how to use it. There is explosion of information and knowledge in this information era. Students have lot of access of knowledge and information such as television, internet, mobile, offline CD, books, journals. There are lots of open-ended source available. Teacher can deliver less amount of information and knowledge compared to these open-ended sources. Therefore, there is no needs to deliver the information only in classroom. Student needs to develop the critical thinking power to judge what is wrong and what is correct. Student needs problem solving skills. Traditional instructional design is not useful to achieve these goals.

The anchored instruction approach is an attempt to help students become more actively engaged in learning by situating or anchoring instruction around an interesting topic. The learning environment is designed to provoke the kinds of thoughtful engagement that helps students develop effective thinking skills and attitudes that contribute to effective problem solving and critical thinking. In this process anchor goes deep and deep in knowledge and skills as soon as students solve the problem through completing activity one by one.

Principles of Anchored Instruction

Learning and teaching activities should be designed around an "anchor" which is often a story, adventure, or situation that includes a problem or issue to be dealt with that is of interest to the students. Instructional materials should include rich resources students can explore as they try to decide how to solve a problem (e.g., interactive videodisc programs) (http://viking.coe.uh.edu/~ichen/ebook/et-it/cover.htm).

Anchored instruction emphasises the need to provide students with opportunities to think about and work on problems, which is an emphasis of cognitive constructivists. Anchored instruction also emphasises group or collaborative problem solving, which is an emphasis of social constructivists. Much of the collaborative problem solving that is at the centre of the problem based scenario, which is an example of applied social constructivism. Story writing is one of the best skilful work of the teacher. In this story teacher present the problem before the student. Student plays the important role to solve the problem and teacher helps them and guides where they face the difficulties.

II. Learning Environment

Maximum Indian families have facilities of entertainment such as television, radio, Direct To Home. Facility has been available in rural India. But there is boring environment not only in classroom of village primary school but also in classroom of colleges in rural areas. The teacher is a single source of skills, knowledge and information in the school as well as in colleges. The textbooks are single channel for teaching learning up to the higher secondary education. In this multi-channel era the students do not feel interesting to use the compulsory channel of textbooks. The circumstances of colleges have not much changed compared to primary school. Students are engaged in farming, business, and daily wages instead of attending the class. Maximum students of degree colleges are only admitted in admission book and pass the examination to cross the class. Professor dictates the notes those who attend the class. We should have to reduce the lazy condition of classroom and create appropriate learning environment with interesting process. In this context, National Knowledge Commission (Report to the Nation, 2007) recommended that use ICT based pedagogy and learning aids, provide broadband connectivity to all the government and government aided secondary schools. NKC has also proposed creating web-based portals on certain key sectors such as Water, Energy, Environment, Education, Food, Health, Agriculture, Employment, Citizens Right etc. The portals would serve as a single window for information on the given sector for all stakeholders; from student to researchers and practitioners in the field (NKC Report to the Nation 2007). Using of broadband connectivity should open the door of enthusiastic learning environment. The alternative media sources are possible solution to quality education for all. The student may select the appropriate alternative channels of learning, which is suitable for him. Som Naidu (2007) gave three suggestions for the type of evidence one should look for in a suitable learning situation, they are:

1. The ability to afford transfer to novel situations

2. The ability to provide meaning for learning
3. The ability to accommodate "anchored instruction"

Technology provides essential tools with which to accomplish the goals of a social constructivist classroom. Here are a few examples of the way information technology can support social constructivist teaching and learning:

Telecommunication tools such as e-mail and the Internet provide a means for dialogue, discussion, and debate — interactivity that leads to the social construction of meaning. Students can talk with other students, teachers, and professionals in communities far from their classroom. Telecommunication tools can also provide students access to many different types of information resources that help them understand both their culture and the culture of others.

Networked writing programmes provide a unique platform for collaborative writing. Students can write for real audiences who respond instantly and who participate in a collective writing activity. Simulations can make learning meaningful by situating something to be learned in the context of a "real world" activity such as running a nuclear power plant, writing up "breaking" stories for a newspaper, or dealing with the pollution problems of local waterways. Learning and development are social and collaborative activity. Teacher plays a role as guide and help whatever student need. Learning should occur in meaningful context and not be separated from learning and knowledge children develop in the "real world". Out-of-school experiences should be related to the child's school experience. (http://viking.coe.uh.edu/~ichen/ebook/et-it/cover.htm)

III. Content Development

Traditional curriculum has been avoided in social constructivist approach and recommended problem based scenario where authentic context, authentic activity, expert performances, multi-perspectives, coaching and collaboration, reflection and articulation all of these are provided in problem based scenarios. When we are going to create the scenario at first we should define the competency and learning outcomes which could be developed through intended course. Learning environment must be predetermined and characteristics of students should be considered when scenarios are being created and mould the content into authentic small activities according to the sequences beyond the subject matter in the scenarios (Tupe, 2008). There are different types of writing scenario such as story writing, research reporting, documentary film, court case and project. In the scenario, problem presents before the learner and learner plays the role according to the context to solve the problem. Context can be: (a) The actual work setting; (b) a highly realistic or 'virtual' surrogate of the actual work environment; (c) an anchoring context such as a video or multimedia programme (McLellan, 1994). In this situation learner completely involved in learning and his or her interest also increased. They realized the problems and motivated to solve it because problems are related to their daily practices (Tupe 2008). Authentic context must be provided for reflecting the way of knowledge will be used in reallife. Another aspect of problem-based scenario is authentic activities. It is an environment where tasks can be integrated across subject areas, and it provides the opportunity to detect relevant and irrelevant material (Brown, Collins and Duguid, 1989), many interactive multimedia programmes are so 'well designed', they fail to account for the nature of real world problem solving. Steps, procedures, hints, suggestions, clues and facts that neatly add up to the 'correct' solution are interspersed within the programme, waiting to be discovered by the learner. Story is one of the best forms of scenario writing. It is developed around the problem and problem is presented before the learner through story. When learner reads the story, he/she realizes the problem and he or she completely involve in solving the problem. Small activities are given in scenario for preparation of major assignment. Learner reflects to the activities and uses the information, knowledge, skills and attitude to complete the activity. In this process, information turn into knowledge, knowledge turn into skills and information, knowledge and skills ultimately turn into attitude.

By lecture method, teacher gives information. In this information era lot of information access have available to student then why should teacher waste his time to deliver the small information in classroom? In problem-based scenario, there is arrangement of sources for easy access of information. Learner gets the information which is necessary to complete the task. In this process, information directly applied for solving the problem. Information goes through analysis, reviewing, sharing ultimately it is turned into knowledge. When this knowledge is applied on application base it is turned into skill. Learner creates something new through his/her vision by using information, knowledge and skills. This process of learning develops a systematic approach and attitude. Scenario building is necessary process in this learning. How to build scenario? It is basic question. Som Naidu suggested some steps in this process such as:

- *Step 1:* Determine the career goals of the students.
- *Step 2:* Determine key attributes of the person who has achieved these goals.
- *Step 3:* Based on these attributes, develop the learning outcomes for your learner.
- *Step 4:* Determine the key events that might occur in the life of a person who has achieved these learning outcomes.
- *Step 5:* Develop a story that will be able to provide the opportunities for these events.
- *Step 6:* Develop the tasks that your students will be required to complete within the context of this story (Som Naidu, 2007). According to these steps author try to develop problem-based scenario in story form as follows:

Example of Suitable Story

Learning Scenario — SPSS SOFTWARE

Dev Research Institution is well known institution in India. This institute works in social research since many years. It became popular for research work. It is widely acclaimed for its very high academic and professional standards, quality of teaching, applied research and effective extension. Students enrol for M.Phil. and Ph.D. degree in this institution. A professor is working in this institute named Mr. Dube. He carries out a research project titled Problems of Ageing. He is principal investigator. He and his research fellows are working on this project since two years. They have taken interviews of senior citizens. Sample size is more about 4000 senior citizens. Huge data has been collected for the study.

Research team could not analyze the data manually. Therefore, the research team took the decision to use the SPSS software for data analysis. But nobody knew the SPSS they could not use the SPSS software. What to do now? One day the question was raised in the meeting of research committee. The Research Team thought that they could complete the work by outsourcing.

Precipitating event they invited a stastistics expert named Mr. More. Mr. More is Head of the Department of the Statistics. Research team put the problem before the expert for outsourcing. He advised research team, "I cannot complete your work because I have no time. Why don't you give that work to your M. Phil. students as a project work? If you give this work to your students as a project I will guide them. In this project your students will learn SPSS as well as your work will be done".

Solution Action Research team agreed to Mr. More and they accepted More's advice. Mr. Dube has taken the decision to give the project to M.Phil. students such as "Data Analysis through SPSS." Research team and M.Phil. students discussed about this scheme. Students were ready to do work under the leadership of one student named Ms. Sunita Shahane. Ms. Sunita Shahane is a statistics student. She is computer expert as well. Your role is of a very sincere student of Dev Research Institute. You have been asked to set up a small task force to complete the project—"Data Analysis through SPSS." You will lead this project and draw upon whoever and whatever you will need to build consensus among students of M.Phil. and resolve the problem that confronts Dev Research Institute.

Learning Activity

1. Identify the actual problem of Research Team.
2. Discuss with research team for which variables they want to analyse.
3. Develop a final proposal of project—Data Analysis through SPSS.
4. How do you compute the new variables demanded by research team?
5. How do you tabulate crossable and analysis the data through SPSS?
6. How do you operate the SPSS for select cases?
7. How do you apply descriptive statistics?

Learning Resources

- Hand Book of SPSS, Statistics Book
- Website, E-mail Chatting
- Discussion Forum
- Video Conferencing (International expert)
- Contact Session
    1. Assignment Submit the Project report of "Data Analysis through SPSS" to head of the department. Marks : 50

IV. Student's Role

In this learning model student is active learner. In lecture model student is passive receiver. Teacher tries to give readymade knowledge to student in lecture method. In constructivist approach, students are the co-builders of knowledge and have to respond to challenges and review their own and others' work/ideas critically. Here the competition is reduced among student and develop the collaboration each other for learning.

In this context Jan Herrington and Ron Oliver stated that, 'However, several research studies have shown that there are clear educational advantages to be derived from collaboration between students who are required to predict and hypothesise, and then suggest a solution. The implications of this for interactive multimedia are that interactions and activities need to be designed to engage higher-order thinking and critical reflection, rather than the rapid-fire question and answer format requiring only a low level factual response or selection. Student apply their knowledge, skills and experience to complete the given task which is based on real life setting. Discussing, critical reviewing, interaction, sharing, analysis—all these learning activities are used to solve the problem. Reflective thinking is rather important than reciting the information. Here student learn to know, learn to be, learn to do and learn to live together.

V. Teacher's Role

Teacher plays the role as a facilitator. He/she doesn't teach but student learn through activities made by him/her. According to Jan Herrington and Ron Oliver, 'The teacher's role in coaching—observing students, offering hints and reminders, provides feedback, scaffolding and fading modelling, and so on—as integral to the learning situation.' Teacher motivate student and give moral support to learning. Teacher always engage to develop learning activity and give continuous feedback while students are completing given task. In this case teacher is a reflective practitioner. Teacher search the learning resources and provide to student when they need. Collins, Brown and Newman (1989) point out that coaching is highly situation-specific and related to problems that arise as students attempt to integrate skills and knowledge. The implication for the instructional design of interactive multimedia is that the teacher's coaching role needs to be acknowledged and addressed, with suggestions and strategies for the implementation of the programme with students. Teacher is not speaker but guide and councellor. A constructivist teacher creates a context for learning in which students can be engaged in interesting activities that encourages and facilitates learning. The teacher does not simply stand by, however, and watch students explore and discover. Instead, the teacher may often guide students as they approach problems, may encourage them to work in groups to think about issues and questions, and support them with encouragement and advice as they tackle problems, adventures, and challenges that are rooted in real life situations that are both interesting to the students and satisfying in terms of the result of their work. Teachers thus facilitate cognitive growth and learning, as do peers and other members of the child's community. Teacher is as a facilitator, as a researcher and expert of extension. But he/she should develop own model of these three aspects of profession.

Conclusion

Present situation of learning is very boring and rigid from K.G. to P.G. education. Students prefer to watch programmes on Television rather than attending the class. Maximum household has a T.V. Set. But school of village has not any T.V. in a good condition. Somewhere T.V., Computer, Radio, and Tape recorder are available but not in use for students. Education does not fulfil the needs of learner because the education is not relevant to real life setting. Poor people do not believe in education. Students dropout due to lack of interest in education, learning disabilities are there in the students even if they go to school for four or five years. Social Constructivist Approach is a way of making education effective, interesting and relevant to real life setting.

Social constructivist approach is considered an active, social process in which individuals actively construct knowledge. This theory proposes learning through analysis, critically reviewing, sharing, discussing, their own and others' ideas and interaction. This approach is often used alongside with task-based approach or problem-based learning approach in classroom practices. Students are the co-builders of knowledge and have to respond to challenges and review their own and others' work/ideas critically. The major role of teachers is to design classroom activities in which students can participate in knowledge co-construction and exploration.

If we want effective results of education in sustainable development we should transform the total education system such as—Teaching methods turn into Teaching models, one way instruction design turn into anchored instruction, lazy environment of learning turn into enthusiastic learning environment, passive learner turn into active learner, teacher turn into facilitator, competitive examination turn into collaborative learning, summative evaluation turn into formative evaluation and formal education turn into non-formal education. The students are capable to construct the knowledge, skills and attitude for solving their day-to-day problems without help of others. Students can become self-reliant by education.

References

1. Atherton, J. S. (2005) *Learning and Teaching: What is learning*? [On-line] UK: Available: file:///H:/New per cent20Folder/What per cent20is per cent20learning.htm (Accessed: 10 November 2008).
2. Brown, J.S., Collins, A. & Duguid, P. (1989) Situated Cognition and The Culture of Learning, *Educational Research,* 18 (1), 32-42. Available online at: http://www2.parc.com/ops/member/brown/papers/situatedlearning.html (accessed 12 January 2005).
3. Conner Marcia, L. (2005). *Andragogy and Pedagogy. Ageless Learner, 1997-2004.* Available online at: http://agelesslearner.com/intros/andragogy.html
4. Collins, A. Brown, J.S. and Newman, S.E. (1989). Cognitive apprenticeship: Teaching the crafts of reading, writing, and mathematics. In L.B. Resnick (ed). *Knowing, learning and instruction: Essays in honour of Robert Glaser,* Hillsdale, NJ: Lea.
5. Dalsgaard, C. & Godsk, M. (2007).Transforming traditional lectures into Problem-based blended learning: Challenges and experiences. *Open Learning,* Vol. 22. No. 1.

6. Dave, P.N. (1992). *Out of School Education in South Asia: A Scenario.* Delhi, NCERT.
7. David Kolb (1984). *Experiential learning: Experience as the source of learning and development.* Englewood Cliffs, NJ: Prentice Hall.
8. Dewey, J. (1916). *Democracy and Education,* New York, The Free Press.
9. Honeben, P.C., Duffy, T.M. and Fishman, B.J. (1993). Constructivism and the design of learning environment: Context and authentic activities for learning. In T.M. Duffy, J. Lowyck, and D.H. Lonassen (Eds.) *Designing environments for constructive learning,* Heidelberg: Springer-Verlag, pp. 87-108.
10. *India* (2001), Publication Division, Ministry of Information and Boardcasting, Government of India, p. 79.
11. Jeong-Im & Michael Hannafin, *Situated Cognition and Learning Environment: Roles, Structure, and Implications for Design.*
12. Jan, Herrington and Ron, Oliver. *Critical Characteristics of Situated Learning: Implications for the instructional design of Multimedia.* Edith Cowan University.
13. Kaushik, Amit, Basic Question on Education, Editorial Opinion, *The Times of India,* Pune, Monday, February 6, 2006.
14. Knowles, M.S. (1980). *The Modern Practice of Adult Education* (revised and updated). Chicago: Association Press.
15. Knowles Malcolm (1990). *The adult learner: A neglected species* (4th Ed.). Houston, TX:Gulf Publishing.
16. Lave, J. and Wenger, E. (1991). *Situated Learning: Legitimate peripheral participation.* Cambridge: Cambridge University Press.
17. Learning: The Critical Technology: A whitepaper on adult education in the information age, *WAVE.*
18. McLellan, H. (1993). Evaluation in a Situated Learning Environment. *Educational Technology,* Vol. 33, No. 3.
19. McLellan, H. (1994) Situated Learning: Cognition the Conversation. *Educational Technology,* Vol.34, No.10,
20. Naidu, Som (2007). *Instructional Designs for Distance Education,* Melbourne University.
21. Naidu, Som (13-1-2007). *Learning Design as an Indicator of Quality in Teacher Education.* pp. 5-6.
22. Naidu, Som (4-9-2007). *Fundamental principles of learning,* Melbourne University, Australia.

23. National Knowledge Commission, *Report to the Nation*, 2007, New Delhi.
24. Robert L. Steinbach (1993). *The Adult Learner: Strategies for Success*. Menlo Park, CA: Crisp Publications.
25. Robert M. Smith (1991, April). How people become effective learners. *Adult Learning*, p. 11.
26. Schultz, R. & Tonnesen, Love Guldbrant (2006). *How can blended learning help to the integration of ICT in adult education?* Elearningeuropa.info.
27. Tupe, Navnath (2008) 'Lifelong Education: Methodology and Tools', Paper Presented in 57th All India Adult Education Conference from 19th to 21st December at Kolhapur, AIEA, Delhi.

4 Need of Lifelong Learning for Neoliterates and Professionals

G.C. Bhattacharya

Lifelong learning is a process of acquisition of personal, social and professional abilities and skills throughout the life span of individuals to enhance quality and status in life. It encompasses all formal, non-formal and informal modes of educational endeavours necessary for attainment of ultimate goals of life and utmost development of personality traits in a way so that social mobility may be ensured as well as formation of 'learning society' may be possible in real sense.

Jessup described it as a temper, a quality of community that evinces itself in attitudes, in relationships and in social organizations (Buwa, 2009). Though, the concept of lifelong learning is not a very recent one and its earlier exposition was made by thinkers like Socrates, Plato and Aristotle through their philosophical views concerned with education (Oduaran, 2000). but actually this concept was propagated by ancient Indian educationists and thinkers who used to be involved in learning and acquisition of knowledge throughout their lives by practicing *yoga* and meditation. Those *'rishis'* and *'munis'* were the ancient lifelong learners who composed the verses of Vedas, Upanishads etc. after enjoying enlightenment on their own ways but never used to be formal in nature. Formal mode of education was delimited by a couple of years in ancient India when pupils were supposed to be in *'gurukuls'* and used to learn observing celibacy or *'brahmacharya'*.

The definition adopted by the General Council of UNESCO in 1976 is more pertinent regarding lifelong education. It is specified that 'Lifelong education and learning denotes an overall scheme aimed both at restructuring of the existing education system and at developing the entire educational potential outside the education system, in such a scheme men and women are the agents of their own education' (UNESCO, 1976).

Some Factors Affecting Lifelong Learning

The definition indicates the pitfalls of the existing system of education in which the formal mode is open for a certain category of learners and for certain age groups but for those who are interested in continuing their education beyond that specification, they are supposed to make use of other modes. Underlying concept is that development of human resource is not possible through the formal mode beyond a certain age limit in the prevailing system of education whereas for professional and technical education, the formal face to face transactional mode is considered always as superior to the other modes, in a contrary. In this situation, adult neoliterates may possibly enjoy a little scope to continue further to be enlightened more. Oduaran (2003) suggested that lifelong learning apparently embraces educational practices and outcomes in both formal and non-formal settings and accepted to include the provision of credit for experimental learning (Kintzer,1997). He clarified well that all learning activities outside the school system need to be articulated and systematically assisted to improve in their operations in order to help...to discover and to develop... potentialities through the acquisition of globalization related knowledge, understanding, value and skills cumulatively and throughout life. So, the existing restrictions in the formal mode of learning is supposed to be a factor hindering the required free support towards the lifelong education for all adults irrespective of their categorization into neo or other types of literates.

Secondly, some socio-cultural beliefs and faiths are also there coming across the way to permit adult neoliterates to enter in classrooms of formal mode like economic and financial issues for those who are the basic earning member of the family and bearing some other family and social responsibilities on account of which time and opportunity both remains limited for adult learners to learn in formal setting in spite of the provision of all motivational and intention based factors.

Somewhere our late Prime Minister Rajiv Gandhi mentioned 'education as a tool for bringing social equality and balance'. According to him 'education must be a great equalizer in our society. It must be the tool to level the differences that our various social systems have created over the past thousands of years'. But in real sense, this process of equalization through education is yet not completed and will never be taken as completed till the formation of a classless learning society is possible.

For this purpose, lifelong education may be treated as the reliable tool for bringing social equality irrespective of the limitations on the basis of caste, creed, religion and age as well as culture of the citizens. Lifelong education ensures continuing of enhancement of knowledge and skills as well as enlightenment of the learners so that attainment of higher social status and better quality of life may be possible but in our country, age factor is considered as a great barrier to ensure lifelong learning as it is presumed that working ability of an individual used to decrease beyond the age of sixty onwards or like that and therefore, retirement from active service is needed making a person pension holder to live in a free but inactive life style. In this condition, the basic presumptions of the lifelong education and learning both are considered as invalid and meaningless on account of motivational point of view. So, aging is accepted as one of the great barrier and demotivating factor in our society where almost each and every adult learner used to raise a question of the need of education and learning at an adult age and about its benefit as it seems to adult illiterates that no monetary gain is possible through such education. So, not only the structure of the system of our education but the whole socio-economic and job set up are required to be modified to float and function the concept of lifelong education well, in India.

Since education will remain as a mere tool to secure better jobs and function as a guarantee card for better possibility of earning, lifelong education will remain an academic issue. Acquisition of life experiences, ensuring maturity of feelings, enhancement of the power of logical thinking and imagination, inculcation of strength of ideas and mind, development of positive and high self concept and raising the level of curiosity and development of the ability to quench the thirst of knowledge and seeking wisdom and accountability etc. remain out of consideration of the functional objectives of education and learning processes, the basic idea of lifelong education and learning both must be rolled back and not to be rooted deeply in the minds of our future citizens, as it is observed in the present situation. For being educated continuously, the strategy of lifelong learning may be required to be used through any mode or media like print or electronic etc. as well as technologies available related with information and communication. In a rigid and non-permissive society, divided into classes and groups, social mobility possesses a little scope which surely hampers the equalizing effect of education and where achievement or success in life is being measured always in terms of efficiency, productivity and financial outcomes, lifelong learning, may not flourish appropriately.

Thirdly, in a society where abilities and efficiency too are being undermined in terms of some other negative factors like politico-social influences of a person or a group of person, significance of approaches and links to earn better, affluences and caste considerations, money and material gains etc. in such types of societies too, lifelong learning is eventually discouraged.

Caste and group based politics germinate a social phenomena called reservation on the same base and that is the another negative factor to demoralize individuals to learn lifelong as for one, all acquisition of knowledge, skills and efficiency is of no use without having reservation facility on account of belonging to a certain category, group or caste. Right to have equal opportunity is hampered when such reservation is imposed and extended from time to time for the sake of vote-bank by the so-called politicians of our country with the logic that backwards may be given extra security to be at par with the advanced group or castes in the society as they remain out of touch of development for a longer period in our history. It may be a truth but at the same time, question arises about the success of reservation policy and requirements of further extension even after the sixty long years of our independence till date and probably beyond that. In such a social set up, it is next to impossible to get motivated for one to be a lifelong learner.

Those who are protected well behind the shield of reservation policy on caste and group basis may not be intended to remain a lifelong learner as they are able to enjoy well all of the required facilities and benefits without enhancement of their basic abilities and skills and at the same time those who are sure that since they are not protected by any such shield, they are bound to fail to get better chance in spite of having better educational and professional qualifications, skills and experiences even at the very younger age of life. So, social mobility is always possibly enjoyed in a learned and classless society and our Indian society was never of this category where degree loaded is countless but educated in real sense are meagre in number. Another significant factor is related with lack of proper guidance and counselling services and facilities for young and neolearners/neoliterates without which selection of right tracks for lifelong education and learning remains a difficult problem. Recently some efforts have been made in this direction by government and non-government organizations, but yet the facility is not availabie at the doorsteps of all those who are in need and on time. Lacking of trained lifelong educators is the issue which may not help us to lead in a better position, too. In this way, it is possible to conclude that there are a number of such factors which are not preparing a very much conducive climate for lifelong education in our country yet after sixty long years of independence.

Need of Lifelong Learning

Conceptually, lifelong education is needed for updating of information and broadening of the knowledge base not only for the neoliterates but also for even well educated on account of continuous expansion of knowledge in all of the fields with scientific development and technological advancement, modernization and constant impact of globalization on economy. Life long learning is inevitable for searching of new opportunities in life and seeking self-employment, too. Due to politico-educational and social factors, availability and opportunity of secured job is diminishing continuously, catalyzed by the worldwide depletion of economic growth which is basically resource based in nature and indication of financial crisis with scarcity of resources for consumption. Though economists are mentioning it as a temporary phenomena but it is not at all so in real sense. Any resource base and consumption oriented culture aspiring for development continuously throughout, is bound to face this sort of crisis as an inevitable consequence. So, for creation of new job opportunities and resources for maintenance of *statu squo* in life, lifelong education has become ultimately a need for all social group and classes as well as for individuals, too.

To use modern technology and media including electronic devices effectively, having knowledge of technical know-how is felt very much needed in order to avoid generation and knowledge gaps. For example, now-a-days, even a school student knows much more about computer operation in comparison to an educated adult as previously, no educational set up with computer application was prevailing in our country ensuring proper use of electronic equipments and devices.

As such, all adults irrespective of their socio-educational status are in need of computer and technical literacy after being literates to keep pace with the younger generation and working system of the modern age like in banks, post offices and other public sectors concerned with their day-to-day life and living. Here, lifelong learning possesses a great scope and chance of intrinsic motivation for learners on account of their daily requirements in life. With the advent of the concept of 'global village', eradication of illiteracy has not only become essential but continuation of learning is also required through lifelong educational activities, for development of international understanding and spirit of 'work culture' lacking in our social setup. In no developed country, work is taken as granted for 'worship' and nowhere is neglected so much, as it is in a country in which it is equated with worship. We have undoubtedly developed a culture to dignify the issue up to the level of heavenly strength and respect which is considered as to be neglected and to sub-humanize. The same is the truth for women too, to whom we have given the label of goddess called '*Devi*' and undermined properly, taken as granted.

Buwa (2009) highlighted some challenges related with lifelong learning related with provision of training of lifelong educators, learner oriented, community level and leadership level challenges. Along with these, neo-learners are really in need of assistance from the trained guidance and counselling personnel for pursuing learning in right and optimally suitable direction on the basis of individual needs and abilities. Provision of proper motivation and feedback to such learners for sustenance of learning throughout their life is also another requirement. In our country since education is not acting as an equalizer in the society but playing a significant role to widen the social gaps between resourceful and resourceless categories, none is interested in learning. The resourceful have no time to spare for it keeping aside their own business and constant earning and unfortunately, the later group is having no resource base and support to learn continually.

Thus, lifelong learning is essentially treated as merely the requirement for the average or middle class people of the society. Quality education is being purchased by resourceful groups as a commodity for their younger generation to ensure better returns in terms of financial output and acquisition of administrative and socio-political empowerment which is somehow beyond the capacity of resourceless social groups and perhaps in view of this discrepancy in the social set up, the policy of caste based reservation emerged and came into function. But even then, with the alarming rate of population growth, tough competition is inevitable in all walks of our life and in such of a situation, survival of the fittest is eventually possible, fittest not in the physical sense but surely in the sense of knowledge and professional abilities, competencies and qualities. Since scientific temper and technological expertise is attainable through lifelong learning and being up to date in terms of new developments, it will be felt needed by the members of all social groups, in no time.

For making proper use of leisure time which is constantly increasing due to mechanization and use of modern technology in all sectors of life and professions, use of lifelong learning is recommended, at all levels—pre-service, in-service or even at post-service level. A literate society may be turned into a learned society eventually due to lifelong learning which is called a continuously supportive process for development of human potentials through acquisition of knowledge, understanding, skills and values and enabling one to apply the same appropriately in real life situation for better outcomes and empowerment of individuals as human resource. This process is helpful for all literates and educated to convert them into highly skilled personnel and to create a social set up in which only accountability and sincerity, efficiency and ability and talents and creativity are being honoured, appreciated and dignified.

It is obvious that this view may encounter a lot of challenges but it is also true that till the entire social setup and its norms, practices, policies, values and culture are not being changed, lifelong learning is not going to seek much impetus and significance, in the prevailing Indian social setup.

Strategies for Lifelong Learning

Even then, some simple strategies were recommended by a small expert group consisting learned workers and personnel working in the field of education in general and adult and continuing education, in particular, invited for providing their valuable suggestions. Some litteratures were also consulted for this purpose to accumulated better suggestions regarding functioning of lifelong learning process and concerned operational strategies. Accordingly, the following provisions are considered as possible to be made to ensure lifelong learning with sharing and shouldering the responsibilities with joint efforts of individuals, government and non-government organizations interested and working in this challenging field:

(i) Use of available media based resources including mass and multimedia as well as electronic media besides print and other traditional one, while ensuring the accessibility of such resources for one and all irrespective of locality concerned. Even in these days, it was observed that in city and town areas some of such facilities are available though at higher charges but in village and remote areas, such facilities are rarely available. This strategy may be termed as formation of media based resource strategy.

(ii) Use of public library based reading material resources may also be facilitated to make available easily in all cities and townships as well as in the rural sectors. For this purpose, community centre and other resource centres may be provided with enriched facilities where learners may join at no or nominal charges to find out and avail the reading materials according to their own needs. This may be termed as reading and learning resource based strategy.

(iii) For ensuring lifelong learning, motivation for enhancement of self-learning habit is considered as essential and therefore, strategies capable enough to provide with intrinsic motivation to the learners may be used which may be initiated with some minimum extrinsic motivational strategies and slowly be culminated into the intrinsic one. For example, in-service education and training in different technical and professional fields may also function as a good tool to function as a strategy to enhance intrinsic motivation during service or self-employment period but is required to be associated with some extrinsic and physical attainment etc. at basic level till formation of 'learning habit' very much needed to initiate the process of motivation. This is known as motivation based strategy.

(iv) Vibrant Quadruple partnership was suggested along with Curriculum Reforms, Scholarship, Netwoks, Micro Enterprises and Managerial Reforms by Oduaran (2003) to bring together the government, corporations, employers, labour unions, institutions of learning, non-governmental organizations and civil society for the purpose of agreeing on a collective strategy for which joint training programmes are required to be worked out with governmental responsibility to coordinate the supply of lifelong learning activities and having provision of regular appraisal and evaluation. For ensuring hand-on-experiences, curriculum reformation was suggested along with proper networking to reduce the scholarship gap in terms of communication, collaboration and cooperation. Enhancing and facilitating the participation of citizens in micro-enterprises was suggested with strengthened managerial skills among personnel to enable them to comprehend the intricacies and effects of globalization.

Conclusion

From above discussion, it is obvious that need of lifelong learning is not only basically required for the Neo-literates but professionals and skilled personnel too and thus it may be taken as granted that government may take care to initiate as well as to coordinate efforts of non-governmental and other organizations and individuals to ensure accessibility of different learning modes and resource bases available and may be made available, easily. With the advent of globalization in one hand and right to education in the other, some strategies are also required to be implemented at national as well as at state and regional levels. Let us make a hope that we may try to follow the African Model of lifelong learning as suggested by Oduaran (2003) and prepared to reposition Africa for globalization through lifelong learning and called lifelong learning discourse model which may outline and explain the contradiction and weakness in Africa's socio-political and economic policies and programmes. For this, a situated lifelong learning curriculum was recommended to conceptualize and address the dominant disruptive circumstances of concerned region including problems of environmental degradation, occupational dislocation arising from the destruction of source of income, unemployment and human misery within environments or even it may focus upon the problems of HIV/AIDS or one related with cultivation of genuine democratic practices, conflicts, resolution and alleviation of poverty, illiteracy, lack of awareness and consciousness among common mass etc.

Discourse or dialogue was given much significance in this model which may be unilateral between government and people of the region or country or even bi- or multilateral in nature. He said that for weal or for woe, there have been gaps in this discussion but this is good for such gaps could be vital for furthering the desirable debate.

So, such model may be eventually be effective for a developing country like India, if practiced to formulate and formalize properly and surely with association of various individuals and organizations.

References

1. Buwa, S.K. (2009) Lifelong Education—Challenges and Opportunities, *Proudha Shiksha*, Vol. 53, Number 1, August, 2009, Indian Adult Education Association, Indraprastha Estate, New Delhi.
2. Kintzer, F.C. (1997) Articulation and Transfer: Critical Contributions to Lifelong Learning, in Hatton, M.J. (ed.) *Lifelong Learning: Policies, Practices and Programmes*, Toronto, School of Media Studies, Humber College.
3. Oduaran, A.B. (2000) Globalization and Lifelong Education: Reflection on Some Challenges for Africa, *International Journal of Lifelong Education*, Vol. XIX, No.3, May-June.

4. Oduaran, A. (2003) Order Out of Chaos: Repositioning Africa for Globalization through Lifelong Learning, *International Journal of Adult and Lifelong Education*, Vol. I., No. 1, January-June, International Institute of Adult and Lifelong Education, New Delhi.
5. UNESCO (1976) 'Recommendations on the Development of Adult Education', Nairobi General Conference, October-November, Paris, United Nations Education, Science and Cultural Organization (UNESCO).

5 Functional Literacy

Asha Patil

India has a long tradition of literacy campaign. Mahatma Gandhi and Tagore, while fighting for independence, realized the importance of literacy. They saw literacy as a tool of liberation from ignorance and poverty. Literacy programme in India has gone through various phases. Literacy campaigns have transitioned from the dictionary definition of the 'ability to read and write' to that of continuing education for adults all through their lives. Mere recognition of letters is not sufficient in today's world to face the economic challenges for social development. Literacy is the first step as it opens the doors for further education, self-development and overall national development too, In today's cutthroat competitive world; there is no scope of growth for an illiterate person. Literacy is crucial for his survival.

Literacy has become a global phenomenon as all the countries have recognized the importance of literacy and its positive implications. Literacy is mandatory in the development of democracy, economic development, alleviation of poverty, etc. Hence, the adult illiterates need to acquire not only the skills of reading and writing, but the functional literacy too. This refers to acquiring practical skills that are basic to the improvement of the quality of life. It is in this context we have to understand the concept of functional literacy and its development in India.

Evolution of the Concept of Functional Literacy: Global Scenario

The First World Conference on Adult Education was organized by UNESCO in Denmark in 1949. It discussed role of adult education in the development of society, polity and economy. The conference stated that, "adult education has the aim to meet the adults' needs and aspirations in their full variety. According to this functional perspective, it neither starts from a previously established programme, nor from the division of knowledge with separate subject matters, but from concrete situations, present problems to which the interested parties themselves must find solution."

William Gray in 1956 defined functional literacy which was widely accepted. He said, 'a person is functionally literate when he has acquired the knowledge and skills in reading and writing, which enables him to engage in all those activities in which literacy is normally assumed in his culture or group.'

The Second World Conference on Adult Education was held in Canada in 1960. In this Conference, once again the major stress was given on the importance of linking adult education to productive activities, work and overall development of a person, which subsequently results in national development.

The World Conference of Ministers of Education on 'Eradication of Illiteracy' was held in Tehran in 1965. This was a milestone in adult education. This conference discussed in detail the linkage of literacy with socio-economic progress. The definition of functional literacy was widened. Functional component of literacy was broadened. It says, 'adult literacy, an essential element in general development, must be linked to economic and social priorities and to present and future needs for labour.'

The report of the conference, in its conclusion, states that '....rather than an end in itself, functional literacy should be regarded as a way of preparing man for a social, civic and economic role that goes far beyond the limits of rudimentary literacy training consisting merely of the teaching of reading and writing. The very process of learning to read and write should be made an opportunity for acquiring information that can immediately be used to improve living standards; reading and writing should lead not only to elementary general knowledge but to training for work, increased productivity, a greater participation in civic life and a better understanding of the surrounding world, and should ultimately open the way to basic human culture.'

Indian Scenario

These World Conferences left a deep impact on the Indian scene of Adult Education. This influenced the thought process of policy planners in this regard.

The Planning Commission organised the Conference of State Education Ministers in June 1965. The Conference discussed various aspects of development. It was noted that, 'one of the reasons for the failure of many development schemes like agricultural production, family planning, cooperatives, Panchayati Raj Institutions was due to the lack of functional literacy among the majority of the population in rural areas.' Hence, it was decided to emphasize on functional approach. This is reflected in the Fourth Five Year Plan as well.

Fourth Five Year Plan

In earlier plans the adult education was considered as a Social Education. It was in the Fourth Five Year Plan, first time, the literacy was looked from its functional perspective. The Fourth Five Year Plan recognized how illiteracy is becoming an obstacle in the way of development—both economic as well as social. Hence, it was decided to make adult literacy more functional in character and be linked to the work and life of the people. Meanwhile, Education Commission, formed under the chairpersonship of Dr. D.S. Kothari, submitted its report. The Kothari Commission Report states that, '...we do not equate literacy with the mere ability to read and write. Literacy, if it is to be worthwhile, must be functional. It should enable the literate not only to acquire sufficient mastery over the tools of literacy but also to acquire relevant knowledge which will enable him to pursue his own interests and ends.'

During this period, Experimental World Literacy Programme was designed by the UNESCO. This provided an opportunity to India to shift from 3Rs to functional literacy. Based on this ideology, the Government of India launched a programme where this concept of functional literacy was translated into action. This programme was known as 'Farmers Training and Functional Literacy Project (FTFLP).' This programme was launched in 1968. This was the Government's first programme in the area of functional literacy, which became a milestone in the field of Adult Education. It was the first time that the three central ministries, namely —Agriculture, Information and Broadcasting, and Education— coordinated their efforts for imparting functional literacy to farmers. It was an integrated approach undertaken for the purpose of rural development. In this project, the functional literacy component was seen from different perspectives—not mere literacy but as a method of training for developmental purposes. The aim of this Project was to improve the efficiency of the farmers for increasing agricultural production in the districts covered under the High Yielding Varieties Programme. The project had three components, namely:

(i) Farmer's training,
(ii) Functional literacy, and
(iii) Farm broadcasting.

For the implementation of these three major components, a variety of activities were organized, e.g. training of farmers, organizing Charcha Mandals, field visits, daily broadcasting for half an hour on All India Radio, imparting reading and writing skills, etc. Separate learning material was prepared for this Project. A book titled '*Kisan Saksharata: Pehali Pustak*' in Hindi was prepared. This was a need based primer. A separate guideline was prepared for teachers, which contained methodology of using the book and correlating agricultural practices with literacy skills.

The literacy component was interwoven in this Project. The purpose of putting this literacy component was to enable the farmers to:

(i) Read and understand the labels written on fertilizer bags;

(ii) Fill up loan application forms, input cards;

(iii) Keep simple account of operations; and

(iv) Read and make use of simple extension bulletins, rural newspapers, etc.

Financial Support

As stated earlier, this Project was a joint venture of three ministries. It received funds from Agriculture Ministry for the farmer's training, Ministry of Education for functional literacy and the Ministry of Information and Broadcasting for farm broadcasting. In addition, the Project also received funding from UNDP, FAO and UNESCO. The functional literacy programme helped the illiterate farmers not only in acquiring literacy in terms of reading and writing skills but also the agricultural knowledge for immediate use in their day-to-day work.

Organizational Structure and Implementation Strategies

The Government of India worked out a separate organizational structure for FTFL Project. From each State, three High Yielding Production Districts were selected. Each district was sanctioned to establish a maximum of 60 centres.

Following human resources were provided to each district :

Project Officer (one) — District level

↓

↓

Part-time Supervisors (six) or — District level
Full-time Supervisors (two)

↓

↓

Instructors (sixty) — Village level

At the district level, one full-time Project Officer was appointed. He was assisted by either six part-time supervisors, who in turn were responsible for ten centres each or two full-time supervisors who were responsible for 30 centres each. Each centre was run by an instructor. The ratio of instructor to learners was 1:30. The part-time supervisors were paid Rs. 50 per month and the instructors were paid Rs. 30 per month.

Duration

The total duration was for one year. It was implemented in two phases—each phase of six months. Each phase was spread over 150 hours of effective teaching. The centres worked daily for an average of one and half hour, throughout the week.

Teaching-Learning Material

A need-based survey was conducted in a few sample districts, where the programme was proposed to be implemented. The main objective was to find out the needs and requirements of farmers cultivating the High Yielding Varieties of crops and applying modern methods and practices with regard to those crops. Based on this survey and inputs from technical, professional and knowledgeable personnel from the field, teaching-learning material was prepared. The materials were region specific and problem oriented.

The Directorate of Adult Education, Ministry of Education and Culture, New Delhi prepared the first book in Hindi titled '*Kisan Saksharta: Paheli Pustak*'. This contained 18 lessons, to be taught within six months duration. Analytic-Synthetic method was followed in lesson preparation. Along with this book other materials such as teacher's guides and other supplementary reading materials were also produced. This material was prepared as prototype and was adapted in other states as per their social, cultural, agricultural and linguistic needs. More than 70 teaching-learning materials in various Indian languages were produced.

Methodology

The curriculum was transacted through various methods, namely oral instruction, discussions, demonstration, practical training and through audio-visuals. The Government of India circulated a detailed guideline of this Project to all the states and requested to follow them.

Evaluation

Initially the pilot Project was implemented only in three districts in 1968. Then it was expanded and implemented in 144 districts of different states of India. It was implemented till 1977. During the Fourth Plan nearly 30 lakh farmers joined the functional literacy classes. The Project was evaluated by national and international agencies at different levels. The Directorate of Adult Education conducted a pilot evaluation study in 1970. The major finding of this study was that functional literacy has contributed a lot in increasing the agricultural production. Drop-out rate was only 17.5 per cent.

Another Evaluation Study conducted in 1977 shows that

- Funds provided at the district level were inadequate.
- Co-ordination among the three departments, namely Agriculture, Education and Information, was not satisfactory.
- Monitoring and supervision did not take place as expected in the project. At many places the supervision was almost non-existent.
- Training, a very important aspect of any successful programme, was neglected. It was further observed that a substantial number of functionaries working at grassroots level did not receive any training.
- Though a separate teaching-learning material was prepared, but it was found that at many places traditional teaching-learning materials were used. Hence, the functionality component was missing.
- In many districts, follow-up programmes for the neo-literates were found to be weak and inefficient.

Limitations

The beneficiaries were mainly from relatively well-off and enterprising farmers. In addition to this they were ready to experiment and introduce new agricultural practices. As a result the programme could not reach to the large masses of the illiterate farmers. The grassroots farmers such as the marginalized ones, the exploited and the landless agriculture workers were totally deprived of the benefits of this programme.

Learning Experiences

Though there were certain limitations, the programme was a great success. There was a shift in emphasis from the traditional 3Rs concept of literacy to the new 3Fs programme:

- Functional literacy,
- Food production, and
- Family welfare.

This also gave an experience of integrating inter-departmental development programmes. This experiment taught us the importance of monitoring, which could strengthen the programme. This resulted in a great learning experience for all the government as well as the beneficiaries.

Other Efforts

Apart from this FTLT Project, many other programmes, during 1970s, introduced the concept of functionality. Following are a few of them—

Functional Literacy for Adult Women

This was an important step taken by the Government of India. It was introduced during 1975-76. In 1977, it was implemented in 23 States/Union Territories. The main aim of this programme was to impart non-formal education using functional literacy as the means, to accelerate participation of adult women in the developmental efforts of the community, to bring about attitudinal changes among women which would enable them to play their role as citizens.

Target Group

The focus was on the adult women from the age group of 15 to 45 years.

Implementation Strategy

This was a joint venture organized by the Department of Education and Social Welfare. For implementation of this programme, experimental ICDS project areas were selected. The Anganwadi workers of Integrated Child Development Services worked as instructors for the functional literacy classes. These Anganwadi workers were paid Rs. 50 per month as honorarium for this literacy work. This was an additional honorarium other than their regular honorarium for Anganwadi work.

The curriculum of this functional literacy class included components on various issues such as health and hygiene, food and nutrition, home management and child care, civic and vocational education. In addition to these programmes, many other positive things happened which helped to carry the literacy programme forward, e.g. in 1969, National Board of Adult Education was established. Establishment of Directorate of Adult Education took place in 1971. Non-formal education programmes also emerged during this period.

Central Advisory Board of Education (CABE)

As early as 1939, the CABE appointed a committee of adult education. This committee met several times and had given many recommendations on adult education.

A meeting of Central Advisory Board of Education was held in November 1974. To improve adult literacy programme, it has given many recommendations. Some of the important recommendations were:

- The exclusive emphasis on formal system of education should be given up and large element of non-formal education should be introduced within the system.
- Multiple entry and programmes of part-time and correspondence education should be developed.
- Functional literacy programme should be planned in relation to various developmental schemes appropriate in rural and urban situations.

The above discussion shows that lots of efforts were made to integrate adult education with a number of developmental programmes during Fifth and Sixth Five Year Plans.

Other Efforts

The Directorate of Adult Education identified 65 schemes/ programmes in different departments of Government of India. For identification/selection the criterion was: each of these schemes had substantial component of non-formal education. The significant schemes included Krishi Vigyan Kendra, Workers Education Programme, Nehru Yuvak Kendra, Satellite Instructional Television Experiment, Shramik Vidyapeeth, Rural Welfare Extension, Family and Child Welfare Project, etc.

The Krishi Vigyan Kendras were concerned with technical literacy. They aimed at imparting education through work experience to rural youth in agriculture and allied subjects.

The Shramik Vidyapeeths were established to serve the industrial workers of urban area. The main objective was to provide integrated education and vocational training to different categories of urban industrial workers. It was intended to improve their professional competency, which will in-turn enrich their lives.

Fifth Five Year Plan

The Plan proposed to extend and expand the Farmers' Functional Literacy Project. This included starting a network of village and block libraries to support the programme of adult education and functional literacy. It was also planned to promote extension education for occupational adjustment and personal development through the universities. For the first time it was decided to involve educational institutions into the programme of adult education through the National Service Scheme (NSS). At many places, the college students worked as adult educators/instructors.

Sixth Five Year Plan

The Sixth Five Year Plan gave a very high priority to Adult Education. The total budget allocated for adult education increased from Rs. 18 crores in the Fifth Five Year Plan to Rs. 200 crores in the Sixth Plan. It emphasized on agricultural and rural development.

Shift in the Concept of Adult Education

Two significant events took place in early 1970s. The first was Paulo Freire's articles on conscientization, which gave a new dimension to this concept of adult education. The second event was International Symposium on Literacy which was held in Persepolis in 1975.

According to Freire, adult education should create an awareness amongst the adult learners, which should lead to action and change. He emphasized on dialogue and participation of learners in learning process. According to him, adult education should not become just the process of learning only 3Rs that is learning the skills of reading, writing and arithmetic but should contribute to the liberation of man and to his full development.

The concept of functionality widened, elaborated in the Declaration of Persepolis. It included all dimensions of human development—political, economic, social and cultural. It states that, "just as development is not only economic growth, so, literacy must aim above all to arouse in the individual a critical awareness of social reality and to enable him or her to understand, master and transform his or her destiny."

Influence on Indian Adult Education Programme

The above two ideas influenced the Indian adult education concept. Till 1977, adult education was mainly confined to functionality component only. From 1978 and onwards, component of liberation was also included in the adult education programme. This led to the formulation of National Adult Education Programme (NAEP).

National Adult Education Programme (NAEP)

One of the most ambitious and revolutionary Adult Education Programme was launched on October 2, 1978. For the first time in the history of India, adult education was put on the educational agenda of the nation. This was the first really serious attempt to meet the challenge head-on.

- Adult Education was defined as literacy, functionality and conscientization (awareness).
- Adult literacy that is 3Rs was the core component of this programme.
- Functionality included teaching practical skills to improve productivity.
- The fourth and the most important component was conscientization.

It was decided to concentrate on poor and the disadvantaged—Scheduled Tribes, Scheduled Castes, and women, and make them literate so that they can contribute in development process. It concentrated on the productive age group of 15-35 years.

Programme Pattern

In the initial phase that is 1978-80, the duration of the programme was for 300-500 hours spread over ten months.

In 1980, the programme was reviewed. Based on this review, it was decided to implement this programme in three stages:

First stage	—	Basic Literacy	—	300-350 hours
Second stage	—	Follow-up	—	150 hours
Third stage	—	Follow-up	—	100 hours

The total duration of the programme was of three years.

During first year emphasis was given on imparting basic literacy skills. It included: 3Rs, knowledge about health, family life, vocations related to the learners' needs and background and laws relevant for family life.

The second and third year was for reinforcement of literacy and improvement in vocational skills.

Functionality was regarded as an essential component of NAEP. This was included to enable the learners to function in a better and effective way, both in their personal life and work situations. It was also decided to increase their professional skills by upgrading them. This could help them to improve their economic conditions.

Meanwhile, the duration of the programme was reduced from three years to two years.

Organizational Structure of NAEP

The NAEP was found to be the most sophisticated planning exercise. It created a potentially effective infrastructure to guide, administer and deliver adult education services to the people.

A network of organizations came into existence during the two years of NAEP (1978-80). This included establishment of National Board of Adult Education and Directorate of Adult Education. These institutions were established at the central/ national level. State Resource Centres (SRCs) were also established in many states. The main roles of the SRCs include production of need-based instructional materials in regional and sub-regional languages/dialects for learners and teachers, provide training to different functionaries at various levels, documentation and research.

For the implementation of NAEP, district level structure was established. Full-fledged District Adult Education Offices were established at the district level. This included one District Adult Education Officer, one Project Officer, Assistant Project Officers (APO) and Supervisors. The number of APOs and the supervisors was dependent on the number of adult education centres sanctioned. The APOs along with the supervisors monitored the programme at the grassroots level. Each adult education centre had one instructor for a maximum of 30 learners.

Evaluation of NAEP

The NAEP was evaluated by many agencies. The findings include:

- The progress and performance of NAEP was very uneven. It was largely based upon the nature of participation of non-governmental organizations in the implementation process.
- The NAEP was envisaged as the first mass programme, after independence, for tackling the problem of illiteracy. But in practice it remained a traditional centre-based programme which was honorarium based, hierarchical, government funded and government controlled.
- NAEP became a typical bureaucratic programme which was also one of the hindrances in its implementation.
- Among the three instructional functions, in the course of operationalization, literacy (3Rs) did the best. Functionality remained at the back. NAEP though emphasized on functionality and social awareness, in

reality it largely confined to teaching rudimentary literacy skills only. Concretization and critical awareness was not visible either in learners or their teachers.

- Structures did get established, but functions were not always performed effectively.
- Decentralization in the production of materials did not work. Follow-up programme almost did not exist.

However, the legacy of poor implementation continued during 1980-1985.

Change from NAEP to AEP

The NAEP was reviewed by a specially established national committee. Based on its recommendations, a few changes were made in NAEP and a new programme, namely Adult Education Programme (AEP) was introduced in 1980. This was at the 16 number of 20-point programme for the removal of poverty (introduced by the then Prime Minister Mrs. Indira Gandhi).

The target group, content, infrastructure established under NAEP remained the same.

Important changes included:

- The burden of funding and implementation was divided between the centre and the states.
- Involvement of students increased.
- Duration of the programme increased from ten months to three years. It was decided to implement this programme in three phases, namely:

  Phase I—300 to 350 hours spread over one year.

  This included basic literacy, general education with emphasis on health and family planning, functional programme relating to learners vocations, and familiarity with laws and policies affecting the learners.

Phase II—150 hours spread over a year.

To reinforce literacy skills and its use in daily life. This phase included appreciation of science in relation to one's environment, components of geography, history and country's cultural heritage, etc. It was also decided to emphasise on vocational skills.

Phase III—100 hours spread over one year.

To achieve reasonable degree of self-reliance in literacy and functionality and better appreciation of the scope and value of science.

This stage emphasized on strengthening of the ability of learners to discuss important problems faced by the individuals, family and the community and take organized action for their betterment.

Linkages with Other Development Programmes and Agencies

In late 1980s, an important decision of establishment of linkages with other development agencies and programmes was taken up. It was also decided to introduce literacy in all labour welfare programmes. Along with literacy, a functionality component was also introduced. This included skill development programmes. Accordingly, a number of programmes were implemented. A few of them were as follows—

1. *Rural Functional Literacy Project* (RFLP)

The scheme of Farmers' Functional Literacy, the Kisan Saksharta Yojana and Non-formal education for the age group of 15-25 were merged in 1978. They were renamed as Rural Functional Literacy Project. For this, the target group was of 15-35 age. All over the country, 452 projects were sanctioned and implemented. Under this project, about 79,000 centres were working till the end of December 1984.

2. *Adult Education through Students and Youth*

The University Grants Commission (UGC) introduced extension as a third dimension in higher education system. It realized the need for carrying knowledge and skills to the people in all walks of life. It was accepted to serve for the community. Hence, it established Centres/Departments of Adult and Continuing Education in the various universities. Under the 20-point programme of Government of India, it involved lakhs of students in adult education programme. They mainly worked as instructors. UGC had given special funds for implementation of this programme.

3. *Nehru Yuvak Kendras*

There were thousands of youth who were not a part of higher education but were willing to serve for the welfare of the community. Their involvement in adult education programme was done through Nehru Yuvak Kendras (NYK).

During 1984, 230 Nehru Yuvak Kendras were provided funds for organizing Adult Education Programme through National Service Volunteers (NSVs). NYK organized about 2500 centres.

4. *Functional Literacy for Adult Women*

This was a special programme to improve the women's literacy rate. This was introduced into the ICDS (Integrated Child Development Services). It aimed at imparting literacy skills to rural and urban women, Scheduled Tribes and Scheduled Castes. It started on the eve of International Women's Year, 1975. It was implemented through the Ministry of Social Welfare. During 1984, about 7800 ICDS areas were having the functional literacy courses.

Seventh Five Year Plan

At the global level, emphasis has shifted towards Human Resource Development (HRD). The focus was on raising actual potential productivity of the population. Also literacy as a central variable in HRD became incorporated into World Bank discourse in 1980.

This change in the shift of literacy definition from development to HRD had a great impact on Indian Adult Education Programme. This reflected in the Seventh Five Year Plan (1985-1990). It stated the need for strengthening the programme for training in functional skills relevant to economic activities. To cover the huge target of illiterates, it was decided to adopt a strategy of mass movement.

In the Seventh Plan it was decided to make adult education as a 'mass programme'. For this a mass approach was proposed. It included mobilization of educated men and women to involve for eradication of illiteracy. It was decided to have a well-planned literacy campaign in which each one who is participating will be assigned a definite responsibility. It was decided to design literacy courses for organized and unorganized sectors separately. It was also decided to involve senior citizens, retired personnel, housewives, ex-serviceman, the students in secondary schools and from higher education institutions as well.

During this plan period, three important events took place, namely:

- Implementation of Mass Programme of Functional Literacy (MPFL).
- Declaration of National Policy on Education (NPE), 1986 followed by Programme of Action (PoA), 1992.
- Establishment of National Literacy Mission (NLM), 1988.

Mass Programme of Functional Literacy (MPFL)

The MPFL was launched on May 1, 1986. This was the first time in the history of adult education that on a large scale college youth were involved in the eradication of illiteracy. During the first year, more than two lakh of NSS students and one lakh non-NSS students from different universities and colleges were involved. The student volunteers taught two to five adult illiterates. At many places it was 'each one teach one' approach where one student taught one adult illiterate. The duration was 150 hours spread over six months. The students taught according to their convenient timings – during Diwali, Christmas and summer vacations as well. The primers were prepared by State Resource Centres and given free of cost to the learners. Students, who participated in this programme, were given thorough training. This included importance of education, how to motivate adult learners, adult psychology, various methods of teaching adults and how to maintain records, etc. At the end of 150 hours of teaching, the learners were evaluated by giving them a literacy test.

National Policy on Education (NPE)

The NPE was declared in 1986. Realizing the importance of literacy, the NPE envisaged that 'adult education would be a means for the end of reducing economic, social and gender disparities and nation as a whole would assume the responsibility for providing resource support.'

Since 1989, UNESCO has been in the process of yet again re-defining its views of literacy in the line with the concept of functional illiteracy which, in addition to a lack of ability in reading, writing and arithmetic, also includes practical skills as well as technological and technical illiteracy. This shift in the definition of functional literacy had impact on framing our new literacy programmes.

The Programme of Action (1992) recommended that 'emphasis in adult education programme should be on skill development and creation of awareness among the learners of the national goals, of development programmes, and for liberation from oppression.'

National Literacy Mission (NLM)

The National Literacy Mission was launched in 1988. It was one of the five Technology Missions. It constitutes a major landmark to combat the evil of illiteracy. NLM aimed at imparting functional literacy to 100 million non-literate persons in the 15-35 age groups by the end of 1997. NLM is based on the premise that literacy is an indispensable component of human resource development. Literacy is an essential tool for communication and learning, for acquiring and sharing of knowledge and information.

Besides achieving functional literacy, NLM was entrusted with other objectives like:

(i) Inculcating a critical consciousness about causes of deprivation and organizing neo-literates for ameliorating their condition through participation in development;

(ii) Imparting skills to improve their socio-economic condition and general well-being; and

(iii) Imbibing values of national integration, conservation of environment, women's equality, observation of small family norms and inculcation of scientific temper.

It was a challenge to NLM to reach its target that is making over 100 million illiterates literate. The constant flow of the un-enrolled and dropouts from the primary education then become adult illiterates, they keep up a daunting size of the target for NLM. The other challenges include multifarious socio-economic deprivations and discriminations along gender, social and regional lines. Illiteracy, especially the size of illiterate population in India, has always a challenge to national conscience. This is because literacy has been considered as indispensable for both personal and national development and well-being. In the last few years, many innovations took place in respect of literacy strategies, methods and contents. There have also been many innovations in combining literacy with life and livelihood skills, in improving the avenues of continuing education and bringing out convergence of different departments and agencies within and outside government to improve the social and economic conditions of the neo-literates and beneficiaries of continuing education programme.

To achieve the goal of imparting functional literacy, NLM adopted mission mode. It opted for Total Literacy Campaign (TLC). Like the NAEP, the TLC is a development oriented adult literacy programme. In most of the districts, it was implemented in the form of a mass movement. It mobilized a large number of literate individuals in a specific geographic area to impart literacy to all the illiterate adults. The essence of the campaign was to generate a positive demand for learning as a tool for social change. For implementation of TLC, the NLM established three-tired structure. At the national and state leveis, National and State Literacy Mission Authority provided the support and direction to the campaign.

At the district level, an autonomous organization called Zilla Saksharta Samiti (ZSS) was registered. The ZSS constituted a mix of government officials, elected political leaders, NGOs and representatives of mass organizations, including women's organizations. In most districts, the collector was the chairperson of the ZSS. The innovating aspect of the TLC model was it emphasized on creation of a favourable environment for literacy. The environment building phase included use of traditional folk media forms and *kala jathas*. Conventional media like the electronic media, posters, banners, hoardings and other non-conventional forms such as *pada yatras, prabhat pheris* were used with great effect.

The SRCs prepared primers based on Improved Pace and Content of Learning (IPCL). These primers had prescribed levels of 3Rs. After completion of three primers the learners were expected to achieve following levels:

Reading

(a) Reading aloud with normal accent simple passages on topics related to the interest of the learners at a speed of 30 words per minute,

(b) Reading silently small paragraphs in simple language at a speed of 35 words per minute,

(c) Reading with understanding road signs, posters, simple instructions and newspapers for neo-literates, etc., and

(d) Ability to follow simple written messages relating to one's working and living environment.

Writing

(a) Copy with understanding at a speed of seven words per minute,
(b) Taking dictation at a speed of five words per minute,
(c) Writing with proper spacing and alignment, and
(d) Writing independently short letters and applications and forms of day-to-day use to the learners.

Numeracy

(a) To read and write 1-100 numerals,
(b) Doing simple calculations without fractions involving addition, subtraction up to three digits and multiplication and division by two digits, and
(c) Working knowledge of metric units of weights, measures, currency, distance and area and units of time.

The instruction period was of 200 hours spread over a period of six to twelve months. It is not clear how the total period required for acquisition of the prescribed levels of 3Rs has been determined. There is no research evidence to support the implicit assumption that the TLC curriculum can be acquired within the stipulated time-period. Volunteer Teachers (VTs) who were taught adult illiterates were trained. In most of the districts, secondary school students and college students worked as Volunteer Teachers.

Characteristics of TLC

The main characteristics of TLC include a strong political will, total and spontaneous participation of the administrative machinery. In addition to this, the state governments took keen interest in this mass campaign, people's participation from all walks of life helped to achieve high success to attain the literacy goal in a short time and at a small cost.

Evaluation

Despite the goal of NLM was to impart functional literacy, the evaluation of TLC districts was on the basis of achievements by learners in 3Rs only. It did not go beyond that. The evaluation guidelines did not specifically mention about other elements of functional literacy including 'skill improvement'. The evaluation of learners' performance which has emphasized in the TLC, measures only the achievement in 3Rs. Evaluation of the other elements of functional literacy did not receive any systematic attention. Most literacy campaigns have generally been dominated by the officials of the district administration despite the establishment of committees with representation of non-officials and the public. The Central Government has retained its control over the policy direction and basic parameters of literacy campaigns, namely training, curriculum, evaluation, etc.

Post Literacy Programme (PLP)

A large number of neo-literates achieved basic literacy through TLC. Without a meaningful Post Literacy Programme, many of these might have relapsed into illiteracy. The literacy achieved through TLC was very fragile, hence, the need for post literacy.

The Post Literacy Programme was based on the following major objectives:

1. Remediation
   - those not covered by TLC to be made literate
   - those below minimum level of learning to be enabled to achieve it.
2. Continuation
   - stabilization, reinforcement and upgradation of learning.
3. Application
   - to living and working conditions.

4. Communalization
   - group action for participation in development process.
5. Skill training
   - life skills, communication skills, vocational skills.

The NLM has de-linked post literacy from continuing education and has been given a separate status. However, retention of literacy after the literacy campaigns is a neglected area of NLM policy. There has been a considerable time-lag between the conceptualization and implementation of PLP. Consequently, many learners have relapsed into illiteracy. Moreover, literacy was not linked with vocational skills.

Scheme of Continuing Education

The NLM had designed a scheme of Continuing Education for neo-literates. This scheme came into force on January 1, 1996, which was later revised in 1999. This scheme replaced the earlier scheme for providing continuing education through the Jan Shikshan Nilayam.

The main objective of the scheme is to institutionalize continuing education for neo-literates. To achieve this, it was decided to establish Continuing Education Centres (CECs). The other objectives of CE scheme include—

- Provision of facilities for retention and reinforcement of literacy skills
- Application of functional literacy for quality of life improvement
- Dissemination of information on development programmes for participation
- Training in vocational skills
- Creation of awareness on national concerns
- Organization of cultural and recreational activities
- Provision of library

The responsibility for the implementation of the scheme rests with Zilla Saksharta Samiti (ZSS). The scheme provides flexibility and freedom to the ZSS for planning and developing CE programmes.

NLM has identified four broad areas, which are also to be implemented through CECs. They are:

- *Equivalency Programmes (EPs)*—alternative education programmes equivalent to existing formal, general or vocational education
- *Skill Development (SD) and Income Generating Programmes (IGPs)*—acquisition or upgradation of vocational skills for income generating activities.
- *Quality of Life Improvement Programmes (QLIPs)*—to equip the learners with essential knowledge, attitudes, values and skills both as individuals and members of the community.
- *Individual Interest Promotion Programmes (IIPPs)*—to provide opportunities for individuals to participate in and learn about their own chosen social, cultural, spiritual, health, physical and artistic interests.

Conclusion

Thus, we see that Adult Literacy in India has come a long way. From the above discussion, we realize that functional literacy has still a long way to go. Unfortunately, the literacy programme is still stuck with the teaching of 3Rs. We have to see that the 3Rs are directly linked with the real life situation. It is high time that efforts should be made to achieve the functional literacy. Otherwise, we would not be able to bring the marginalized strata of society that is adult illiterates (both men and women)—into the mainstream of national development. For this we have to create the need for literacy among the psyche of people. Otherwise the dream of Total Literacy would remain a dream.

References

1. Adiseshaiah, Malcolm (1992) *The Total Literacy Campaign: Strengths and Weaknesses, The Turning Point—Some Thoughts on Adult Education,* Directorate of Adult Education, New Delhi,
2. Bhola, H.S. (2000) Functional Literacy, Workplace Literacy and Technical and Vocational Education: Interfaces and Policy Perspectives, Education for All. *Spotlight on Adult Education,* UNESCO, New Delhi
3. Chatterjee, Bhaskar (2000) 'Strategies for Post Literacy in the Next Decade, Adult Education in India'—Selected Papers, UNESCO, New Delhi,
4. Daswani, C.J. *Changing Concepts and Shifting Goals: Post Literacy and Education.*

ROLE OF MEDIA IN ADULT EDUCATION

6 Role of Media in Social Change

Anjali Pattanaik
Gunum Pattanayak

Development means a change in the society. In the context of our nation when we are more concerned about rural development, as 75 per cent of its population lives in rural villages, emphasis on change in the rural society is a necessity. Development refers to basically, social and economic development, which can be possible through IEC. It is the communication process/media without which no progress is possible. There is a great number of information for the rural development like health and hygiene, agriculture, animal husbandry, adult literacy and entrepreneurship etc. from different sources which need to be transferred to the rural communities through proper transfer mechanism. A big jump from rural communication to satellite communication is a blessing in disguise to the whole mankind. This development in communication is mainly intended to promote human development, which basically means communication that will help to reduce poverty, unemployment and social inequality. It is communication with a social conscience (Gupta, 1999). Thus mass media is a great catalyst in creating awareness among the people about policies and programmes. During the past decade there has been a rapid explosion of media that still remains inaccessible to many of the people in the rural communities. The Indian Readership Survey 2001 (IRS) announced that the reach is 15.8 per cent for radios, 33.3 per cent for press and 49.4 per cent for TV (Ninan, 2001).

Thus in the above context this study is a maiden venture to assess the precise role of media in social change in the rural setting. However, the study sought to achieve the following purposes:

- To study the socio-economic background of the respondents.
- To ascertain the level of exposure to different types of media.
- To ascertain the level of adoption of various developmental information.
- To study different sources of information.
- To draw the opinions of respondents in respect of different social welfare aspects and suggest certain steps towards improvements in media exposure for the rural community.

Design

The present study is an empirical study where an empirical survey was conducted in two villages of Khallikote block of Ganjam district of Orissa state. Two villages Kushudhipa and Manapalli were equidistant from the block headquarters were selected. 150 numbers of respondents (45—Scheduled Caste and 105—General Caste) were selected on the basis of judgement sampling method so as to include agriculturists, beneficiaries of rural development programmes etc. A pre-tested structured interview schedule was used to collect the required information. After compilation the data were analysed by using statistical methods like percentage and correlation of co-efficient.

Result and Discussion

Results of Table 6.1 show that a majority of the samples were taken from the general caste in all the three age groups and only lesser per cent of samples were taken from scheduled caste.

Table 6.1: Distribution of Respondents by their Socio-Economic Status

Variables	*Scheduled Caste*	*General Caste*	*Total*
Age Groups			
20—40 years	23 (15.0%)	67 (45.0%)	90 (60.0%)
40 — 60 years	22 (14.6%)	34 (22.6%)	56 (37.2%)
> 60 years	--	04 (2.6%)	04 (2.6%)
Level of Education			
Illiterate	11 (7.3%)	02 (1.3%)	13 (8.6%)
Primary	17 (11.3%)	11 (7.3%)	28 (18.6%)
Secondary	03 (2.0%)	33 (22.0%)	36 (24.0%)
Higher Secondary	14 (9.3%)	59 (39.3%)	73 (48.6%)
Source of Income			
Cultivation	45 (30.0%)	105 (70.0%)	150 (100.0%)
Cultivation + Service	04 (2.6%)	29 (19.3%)	33 (22.0%)
Cultivation + Other	37 (24.6%)	21 (14.0%)	58 (38.6%)

As far as education of the respondents was concerned it could be found that the level of education of samples of general caste was better than Scheduled Caste, and also the number of illiterates was negligible in both the categories of samples. While looking into the sources of income of the respondents, it could be observed that all the respondents were depending mostly on cultivation as their source of income. Some of the samples from both the categories were also earning income from services and other sources apart from their agricultural sources.

Table 6.2 focuses on the distribution of respondents on the basis of their media exposures. It was found that maximum numbers of respondents in Scheduled Caste were listening to radio whereas 16.6 per cent did not have any such exposure. But, in general caste group majority were exposed to both radio and television, only 10.6 per cent did not have any such exposure.

Table 6.2: Distribution of Respondents in respect of their Media Exposure

Variables	*Scheduled Caste*	*General Caste*	*Total*
Ownership of Radio/TV sets			
Radio	19 (12.6%)	29 (19.3%)	48 (32.0%)
Radio & TV	1 (0.6%)	60 (40.0%)	61 (40.6%)
Nil	25 (16.6%)	16 (10.6%)	41 (27.3%)
Newspaper Readers			
Regular Readers	21 (14.0%)	79 (52.6%)	100 (66.6%)
Occasional Readers	02 (01.3%)	10 (06.6%)	12 (8.0%)
Preference for Different Programmes in TV			
Educative	—	17 (11.3%)	17 (11.3%)
Informative	23 (15.3%)	78 (52.0%)	101 (67.3%)
Entertaining	39 (26.0%)	105 (70.0%)	144 (96.0%)
Others	16 (10.6%)	20 (13.3%)	36 (24.0%)
Development Programmes			
IRDP	17 (11.3%)	07 (4.6%)	24 (15.9%)
TRYSEM	5 (3.3%)	5 (3.3%)	10 (6.6%)
Co-operative Loan	20 (13.3%)	51 (34.0%)	71 (47.3%)
Other	45 (30.0%)	105 (70.0%)	150 (100%)

It was found that newspapers had already found their way into the area of study. Three daily newspapers, namely "The Samaj", "The Prajatantra" and "The Dharitri" were in circulation. It is evident from the table that around 50 per cent of respondents of both the group were reading newspaper regularly whereas the number of occasional readers was few. So far as their preference for different programmes in radio and television were concerned, it could be observed that only in general caste group 11.3 per cent of respondents preferred educative programmes whereas maximum number of respondents from both the groups liked entertaining programmes followed by informative programmes.

Observation of exposure to developmental programmes shows that maximum samples of Scheduled Caste group as well as general caste group were assisted by cooperative loan followed by IRDP (Integrated Rural Development Programme). A small number of respondents of both the categories were benefited by the TRYSEM programme. There were some other developmental schemes apart from co-operative loan, IRDP and TRYSEM programmes, which were also providing benefits to all the respondents.

Table 6.3 focus on the adoption practices of better inputs in agriculture. As is evident from the table almost all the samples from both the target groups had adopted the improved agricultural practices such as HYV seeds, fertilizers, pesticides, tractors and pump sets. So far as adoption of family planning measures was concerned it has been found that maximum number of samples from both the groups had adopted sterilization method followed by adoption of loop and copper-T. Other measures such as Nirodh and Pills had been adopted by very few samples of both the groups whereas in Scheduled Caste group herbs were also used as measures of family planning.

Table 6.3: Distribution of Respondents on the basis of their Adoption Practices

Variables	*Scheduled Caste*	*General Caste*	*Total*
Better Inputs in Agriculture			
HYV Seeds	45 (30.0%)	105 (70.0%)	150 (100%)
Fertilizers & Pesticides	45 (30.0%)	105 (70.0%)	150 (100%)
Tractors/Pump sets	15 (10.0%)	47 (31.3%)	62 (41.3%)
All of the above	5 (3.3%)	18 (12.0%)	23 (15.3%)
Family Planning Measures			
Sterilization	20 (13.3%)	60 (40.0%)	80 (53.3%)
Nirodh	--	16 (10.0%)	16 (10.0%)
Pills	10 (6.6%)	9 (26.0%)	19 (32.6%)
Loop/Copper-T	5 (4.0%)	20 (13.3%)	25 (17.3%)
Herbs	10 (6.6%)	--	10 (6.6%)

Table 6.4 depicts the sources of information of the respondents regarding various aspects. As is evident from the table that most

of the respondents were getting information regarding different rural development programmes from government sources, mass media like radio/television and print media, but all the samples were relying more on their neighbours/villagers for information. So far as information regarding the political activities was concerned it was found that maximum number of samples were getting such information from radio followed by newspapers. The role of opinion leader was found better in providing information as compared to television.

Table 6.4: Sources of Information of the Respondents about Various Aspects of Activities

Aspects of Activities	*Scheduled Caste*	*General Caste*	*Total*
Rural Development Programmes			
Radio/TV	27 (18.0%)	81 (54.0%)	108 (72%)
Government Officers	43 (28.6%)	92 (61.3%)	135 (89.9%)
Newspaper	23 (15.3%)	89 (59.3%)	112 (74.6%)
Other Villagers	45 (30.0%)	105 (70.0%)	150 (100%)
Political Activities			
Radio	24 (16.0%)	91 (60.6%)	115 (76.6%)
TV	9 (6.0%)	43 (28.6%)	52 (34.0%)
Newspaper	17 (11.3%)	82 (54.6%)	99 (66.0%)
Opinion Leader	33 (22.0%)	39 (52.6%)	72 (74.6%)
Health & Sanitation			
Radio/TV	18 (12.0%)	55 (36.6%)	73 (48.6%)
Newspaper	17 (11.3%)	24 (16.0%)	41 (27.3%)
Health Visitor	29 (19.3%)	86 (57.3%)	115 (76.6%)
Others	16 (10.6%)	24 (16.0%)	40 (26.6%)
Family Planning Measures			
Government Campaign	31 (20.6%)	99 (66.0%)	130 (86.6%)
ANM/Health Assistant	29 (19.3%)	86 (57.3%)	115 (76.6%)
Mass Meetings	27 (18.0%)	59 (39.3%)	86 (57.3%)
Bill Board	18 (12.0%)	55 (36.6%)	73 (48.6%)
Others	16 (10.6%)	24 (16.0%)	40 (26.6%)

(Contd.)

Table 6.4 (*Contd.*)

Aspects of Activities	*Scheduled Caste*	*General Caste*	*Total*
Use of Better Inputs in Agriculture			
Radio	24 (16.0%)	91 (60.6%)	115 (76.6%)
TV	8 (5.3%)	43 (26.6%)	51 (34.0%)
Newspaper	17 (11.3%)	82 (54.0%)	99 (66.0%)
Other Sources	33 (22.0%)	79 (52.6%)	112 (74.6%)

While looking into the sources of information of the respondents on health and sanitation aspect, it could be observed that majority of respondents were influenced by health visitors than radio, television and newspapers. It was also observed that maximum sample population relied on government campaign, ANMS and health assistant for getting information about family planning measures. The study also focuses on different sources of information of the respondents regarding better inputs in agriculture. Maximum samples relied on radio than newspaper and television to know about the use of better inputs in agriculture.

Table 6.5 focuses on the distribution of the respondents in accordance with their opinion on different activities. As is evident from the table that all the respondents were of the views that deforestation and shifting cultivation were not good practices. They opined that media campaign was effective in respect of agriculture.

So far as their opinions on some social issues were concerned it was found that almost all the samples opined against untouchables and dowry system. Also, all the respondents believed in modernization of agriculture and higher education for children.

Correlations of co-efficients were computed to find out the relationships between the independent variables as (education and monthly income of the respondents) and dependent variables (media exposure of respondents in respect of agriculture, rural development, social forestry, socio-political awareness, health and sanitation and family and child welfare).

Table 6.5: Opinion of Respondents about Different Aspects

Different Aspects		*Scheduled Caste*	*General Caste*	*Total*
Deforestation				
Good		—	—	—
Bad		45 (30.0%)	105 (70.0%)	150 (100%)
Shifting of Cultivation				
In Favour of		—	—	—
In Against of		45 (30.0%)	105 (70.0%)	150 (100%)
Media Campaign on Agriculture				
Yes		45 (30.0%)	105 (70.0%)	150 (100%)
No		—	—	—
Social Issues				
Untouchabilities	Good	—	2 (1.3%)	2 (1.3%)
	Bad	45 (30.0%)	103 (68.6%)	148 (98.6%)
Dowry System	Good	—	2 (1.3%)	2 (1.3%)
	Bad	45 (30.0%)	103 (68.6%)	148 (98.6%)
Modernization of Agriculture	Good	45 (30.0%)	105 (70.0%)	150 (100%)
	Bad	—	—	—
Higher Education for Children	Good	45 (30.0%)	105 (70.0%)	150 (100%)
	Bad	—	—	—

It was found from the result that all the correlations were strongly positive with high level of significance (0.001P < level). Table 6.6 shows a good association between both categories of variables.

Table 6.6: Correlation Co-efficient between Independent and Dependent Variables

Dependent Variables	*Independent Variables*	
	Education (r' value)	*Monthly Income (r' value)*
Agriculture	0.81	0.80
Rural Development	0.61	0.90
Social Forestry	0.80	0.64
Social Political Awareness	0.80	0.78
Health and Sanitation	0.84	0.64
Family and Child Welfare	0.78	0.68

Note: All the correlations are significant at 0.001 per cent level.

Conclusion

Illiterates and less educated respondents had failed to realize the developmental roles of media and till today most of them think media only in terms of entertainment. Most of the respondents opined that media is important in spreading new possibilities and practices but at the stage where decisions were being made about what to do and what not to, the role of interpersonal channel was mostly admired. The study also have brought forth the fact that media had played a praise worthy role in extending information to the rural people regarding various welfare oriented schemes of the government. In case of family welfare measures, the role of media to change the attitude of the mass was felt significant. Media have been influencing extensively the level of socio- political awareness among the respondents. In the field of child welfare and health and sanitation also the role of media could not be denied.

Now the challenges are before the policy-makers, administrators, government and non-government organizations and the media planners to make the media accessible to rural community by developing appropriate media technology which would be gearing up to the needs of rural people.

References

1. Gupta, V.S. (1999) *Communication Technology, Media Policy and National Development*, Concept Publishing Company Pvt. Ltd., New Delhi.
2. Ninan, Seventi (2001) Tune into Quality, *The Hindu*, July 29.

7 Media as a Partner in Adult and Non-Formal Education

Manoj Dayal

It is an undisputed fact that liberation from oppression and anomaly is the primary function of education. No doubt education acts as a force towards the formation of an oppression free society. Education not only provides us job and livelihood, but also develops our personality. It shapes our character. It makes us mannered and cultured. It expands the intellect of mind. It helps us to stand on our own feet. It develops a feeling of self-reliance and self-confidence. It inculcates the quality of leadership. It makes us gregarious and co-operative. It promotes team spirit. It generates patience and leads us to perfection. It controls our mind and heart leading to overall self-control. It takes us from dark to light, from untruth to truth and from wrong to right. It is the cornerstone of democracy and the soul of an egalitarian society. Further, it motivates the right kind of attitudes and values in the individuals to fulfil their social obligation.

Concept of Education

Before any further analysis of Adult and Non-Formal Education, it is pertinent here to comprehend the real concept of education. The word Education has been derived from Latin word "Educere" which means to develop and the Greek word "Educare" which means to nourish. Hence, Education strengthens the human resources and for overall growth of our society, we do not have any magic before us except the occasional magic of human mind, human capital, human resource and human personality. Education not only develops human but humanity also. It plays a vital role in sensitizing the youth human resources about the real socio-economic development. Here the young men and the young women can break fresh ground with their scientific temper and ethos. In social life, the deep-rooted prejudices including those based on caste, creed and religion and several other social overdues can be removed by young people by promoting feeling of fraternity and by enlighting people about the changed conditions as well as all-round progress of the world.

Sustainable Development

In a developing economy like India, the sustainable development is the major challenge before any education including Adult and Non-Formal Education. Sustainable development is that which is long-lasting and which also cares for the future generation. In this context, the elimination of poverty, malnutrition, ill-health and unemployment should engage the serious attention of educators. Education of various subjects should keep the national socio-economic priorities before the students so that the real issues are not lost. Even academic profession is not merely a career or a way of earning a livelihood. It implies commitment to a distinct set of high ideals and values. It is because of this commitment that the academic profession has been called a noble profession and accorded higher respect. However, to make it a living force, these values need constant emphasis and nourishment.

Education is the cornerstone of socio-economic development of a country. Several educationists, national leaders and international experts have stressed the vital role of education in developing a human being. We have many engineers, doctors, historians, economists and political scientists with profound knowledge and expertise. But even optimists find it difficult to agree that we are really moving towards creating good and happy society. Professionals, administrators, politicians, businessmen are all exploiting their education, knowledge and skills for merely personal gains. There education in them has not infused in them a sense of responsibility to work for the common good. All great educationists of modern India like Pandit Madan Mohan Malviya, Annie Besent, Ravindra Nath Tagore have emphasized on character building as an important component of education. Yet integrated personality development remains a neglected aspect of our education system. Value-based education is a holistic approach to develop the social, cultural and moral personality of a student. It keeps in developing sensitivity of human values and ideals. When these ideas are internalized and habitually practiced, they give right directions to desire, emotions and outward behaviour of individuals and are reflected in the total personality. Only such person can lead a good life and create a good society. It is bad and sad to note that there is crisis of ideas and no interest to chalk out plans for value education.

Analytical and Synthetic Skills

The main purpose of Adult and Non-Formal Education is to bring about natural curiosity and creativity to develop their analytical and synthetic skills. It should also train them for self-learning. It is intellectual training and development of right attitudes which are far more important than merely information dissemination. Most unfortunately, it is not the teaching-learning process, but the examination which is considered to be more important in our education system. The teacher delivers knowledge to the students so that they could pass examinations and then the students often use all possible means to do so. Most of the questions are generally based on memorizing and then vomiting in the examination. Higher level of academics, competence, comprehension, analysis, synthesis, evaluation and judgement are rarely tested. The undue importance on degree distribution is the reason behind many ills and maladies in the academic arena including students' unrest, moral degradation, examination scandals and so on.

Value Dimension

The complete negligence of value dimension and character formation aspects of our education system is the main reason of value crisis. While education is the joint venture of both teachers and taught, it can succeed only through their mutual understanding and co-operative partnership. The task of mutual respect trust and goodwill appears to be difficult because of poor interpersonal communication. The art and craft of receiving good education, of being good students, has to be effectively communicated to the students through demonstrations and deeds. But hardly any attempt is made to develop social, ethical, cultural and human personality of the youths passing out through the portals of our examination system. There is hardly any motivational force for cultivation of virtues, formation of character and pursuits of ideals. Pandit Madan Mohan Malviya has aptly remarked, "Formation of character is even more important for the well-being of individual and of the community than cultivation of intellect." More industrial advancement cannot ensure happiness and prosperity to any people. And even industrial development cannot be achieved without mutual co-operation among all concerned and these can only prevail among those who are fair in their dealings and loyal to truth. Hence our education system has placed formation of character of youth as one of the principle objects. It will seek not merely to turn out man as engineers, scientists, doctors, merchants and technocrats but also as men of high character, dignity and honour. It will be a nursery of good citizen instead of only a mint for hallmarking as certain standard of knowledge. The main function of this value-based education system is to involve students in an exploration of various value dimensions of life which go into making a "good" man, "good" life leading to a "good" society. The idea is not to convert students to any particular "ism" or "ideology" but to give them a conceptual framework for understanding and cultivating their own value standards. The education should be practical, man-making fruit-bearing and useful for the society.

Global Importance of Our Primitive Education

Our primitive higher education has already earned an international image and identity. That is to say that before Fifth century AD, our education system was so excellent that students from all over the world used to come to India to study Philosophy, Science, Yoga, Arts and Culture, Literature and Mathematics to our Nalanda University, Vikramshila University and Takshashila University. After the setting up of Allahabad University, Bombay University, Calcutta University and Madras University during the second half of the Nineteenth century, the academic climate of India was so good that there was hardly any brain drain. This trend continued till 1950s and 1960s. But after that massive brain drain started from India and our higher education started loosing its own credibility. Many Indian scholars started believing in the slogan: "It is better to have brain drain than to put our brain into drain."

Cost Ineffectiveness of Higher Education

Comparative studies in India were conducted in 1950s, 1960s and 1970s and it was observed that primary education is cost-effective whereas higher education is cost-ineffective. As a result, universalisation of primary education, vocationalisation of secondary education and specialization of higher education became the theme of our New Education Policy and the Government started diverting funds from higher education to primary education. Several research studies have also revealed the fact that beneficiaries of higher education are students belonging to higher socio-economic section of the society. Another finding of interest is that cost of educating one student of higher education is equal to the cost of educating of six students at primary level.

Rig Ved Message on Education

In addition to universalisation of primary education, vocationalisation of secondary education, specialization of higher education and strengthening of professional education, technical education and distance education, boosting Adult Non Formal Education are all very important in desirable proportion for good, healthy and illuminating prospects of our society. According to Rig Ved, *"Satyat na parmadhitabhayam; Dharmat na parmadhitabhayam; Swadhyay Parvach-anabhayam na parmadhitabhayam"*. That means do not deviate from truth, do not deviate from duty and do not deviate from teaching and learning. This is because teaching-learning based complete education is extremely vital for healthy personality, sound character, bright career and prosperous future.

Media as a Partner

In boosting Adult and Non-Formal Education media can turn out to be a big partner. But media gives very little time or space to educational issues, educational policies and strategies and importance and relevance to education. Media is both mirror and torch of the society. News media, whether it is newspapers or news magazines or news bulletins or news channels, works like a mirror. But a mirror should work like a plain mirror which should reflect the exact picture of the society. But many a time media works like a concave or convex mirror which reflects the enlarged or reversed or imaginary picture of the society. Today the rate of growth of yellow journalism is much faster than the rate of growth of investigative journalism and there has been more yellow journalism in the name of investigative journalism. Media is turning from mission to profession, from profession to sensation and from sensation to commission. Today the theory of commerce is more applicable to media than the theory of journalism and mass communication. So media is deviating from its main objectives. Today developmental aspects are neglected in media whether it is print media or electronic media or web media. Media is no doubt a mirror. But it is very much influenced by the Western media. It often copies the critical and negative style from the Western media. John B. Bogart of England emphasized that we should report the events as it is. We have nothing to do with its consequences. But in Indian context this blind imitation of the West appears to be wrong. The Western philosophy is based on materialistic pleasure whereas Indian philosophy is based on spiritual pleasure. If the glass is half empty, then this is also true that the glass is half full.

Therefore, for Adult and Non-Formal Education, our outlook should always be positive. Our media no doubt is highlighting the achievements of education but not able to motivate people to participate in educational activities.

Recommendations

First, media should often play a creative constructive and positive role and emerge as a partner in a sensitive matter like Adult and Non-Formal Education. Yes, in some exceptional cases like reformation of Adult and Non-Formal Education, media may play a critical role under some special circumstances.

Second, Adult and Non-Formal Education should get more space in print media and more time in electronic media.

Third, instead of highlighting the achievements of Adult and Non-Formal Education, media should highlight those aspects which motivate people to participate in Adult and Non-Formal Education.

Fourth, for boosting Adult and Non-Formal Education, media should work like mirror and torch. The form of the mirror should not be like concave or convex, or lens, but it should be like plain mirror.

Fifth, when we talk of value based Adult and Non-Formal Education, we should also provide value based administration. And again media can play a vital role here and emerge as a partner.

Sixth, the Government should give more advertisements to those media which are giving more space or time to Adult and Non-Formal Education.

Seventh, the Government and different educational bodies should annually give prizes for excellent writing and journalism relating to Adult and Non-Formal Education.

Eighth, in this context, the schools, colleges and universities should not only encourage their teachers for research writing but also for writing popular articles and features relating to Adult and Non-Formal Education. They should be equally encouraged for giving their programmes or producing programmes for electronic media on Adult and Non-Formal Education.

Ninth, regarding Adult and Non-Formal Education, the Bullet Theory or Hypodermic Needle Theory of Mass Communication should be applied. Adult and Non-Formal Education is so important for development of our nation that such messages can work like "bullets" and the media can work like a "gun". Media can never work in a vacuum. It always needs a thematic support in the form of subject of messages. Hence, it is imperative to inject the messages of Adult and Non-Formal Education into the veins of the target audiences so that these messages can be internalized into their hearts and minds.

Tenth, such messages of Adult and Non-Formal Education should be given with effective communication and appealing presentation. The raw editorial matter should be converted into something worth-reading, worth-listening, worth-viewing and worth-using. Finally, the messages of Adult and Non-Formal education should be given in a featurised manner so that these can be interesting, lively, appealing and easily understandable to masses. For that there should be conceptual and linguistic clarity, conciseness, continuity, correctness, commonness, credibility and completeness. Further, it is recommended that more knowledge based Radio programmes, TV programmes and films should be produced and telecast which would help the students of Adult and Non-Formal students to enhance their knowledge in relevant subject area.

References

1. Sodha, Mahendra and Srivastava, Kamna (2000) "Primary Education in India" published in *University News*, Vol. 16.
2. Shiralashetti, A.S. (2007) "Progress and Prospects of Higher Education in India", published in *University News*, Vol. 45 (10).
3. Dayal, Manoj (2008) "Importance and Universalisation of Education: The Role of Media" published in *University News*, Vol. 46 (28).

8 Communication for the Development and Food and Nutrition Security of India

Vanisha S. Nambiar

Food and nutrition security is influenced by several factors ranging from income, poverty, education, employment, availability of resources, gender bias, beliefs and attitudes, available accessible and affordable health care. However, the most crucial among these is the knowledge, attitude and practice among the population. Nutritional deficiencies contribute to a large percentage of deaths associated with the other child survival interventions. Every child, woman and man should have the opportunity for a productive and healthy life. This will be possible only if we integrate cutting-edge science and technology with dying wisdom and vanishing useful traditional knowledge, culture and practices and preservation of indigenous crops of India. The past three decades have seen a quiet but dramatic revolution in health education programmes. Behavioural challenges are the most diverse of any health area. Interventions are often launched parallel to child survival efforts and parallel to each other. To meet the Millennium Development Goals, India needs to focus on the use of agricultural biodiversity to enhance nutrition and improve livelihoods. Social marketing and extension of education, therefore, would be important tools to achieve our targets.

International health organizations have recognized not only the essential role that prevention and health promotion play within health care systems, but they also recognize the contribution that a modern health communication methodology offers to these programmes and to the well-being of their people. The challenge now is how to carry out effective Health/Behaviour Change Communications Programmes.

We initiated a process of advocacy, capacity building and used positive deviance as a method for Behaviour Change Communication for improvement of the Mid Day Meal Programme (MDMP) of Gujarat (Nambiar, Gandhi and S. Nithya, 2008). Advocacy is an action directed at changing the policies, positions or programmes of any type of institution. Advocacy is pleading for, defending or recommending an idea before other people. Capacity development *via* adult education programmes can be used effective for training of Government employees dealing with National Programmes. Educational materials were developed which included an audio VCD, training manual, calendar and posters which were personally disseminated by the team through various training programmes organized in various districts of Gujarat. Simple steps on how MDMP can be improved were highlighted in this advocacy.

Advocacy is generally a necessary first step for any nutrition intervention. Decision-makers must be convinced of the epidemiological need, the feasibility, and the cost-effectiveness of new directions. Nutrition health education imparted as a part of non-formal education or as adult education, if imparted appropriately leads to an increase in knowledge, change in

The Dynamic Advocacy Process

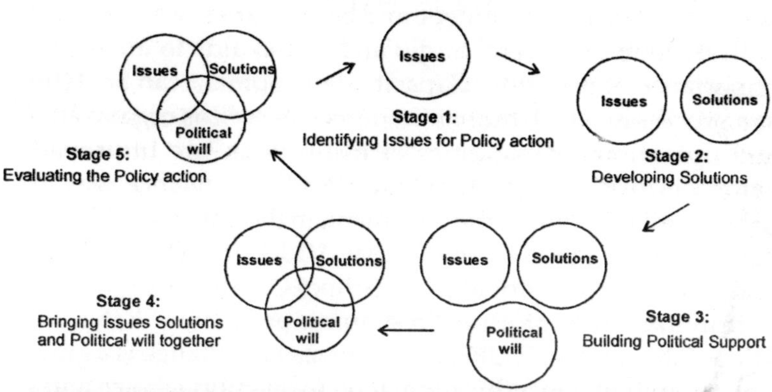

Source: Adopted from Knowledge Utilization and the Process of Policy Formulation: Towards a Framework for Africa.

attitude and initiation of a practice which is good for the improvement of their health and nutritional status.

The Positive Deviance approach looks for solutions within the community, and also focuses on the community as the means of rehabilitation. It includes two phases. Formative research consists of nutrition and health assessments as well as a participatory process that helps the community identify conditions which are favourable. These are the "positive deviants." The second phase consists of demonstrations of these positive deviants in the community. Such an example from within the community is helpful in implementation as it can be easily replicated. The second example is of a study conducted to assess the process of augmentation of vegetables in the Mid Day Meal Scheme (MDMS) along with nutrition communication in urban Vadodara (Nambiar V.S., Gandhi N. and Nithya, S. 2008).The new MDM recipes were developed in the Foods and Nutrition Department Laboratory with the inclusion of seasonal vegetables within the cost limits provided by the Government (with no extra cost). The menu provided extra nutrients of 13.5g protein, 16.4g vitamin C and 5.9g iron. Health systems research was conducted to assess the entire system of MDM and the lacunae were identified. Behaviour change communication strategies included capacity development with the help of training programmes with the policy makers, implementers, and beneficiaries were conducted with the help of several audio and visual aids to enhance the importance of nutrition. Capacity development can be defined as a process in which human resources, as well as organizational and operational capabilities of institutions, are improved to better perform priority functions. Positive deviance was used to help and implement the new menu in the entire MDM centres run under the jurisdiction of urban Vadodara. The third study assessed the feasibility of using School Children as Scouts for a Nutrition Communication Programme on Vitamin A (Nambiar, V.S. and Kosambia, P., 2004). Positive dietary change is a gradual process initiated by education, food availability/choice and has been given low priority in most vitamin A (VA) intervention programmes. The present study aimed to assess the impact of a Nutrition Communication Programme to increase awareness of VA rich foods in school children. A sample of 105 schoolboys and girls (7-13 years) were enrolled from two different primary Municipal schools of urban Vadodara. Baseline data on the socio-economic status, dietary intake, attitudes and beliefs about VA food and feeding behaviours of the target groups was collected. This formative research data was used to develop Nutrition Communication Programme, which included (1) Participatory, (2) Instructional, and (3) Child-to-child approaches wherein slides on VA, posters, charts and pictures were used as audio and visual aids. Teachers were also trained for this interpersonal communication and they acted as Agent Communicators during the one-month intervention period. Results revealed several community risk indicators of vitamin A deficiency such as unhygienic sanitary conditions, clustering, female illiteracy, traditional beliefs, negative attitude and a low priority given to carotene rich plant foods specially green leafy vegetables among the target group and their families. Results of nutrition intervention revealed a significant increase in the knowledge about VA, its sources, importance and consequences of not consuming it. A combination of approaches rather than a single approach and involvement of teachers as agent communicators had a positive impact. School teachers and children in India, thus, are the most often first-generation givers and learners and can be trained to be 'change agents' of the community. Also, it can be suggested that school children in India are the most often first-generation learners and can be trained to become 'change agents' of the community. School programmes will have greater impact and be sustained longer if they are tied to community activities, programmes, and other private and non-governmental organizations. School health education demonstrates that the primary school stage provides an ideal time to prepare children to assume primary responsibility for their own and their community's health. Thus, the challenge for the new system will be to find a way to develop nutrition education intervention measures which would become part of the social structures influencing nutrition behaviour and which would reach large number of people.

Household approaches include promoting consumption of vitamin A-rich foods and preservation techniques. Successful programmes often collaborate with agricultural extension activities, especially kitchen garden or animal husbandry efforts. The objective of this forth study was Assessing the feasibility, acceptability and impact of introducing dehydrated drumstick leaves (DDL) (*Moringa oleifera*) into the salty recipes provided by the supplementary food (SF) component of the Integrated Child Development Scheme (ICDS) as a source of Vitamin A along with nutrition health education (NHE) (Nambiar, Bhadalkar and Daxini, 2003).

An integrated approach was adapted in this study. Comprehensive training sessions were organized for the staff of the ICDS and Non-government Organizations (NGOs) involved in the food preparations. Nutrition heath education: A pretested semi-structured questionnaire was used to elicit data regarding their baseline KAP. Thereafter, some counselling materials with clearly defined messages for the target audience (mothers and children), were developed, which included four posters developed in local language (Gujarati). These messages were developed based on the results of the initial KAP scores of the children and their mothers. The theme of the posters were: sources of Vitamin A rich foods, importance of market visits to create awareness regarding the Vitamin A rich foods such as GLVs and yellow fruits in the children, promotion of home gardening for Vitamin A rich foods, and the best cooking methods for maximum retention of Vitamin A. The posters were pretested with 20 children (1-5 years) other than the experimental or the control group. Prior the acceptability trials, data were elicited on the socio-economic profile and knowledge about Vitamin A, from 60 children 1-5 year of age attending two anganwadi centres of the ICDS. From these, 40 children attending one anganwadi were supplemented with pretested DDL incorporated recipes (5-7gm DDL/100gm product) and NHE for a period of one month. Spot observations and organoleptic evaluation results indicated high compliance of the DDL-recipes by the children. Our results also indicated that the recipes were highly acceptable to the ICDS authorities as well as the NGO staff. NHE sessions also had a positive impact on the mothers (17% increase) and children (60% increase). The study indicated that introducing DDL into the ICDS-SF, along with NHE sessions can be a cheap, non-toxic and practical approach to overcome Vitamin A.

The above study highlights on Human capital and involved the development of human skills capacity, and the effective use of managerial, professional and technical staff, and beneficiaries. It includes identifying the right people to be trained; developing and delivering training strategies that are responsive to the needs of the target audience; providing an appropriate learning environment for training and education; ensuring in-service/field supervision for continued skills transfer. Action research challenges traditional social science, by moving beyond reflective knowledge created by outside experts sampling variables to an active moment-to-moment theorizing, data collecting, and inquiring occurring in the midst of emergent structure. At the present time, there is a need for a comprehensive approach for a nutrition communication intervention to be fully effective as an action oriented strategy for nutritional development especially in India, where large segments of the populations are still uneducated, deprived of their basic needs and are the target of the political corruption. Thus it is imperative that the researches conducted in the laboratories and stored in the libraries be disseminated to the field. There is an urgent need to transfer the technology from laboratory to the field. India needs good educators and its time that academicians move out of their classrooms towards community development.

Research—Extension of Research—Applications—Formulation of Policies—Implementation of policies—Monitoring—Evaluations = Development of India

References

1. Achterberg (1993) Qualitative research: What do we know about teaching good nutritional habits? *J. of Nutrition* 124.

2. Green, L.W. (1980) To educate or not to educate: Is that the question? *Am. J. Public Health* 70.
3. Kuhnlein, H.V., Receveur, O.R, (1996) Dietary change of traditional food systems of Indigenous Peoples. *Am. Rev. Nutr.* 16.
4. Nambiar, V.S. and Kosambia, P. (2005). School Children as Scouts for a Nutrition Communication Programme on Vitamin A. *Journal of Indian Dietetic Association.* Vol. 30 (No. 1 & 2),
5. Nambiar, V.S. and Kosambia, P. (2004). Communication Programme for promoting increased awareness about plant sources of vitamin A. *Sight and Life Newsletter.* A humanitarian initiative of DSM, Basel, Switzerland. Vol. 3, 2004.
6. Nambiar, V.S., Bhadalkar, K. and Daxini, M. (2003). Introduction of Dehydrated Drumstick Leaf Powder into the Salty Recipes of the Supplementary Feeding Programme of the ICDS – Feasibility and Acceptability Trials—A Pilot Study. *Indian Journal of Peadiatrics,* 70 (5):11-15.
7. Nambiar, V.S. (2002). Use of posters developed for the Sight and Life drawing competition for increasing the awareness on vitamin A in children. *Sight and Life Newsletter* 2, 2002.
8. Nambiar, V.S. (2008). *Nutrition Health Education—Teaching Modules* (Gujarati). Anada Publications. Ahmedabad.
9. Nambiar, V.S., Natasha, G. and Nithya, S. (2008). A Project report on Augmentation of vegetables in the MDMS and fortified Atta in the SPF-ICDS on selected children of urban Vadodara. Submitted to Dr. S. K. Nanda (IAS), Principal Secretary, Food and Civil Supplies Division, Government of Gujarat, Gujarat, India.
10. Nambiar, V., Gandhi, N. and Nithya, S. (2008). A training manual for the Mid-Day Meal functionaries of Gujarat. Department of Foods and Nutrition. The M.S. University of Baroda and Mid Day Meal Section, Department of Education. Government of Gujarat, India.
11. Nambiar V., Sharma, K. and Gandhi, H. (2005). 'Food Based Approach to Combat Vitamin A Deficiency'. UGC-DSA Monograph Series No. 3. Department of Foods and Nutrition, The M.S. University of Baroda, Vadodara-390002.

9 Educating the Adults : Communication to Strengthen Interpersonal Relationship

Sarjoo Patel
Maneesha Shukul

Communication is a process by which people seek to share meaning *via* the transmission of symbolic message. It is essential element in building healthy relationship between individuals (Stone and Freeman, 1988). Communication in the family is essential to satisfy the needs of inclusion, control, affection, expression, affiliation and identification (Mehta, 1997). It is through the communication that the family members share their experiences, ideas and personal views. Communication in the family life is essential for the management of its resources. Communication is also basic to the management of family resources which include decision-making related to planning and controlling resources, establishing goals, decisions related to choice making etc. When the family begins, the goals are set, the family members communicate their needs, desires, likes and dislikes, approval or disapproval of goals and related decisions. Plans are made to use the resources to achieve the set goals and the delegation of responsibilities for each action. Decisions are made as to when, where and how each action will take place, such organizing consists of dividing, delegating and grouping activities and assigning them to the family members, usually the parents and grandparents have the responsibility of doing this. Controlling of activities becomes necessary once they are organized. Controlling in the management process is the activity that aids in putting and keeping the plan in action that keeps the family going on its planned path. Here the energizing phase becomes important where the parents and grandparents help the youth to start the work and motivate for initiating the task assigned to them. Generally, the youths have a feeling of laziness to get started. This can be overcome by energizing. The adults frequently keep checking the progress of children by guiding and supervising them. Each of this can be done only through effective communication. It is needless to say that communication is an essential component of management. It is also essential among family members in the course of their performance of the managerial activities of the household. It keeps the family moving on its day-to-day course. One of the purposes of communication is to promote future oriented managerial process (Gross, Crandall and Knoll, 1980) whereby the family members need to communicate with each other in order to make decisions regarding use of resources not only for the present but also for future use. So to effect good management interpersonal communication, which requires the family members to treat each other with understanding, is essential. The sharing of communication is assumed to be a dynamic force, which influences family's style of management. Communication between the family members fosters interaction between them, which helps to exchange information regarding goals, values, standards and the managerial aspects essential for family living and which are unique for each family. These are transmitted in a family from generation to the other through the communication. For promoting training and socialization of children communication plays an important role. It is through the communication that they teach their children to perform various activities, especially the managerial tasks.

As in all communication groups, barriers may interfere with communication among family members by preventing message from getting through to each other. Within families, variations are found in age, status (between parent and child), value and language. Word meanings become altered and teenage speech often differs from speech of middle age. Such discrepancies are communication barriers for members of the family (Deacon and Firebaugh, 1975). Also it is seen that if communication lacks and misunderstanding prevails the relationship between adults and children is not a positive one. The home atmosphere also plays an important role in good interpersonal communication. If home atmosphere is healthy, it fosters family interaction. More discrepancies between the individuals lead to more conflicts.

It is usually observed that when a number of people live together under a common roof conflicts are bound to occur. A conflict is a struggle with values, with power, or with resource allocation. People who interact across time are bound to have differing opinions or perceptions about some aspects of family life (Nickel, Rice and Tucker, 1976). Conflicts occur because every person has his/her own personality and thinking which differs from the other person. Conflicts may affect his/her peace of mind, create tension and also affect the health. The family's co-operation for smooth functioning of household is negatively influenced by conflicts. Conflicts are more evident where members of various age groups reside together such as parents, grandparents and young children.

Since the time immemorial, it has been observed that there exists a constant and consistent rift between the younger and older generations. There was a time when "gray hair" was respected as they were able to give guidance based on their own past experience. But at that time the areas of experience were more limited than today. Now the child may have more exposure to outer world than his parents and/or grandparents. The refusal to go by the parents' experiences creates misunderstanding between both the generations (Hurlock, 1955) life style, habits, patterns of behaviour, modernization, norms and values of the older generation are felt as inadequate and irrelevant to the aspiration and expectancies of the newer generation. The youth in every era has regarded the old as outdated, old-fashioned, conservative and lacking in understanding. The son complains that his father cannot "understand him". On the other side, the older generation has felt the young as lacking in respect and radical in outlook, which is bound to mismanage the affairs of the world.

Due to advance of science and technology the gap between the older and the younger generation has become vast and the problems created by it have baffled all the concerned people. Today, there are less common ground between the ideas and the ideals of adults and the younger generation.

To avoid conflicts person should have control on his/her self for anger and should not loose temper. Conflicts can also be avoided by discussing and sharing problems in a group. Empathizing, and seeing the situation from the other person's point of view and delaying reactions until the relevant information is weighted will help to reduce conflicts (Stone and Freeman, 1998).

In some families where authoritarianism is prevalent parents use dominance methods for resolving conflicts where they want the children to voluntarily submit their wishes/desires or let go their point of view. The families which believe in the democratic pattern of living, conflicts are resolved by compromise where the parents and children, both, let go some of their wishes or desire. Such families may also follow integration method where a totally new solution is found out by which both parents and youths, each one is satisfied. These methods call for open and free communication between parents and youth.

It should be noted that developing communication skills is very essential for smooth and healthy relationship. Improvements in the communication skills are very reinforcing. When one communicates well, people generally respond one in a positive way, even if they are not totally happy with the message. Poor communication can provoke a negative response that is self perpetuating, in that it leads to even poorer communication. For effective communication it is essential to take time, accept the other person, listen actively, show empathy, and give timely and specific feedback, recognize differences and watch one's language (Tyagi, 1997).

It is also important that the adults should appreciate that in fast changing society they should keep their minds open and be ready to sort out the differences with the children. On the other hand, the youths should also have respect for older generation. For healthy communication the adults should create such home environment in which the adolescent feels protected; a home, which fosters love, the stimulation encouragement and appreciation. The home should provide the opportunity for adopting varieties of practice, experimentation and experience which prepare him to emerge later with an assurance and confidence into the larger world which is ruthless and impersonal. For successful communication between adults and children, it is important that the willingness to communicate with each other is accompanied by parental respect for the child's opinion and child's respect for parent and grandparents for their valued guidance. Thus effective communication practiced will surely foster good interpersonal understanding in the family. One needs to recognize communication as an often overlooked but dynamic force in human development and interaction.

Communication thus becomes the crux to the relationship between adults and children. There is really no gap between generations, only a gap between talking and thinking and thinking and doing, that is indeed a "communication gap".

For this purpose, the case studies were undertaken of selected families to understand the dynamics of interpersonal communication among the adults and youths.

Methodology

Descriptive research design was used for the study. A survey was conducted on 50 three generation families living in Baroda city, selected through purposive sampling technique. Case studies were undertaken for those families in which extent of communication was found to be low. Interview schedule was used as an instrument for gathering data.

Case Studies

In 20 per cent of the families the extent of communication was found to be low. In order to help these families to improve their interpersonal communication an in-depth analysis was done through case studies and reasons traced out for the low extent of communication.

Major Findings

The reasons for the low extent of communication between the adults and youth were mainly the busy schedule of the youth, age difference between the three generations, poor parent-child relationship and poor perception of home environment on the part of the youth. Also it was observed that difference in the values of three generations affected their communication. Taking all this into consideration booklet was developed which included guidelines for the adults for improving their interpersonal communication and counselling sessions were held with these families so that these families can also have good interpersonal communication. Through the counselling sessions the adults were informed and made aware of various barriers which hindered the communication between family members, to facilitate effective interpersonal communication guidelines were given to them for developing effective interpersonal communication and improving communication in families which are given as under :

Barriers to Communication

Various aspects act as barriers to communication, i.e. they hinder or reduce the communication between the family members. They are due to:

(1) Difference between youths and elders like difference in—

- Age
- Values
- Educational level
- Knowledge
- Personality
- Attitude
- Expectations
- Standards
- Goals
- Sex

(2) Due to lack of something like lack of—
- Time
- Understanding for others
- Compromising nature
- Clarity in idea or purpose
- Concern for family members
- Affection for family members
- Patience
- Co-operativeness

(3) Due to differences in mental abilities—
- Inattentiveness of member
- Poor listening capability
- Poor retention
- Not using proper words to express oneself
- Wrong interpretation of meaning of message of communication
- Using harsh language

(4) Due to differing nature—
- Authoritarian behaviour
- Aggressive nature
- Short temper

(5) Due to uncontrollable situations—
- Interruptions by outside factors
- Improper place, surrounding and environment for communication

Facilitators for Effective Interpersonal Communication

The adults and the youths should keep in mind the various facilitators for effective interpersonal communication and make it a point to use them in communication with others. They are as follows:

- Understanding power

- Polite tone of voice
- Good listening habits
- Trust in others
- Respect for others
- Positiveness
- Handling of anger
- Flexibility
- Appropriate language
- Clarity in idea or purpose
- Adequate time for communication
- Supporting words with action
- Showing concern for others
- Good retention
- Compromising/adjusting nature
- Ability to communicate in straightforward manner
- Correct interpretations of meaning of message of communication
- Harmony between sender and receiver of message
- Using suitable mode of communication for the person and purpose
- Using proper words to express oneself
- Develop healthy/good relations
- Proper timing of communication
- Developing empathy

Guidelines for Effective Interpersonal Communication for Adults

There is really no gap between generations. It is only a gap between talking and thinking and doing that is indeed a communication gap:

- Have frank and open discussion amongst you regarding disciplinary techniques, socially desirable behaviour, and family norms through explaining and reasoning

- Develop an insight in the relationship and the personality of each individual in the family
- Realize that spending leisure time together fosters a feeling of mutual understanding
- Use a combination of verbal and non-verbal communication
- Have an intimate, deeper and continuous dialogue amongst you
- Develop ability to communicate in straightforward manner
- Develop good understanding power
- Develop good listening habits
- Learn handling anger
- Use appropriate language to communicate
- Develop compromising nature
- Try to use proper words to express yourself
- Use suitable mode of communication
- And most important of all it should be understood that

  "There is no conflict on the earth which cannot be solved when there are noble intentions on both the sides".

Guidelines for Adults for Improving the Interpersonal Communication with Youths

- Create such home environment in which the adolescent feels protected
- Have a home which fosters love, the simulation, encouragement and appreciation
- Provide the opportunity for variety of experimentation and experience which prepare him to emerge later with

an assurance into the large world which is ruthless and impersonal

- Treat both the children, male and female, alike in all respects
- Each one of you should equally involve in child rearing to increase the communication with children
- Introspect yourself regarding the needs of the children
- Adapt yourself to the fast changing world
- Be ready to set out the differences with the children
- Do not scold children in front of others
- Consider youths as your friends
- Select proper time, place and tone for pointing out mistakes of children
- Talk openly with the children
- Answer the questions of children carefully and honestly admitting when you do not know the answer
- Develop an ability to withdraw yourself to a certain distance when youths indicate that they want to be on their own
- Use less authority
- Show understanding and skilfully guide him/her to make a choice
- Show love and sympathy with children
- Keep the channels of communication open in depth
- To reduce tensions be open to teenager's point of view
- Provide opportunities for sharing ideas and problems.

Conclusion

Through this study remedial measures by providing guidelines through the medium of booklet and counselling session were given to adults for improving interpersonal communication in Indian families and a positive response was received from the adults. The findings of the study brought out a number of implications for the government, educational institutions and NGOs. The NGOs and government can publish booklets wherein the problems of generation gap are discussed in a simple language and in a style which attracts the common people. Such booklets would go a long way in making the families relatively free from the avoidable tensions owing to generation gap. Voluntary organizations can open counselling centres to improve interpersonal communication among three generation families. Educational Institutions can open counselling centres for youth, and elders to improve their interpersonal communication and to resolve their conflicts. The educational institutions can also strengthen their curriculum for improving interpersonal communication skills, to sensitise youth towards problems and feelings of their grandparents. At present it is an integral part of the curriculum of Home Science, Sociology and Psychology but students from other disciplines can also be made aware of this aspect. Since the field of Home Management is concerned with the interplay of components of management in people's life, the present study has thrown light on the place of communication for the purpose of management in the home. It was found that very less interpersonal communication was done in relation to decision making and management of home. This has widened the data base. The experts from the Field of Home Management can provide counselling to the families to include youth in major decision making, participation in household work which may provide ample opportunity to increase interpersonal communication between family members.

References

1. Deccan, R.E. and Firebaugh, F.M. (1975): *Home Management Context and Concepts*, Haughton Miffin, London.
2. Deacan, R.E. and Firebaugh, F.M. (1981): *Family Resource Management*, Allyn and Bacon Inc., London.
3. Gross, I.H., Crandall, E.W. and Knoll, M.M. (1980): *Management for Modern Families*, Fourth Edition, Prentice Hall Inc., Englewood Cliffs, New Jersey.

4. Hurlock, E. (1955) *Adolescent Development,* McGraw Hill Book Co. Inc., New York.

5. Mehta, N. (1977): *Communication : Plugging the Basics,* Manan Copiers, Department of Extension and Communication, Faculty of Home Sciences, The M. S. University of Baroda, Vadodara.

6. Mehta, M. (1990): "Grandparent's Role in Today's Families", Unpublished Masters thesis, Faculty of Social Work, The M.S. University of Baroda, Vadodara.

7. Nickell, P., Rice, A.S. and Tucker, S.P. (1970): *Management in Family Living,* 5th Ed., John Wiley and Sons Inc., New York.

8. Stone, J.A.F. and Freeman, R.E. and Gilbert, J.R. (1998): *Management Prentice,* Hall of India Private Limited, New Delhi.

9. Tyagi, A. (1977): *Organizational Behaviour,* Excel Books, New Delhi.

ADULT AND NON-FORMAL EDUCATION

10 Dietary Pattern and Nutritional Deficiencies in Rural Areas of Shimla District

Anjali Dewan

Diet and nutrition are important factors in the promotion and maintenance of good health. The health and nutritional status of rural women who form the vulnerable group of India's population is far from satisfactory. In the rural areas of Shimla, they work as homemakers, farmers, food providers, fuel gatherers and animal feeders. Diets evolve over time, being influenced by many factors and complex social interactions. Such as income, prices, individual preferences and beliefs, cultural traditions as well as environmental, social and economic factors all interact in a complex manner to shape dietary consumption patterns.

The results of various surveys reveal that the diets of rural women are mainly based on cereals and are deficient in vegetables and fruits. The low intake of these protective foods results in nutritional deficiencies. Keeping this in mind, the present study has been undertaken with the following objectives:

- To find out the anthropometric measurements consisting of weight, height and Body Mass Index.
- To determine and compare the nutrient intake with the recommended quantity.
- To examine the clinical signs and symptoms of nutritional deficiencies.
- To assess the blood parameters of the rural women.

Locale of the Study

The study was conducted in the villages of Malliana, Pujrali, Badagaon, Kiari of Shimla district in the state of Himachal Pradesh.

Material and Methods

A well structured interview schedule was developed considering the specific objectives of the study. A sample of 500 rural women in the age group of 20-35 years was randomly selected for the study from the four villages. The food consumption of the subjects was recorded by 24-hour recall method for three consecutive days. The cooked dishes were converted into raw foods with the help of *katories* to facilitate the calculation of nutrients in the diets. From the actual consumption of foods daily by the respondents, the energy, proteins, iron, calcium, vitamin A (Retinol), thiamine, riboflavin, niacin and ascorbic acid content was calculated using food composition tables. The percentage adequacy of the diets was also calculated. Body mass index was calculated using the formula given by Wyngaarden, as cited in Srilaxmi (2002).

$$\text{B.M.I.} = \frac{\text{Weight (kg.)}}{\text{Height in metres}}$$

The blood samples of the respondents were checked for haemoglobin by cyanmethaemoglobin method of Dacie and Lewis (1966) and Packed Cell Volume (PCV) by Hunter and Bomford (1967). The results were statistically analysed. The morbidity symptoms and the information regarding the illness suffered by the women since past three months were noted down. All the women were clinically examined using the ICMR schedule. The presence or absence of the clinical deficiency symptoms was recorded.

Results and Discussion

The results obtained of the study are as follows:

Dietary Intake

Nutritional status is usually influenced by a large number of factors. One of the important factors is food consumption. The diet of rural women was monotonous and lacking in variety. They were more concerned about the quantity than quality of the diet. The common menu was cereal for breakfast and rice with dal or vegetable for dinner. The average daily intake of nutrients by the rural women is presented in Table 10.1.

Table 10.1: Mean daily nutrient Intake of rural women in comparison with RDA

Nutrient	*RDA*	*Mean value ±SD*	*% Diet Adequacy*
Energy (Kcal.)	2225	1894 ± 241	117.47
Proteins (gm.)	50	41 ± 3.69	121.95
Fats (gm.)	20	11.4 ± 1.15	175.40
Iron (mg.)	30	23 ± 1.99	130.43
Calcium (mg.)	400	342 ± 31.0	116.95
Vitamin A (µg.)	600	425 ± 51.3	141.17
Thiamine (mg.)	1.1	0.6 ± 0.1	183.33
Riboflavin (mg.)	1.3	0.7 ± 0.2	185.71
Niacin (mg.)	14	9.3 ± 1.03	150.53
Ascorbic acid (mg.)	40	30 ± 5.6	66.66

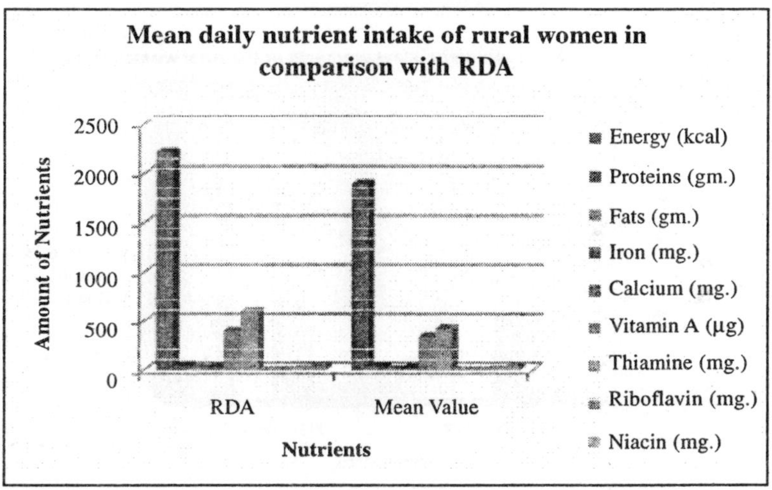

The adequacy of nutrients was below the RDA's for all the nutrients. The mean daily energy and protein intake by the respondents was 117.47 and 121.95 per cent adequate as compared to the RDA (ICMR, 1990). The mean daily intake of iron intake among the subjects was 23 mg. which was 130.43 per cent of the RDA for iron. The low iron intake was due to insufficient intake of green vegetables, absence of sprouts. The mean values of thiamine, riboflavin, niacin in the daily diets of the respondents were inadequate as compared to the RDA's. This has also been reported by Oyarzun & Sanjur (1993). The intake of Vitamin C with the mean value being 30 mg. was less as compared to the RDA. A low consumption of Vitamin C among women of low income has also been reported by Gibney & Lee (1993).

Anthropometric Measurements

The average weight and height of the subjects is shown in Table 10.2. The average weight of the rural women ranged from 35 to 55 kg. whereas the range of height was from 115 to 150 cm.

Table 10.2: Anthropometric Measurements of the Rural Women

Parameters	*Mean value*	*Normal value*
Weight (kg.)	40 ± 1.8	50*
Height (cm.)	141 ± 7.9	156*
B.M.I.	16 ± 0.8	18-23**

* ICMR, 1990 **Srilaxmi, 2002

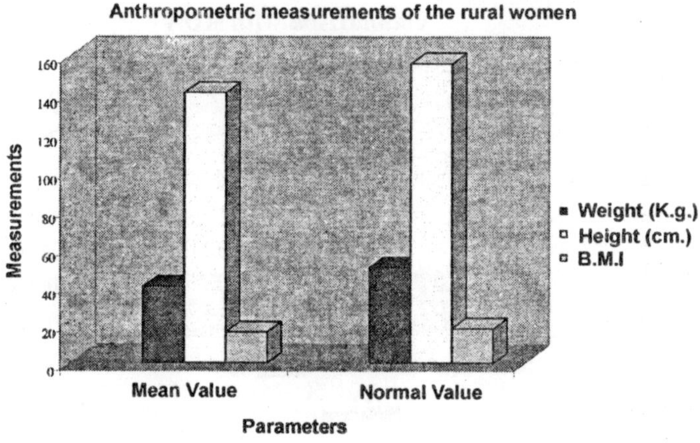

The results showed that the rural women were of less height, weight and B.M.I. than the normal values. The low B.M.I. was an indicator of malnutrition among the rural women.

Morbidity and Clinical Symptoms

Table 10.3: Existing illnesses and other clinical symptoms among rural women

S.No.	*Symptoms*	*Number of subjects (N=500)*	*%*	*Rank*
1.	Cold	98	19.6	5
2.	Cough	107	21.4	4
3.	Diarrhoea	43	8.6	7
3.	Fever	65	13.0	6
4.	Headache	119	23.8	3
5.	Pain in hands and legs	150	30	2
6.	Backache	202	40.4	1

Existing Illnesses and clinical symptoms among rural women

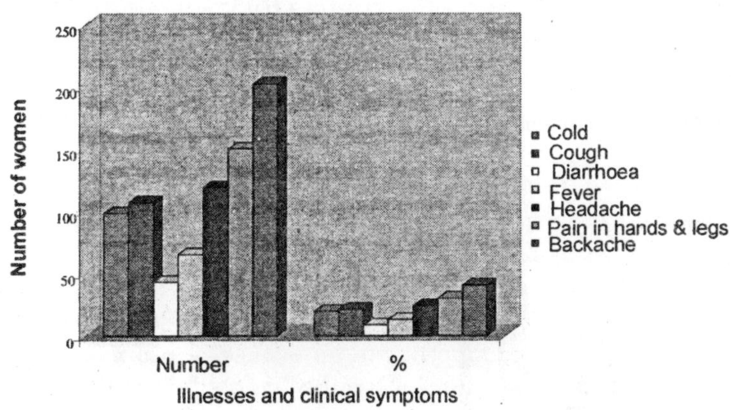

The illnesses and other clinical symptoms reported among this study were backache, headache, pain in the legs and hands, diarrhoea and fever as shown in Table 10.3. This may be due to the considerable workload for women who spent 8-9 hours at work, continued their work at home also and consumed less food. This led to dietary inadequacies.

Anaemia was rampant as shown in Table 10.4. Clinical symptoms of anaemia such as paleness of conjunctiva and skin, pale and smooth tongue, koilonychias (flat and spoon shaped nails) and fatigue were observed among the rural women. 82 per cent of the respondents complained of lethargy. Symptoms of other nutritional deficiency diseases such as pale eyes, scarlet raw tongue, angular stomatitis, cheilosis, mottled enamel, dental caries, phrynoderma, scurvy were observed among the rural women as shown in Table 10.5.

Table 10.4: Clinical Symptoms of Anaemia Among Rural Women

Symptoms	*Number of subjects (n=500)*	*%*
Pale conjunctiva	218	43.6
Paleness of skin	106	21.2
Pale & smooth tongue	76	15.2
Koilonychia	297	59.4
Feeling of lethargy	410	82

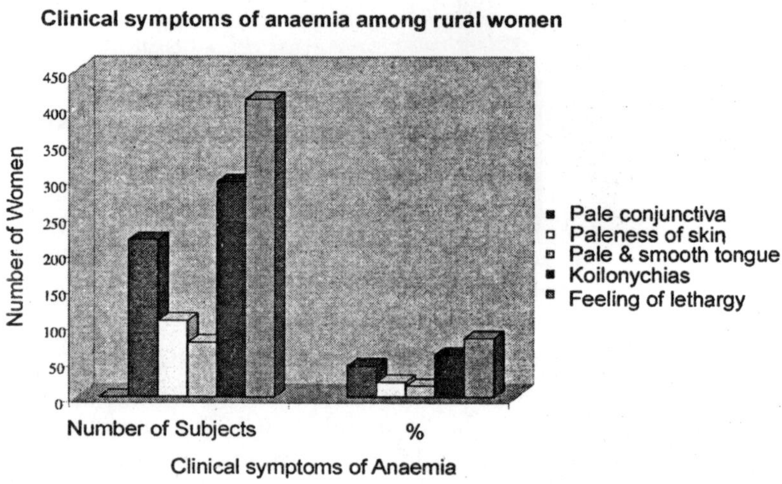

Table 10.5: Clinical symptoms of other nutritional deficiencies among rural women

Symptoms	*Number of subjects (n=500)*	*%*
Pale eyes	10	2
Scarlet raw tongue	25	5
Angular stomatitis	43	8.6
Cheilosis	52	10.4
Mottled Enamel	103	20.6
Dental caries	291	58.2
Phrynoderma	8	1.6
Scurvy	38	7.6

Data showed that 58.2 per cent rural women had dental caries. Mottled enamel was observed in 20.6 per cent subjects. The symptoms of B-complex vitamin deficiencies like scarlet raw tongue, angular stomatitis, cheilosis were present in some women though the number of subjects who were suffering from these deficiencies was not high. Bleeding gums, loose teeth which are the characteristic symptoms of scurvy were present in 7.6 per cent respondents.

Clinical symptoms of other nutritional deficiencies among rural women

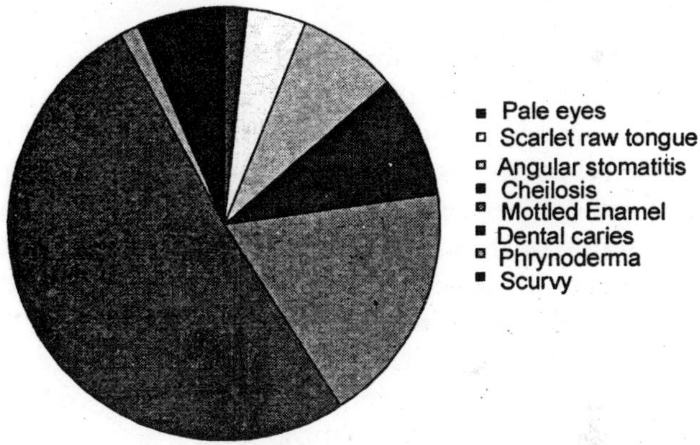

Clinical symptoms of other nutritional deficiencies among rural women

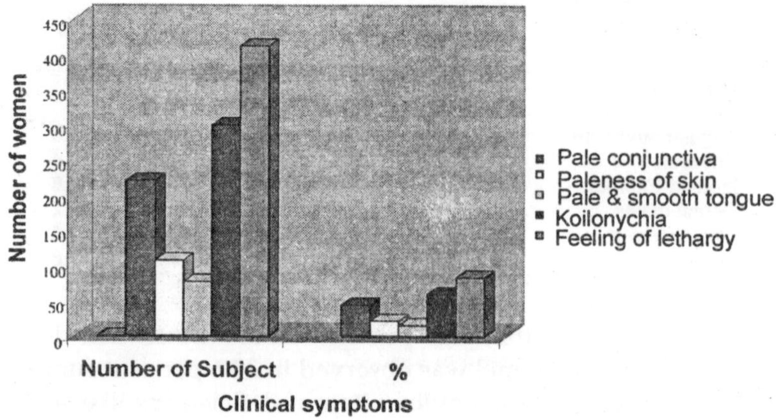

Gangadharappa *et al.* (2003) found the common deficiency signs and symptoms of B-complex vitamins among adult women in South India. The results of the present study indicate that the rural women consumed inadequate amounts of iron, calcium, B-complex vitamins and vitamin C.

Blood Parameters

The blood haemoglobin (Hb) level, packed cell volume (PCV) and mean corpuscular haemoglobin concentration (MCHC) values ranged from 7-12gm./dl, 25-42 per cent and 22-37 per cent respectively. The mean Hb value of 9.8 gm./dl and of MCHC 28 per cent were below normal limit confirming the presence of iron deficiency anaemia as shown in Table 10.6. However, the average value of PCV which was 36.7 per cent obtained in the present study lies within the normal range. According to WHO (1970), the percentage prevalence of anaemia was 83 per cent and only 17 per cent of the subjects had normal level of haemoglobin.

Conclusion

The present study revealed that most of the rural women in villages had education only till the primary level. They were

Table 10.6: Blood Parameters of the Rural Women

Blood Parameters	*Mean ± S.D*	*Normal Value*
Haemoglobin	9.8 ± 0.4	12.0*
Packed Cell Volume %	36.7 ± 0.8	32-38**
Mean Corpuscular Haemoglobin Concentration %	28 ± 0.2	32-38**

* WHO (1970)

** Hunter & Bomford (1967)

ignorant about personal hygiene and cleanliness of the surroundings. The consumption of milk and milk products, vegetables and fruits was much less than the RDA proposed by ICMR (1990). The body weight, height and B.M.I. of the rural women were below normal. There were clinical signs and symptoms of anaemia, B-complex vitamin deficiencies. The dietary inadequacy of iron seemed to be the main causative factor of anaemia. The rural women are a vulnerable section of the society. They suffer from various health problems. Promoting healthy diets and lifestyles to reduce malnutrition and non-communicable diseases requires a multisectorial approach. The strategies must not only be directed at ensuring food security for all but the rural women must be encouraged to consume adequate quantities of safe and good quality foods. Nothing short of radical change will help in raising the health and nutritional status of the rural women.

References

1. A global agenda for combating malnutrition: Progress Report (2000). World Health Organization, Geneva.
2. Dacie, J.V. & Lewis, S.M. (1969). *Practical Haematology*. p. 216. English Language Book Society and J.A Churchill Ltd., London.
3. Gangadharappa, N.R., Vijayalakshmi, D. *et al.* (2005). *Dietary Habits and Nutritional Deficiencies—An Appraisal of Trends in South India.* Gandhi Krishi Vigyana Kendra. University of Agricultural Sciences, Bangalore.

4. Garrow, J.S. (1981). *Treat Obesity Seriously: A Clinical Manual.* Edinburgh Churchill Livingstone.

5. Gibney, M.J. and Lee, P. (1993). Patterns of Food and Nutrition intake in suburbs of Dublin with chronically high unemployment. *J. Numun. Nut. Dietet.* Vol.6 (1):13-22.

6. Hunter, I. Bomford, V.N. (1967). *Clinical Haematology.* p.11. Academic Press, New York.

7. Indian Council of Medical Research (1990). *Nutrient Requirement and Recommended Dietary Allowances for Indians.* National Institute on Nutrition, Hyderabad.

8. Jellife, D.B. (1966). *The assessment of nutritional status of community.* p. 74. World Health Organization, Geneva.

9. Nagi, M. and Mann, S.K. (1991). Nutrient intake of Punjabi women with special reference to iron availability. *J. Food Science Technology,* Vol.4 : 230-233.

10. Oyarzun, M.T. and Sanjur, D. (1993). Diet of low income urban women in Central Chile. Rewisia. *Chiene-de-Nutrition,* Vol. 21 (2) : 87-97.

11. *The World Health Report 2002: Reducing risks, promoting healthy life.* World Health Organization, Geneva.

12. WHO/UNICEF/United Nations University (2001). *Iron deficiency anaemia assessment, prevention and control: a guide for programme managers.* World Health Organization, Geneva.

11 Need of Consumer Education in Non- formal Education

Sheetal Helaiya

In Sanskrit *"Jiva jivya jivanam"*, it means to survive on the earth every living being depends on each others. In Stone Age, to survive human beings were hunting animals than later on discovered agricultural foods. As the society developed, their necessities had increased. In Stone Age, their requirements were limited like food, shelter and clothes and lived like animals. Then later on they had developed own society near to river and started cultivating agricultural products. Due to that reason their necessities increased. In the case of food choices were increased and same way for shelter and cloth. The basic requirements also changed with the change in time. An individual is not able to satisfy all his need own self by making their production. So, society had develop Batter System where individual exchange goods/services against goods/ services. But Barter System has its own limitations and overcame those limitation money/exchange medium introduced to make trading function easy.

To survive and live life happily individual needs to depend on each other. He cannot satisfy own needs without help of others. He needs to purchase goods and services for satisfying own needs. In commercial terms every individual is a consumer, regardless of occupation, education, age, gender, community or religious affiliation. From the birth till the death he performs role of consumer and consume different services and goods. An individual plays the role of consumer in his life such a way that now it has become part of his life. Consumer has some rights and duties which sometimes performed by him knowingly or unknowingly.

Due to globalization, more number of branded products is available with duplicate products in the market. Now-a-days, on one side consumer has more varieties of goods and services for satisfying own needs and on other side it become riskily if he is not aware about own rights and duties he may be exploited in the market. He needs to get aware about his rights and duties.

Meaning of Consumer

In layman language consumer means people who buy goods and services to satisfy their needs. In commercial terms Consumer means any person who buys/hires goods/services against money or money worth. But as per the Act, a 'Consumer' has been defined as:

- Any person who buys goods for consideration, and any person who uses goods with the approval of the purchaser.
- Any person who hires any services for a consideration and any beneficiary of such services, provided the service is availed with the approval of the person who had hired the service for a consideration.

Moreover, the consideration for either the goods or services may be either paid or promised, or partly paid or promised, or provided under a system of deferred payment. It means consumer is any person, i.e. individual or legal person who purchases or hires goods or services by making payment or promises to make payment in future fully or partial. They all have rights and duties under Consumer Protection Act, 1986. These rights and duties are provided in the Act for the welfare of the consumer and society at large. As per requirements of time this Act is modified.

Consumer Protection Act (1986)

This Act clearly defines consumers' rights and duties/

responsibilities. It seeks to provide consumers with quick, easy and inexpensive redressal of their genuine complaints, under this Act, the consumers can file complaints against goods and services provided by not only private companies but also the government departments. For the legal settlement of complaints, courts have been set up at the district, state and national level, such courts are called consumer redressal forums. The Act envisages the promotion and protection of the following rights of consumers:

Right to Safety

Means right to be protected against the marketing of goods and services, which are hazardous to life and property. The purchased goods and services availed should not only meet their immediate needs, but also fulfil long term interests. Before purchasing, consumers should insist on the quality of the products as well as on the guarantee of the products and services. They should preferably purchase standardization/ quality marked products such as ISI, AGMARK, etc. Consumers should be well guarded from any physical damage or difficulty or discomfort due to poor quality or sudden failure of the product. Consumers are assured of quality, reliability and performance by this right.

Right to be Informed

Means right to be informed about the quality, quantity, potency, purity, standard and price of goods so as to protect the consumer against unfair trade practices. Consumer should insist on getting all the information about the product or service before making a choice or a decision. Right of information can be interpreted considering dual facts. First, consumers should be given complete information of all the aspects of the product and second, the information should be correct, reliable and up-dated. The consumer must be informed not only about basic information such as price, size, weight, ingredient, standardization or quality marks, manufacturers but also about safety aspects, hazards involved and measures to avoid them.

He must also know whether the item he selects is the best for the money he spends. He would also like to know after sales service would be available or not. He should have complete knowledge about the safety and durability of the product he purchases. This will enable him to act wisely and responsibly and also enable him to desist from falling prey to high pressure selling techniques.

Right to Choose

Means right to be assured, wherever possible of access to variety of goods and services at competitive prices and whenever not possible, government should assure the consumers of good quality and controlling the prices. In case of monopolies, it means right to be assured of satisfactory quality and service at a fair price. It also includes right to basic goods and services. This is because unrestricted right of the minority to choose can mean a denial for the majority of its fair share. This right can be better exercised in a competitive market where a variety of goods and services are available at competitive prices. This right accelerated the economic growth and healthy competition in the market thereby improving the quality and controlling the prices. In other words, this right can be better exercised in a competitive market where a variety of goods and services are available at competitive prices.

Right to be Heard

Means that consumer's interests will receive due consideration at appropriate forums. It also includes right to be represented in various forums formed to consider the consumer's welfare. This right also means to be assured that consumer interest will receive full and sympathetic consideration in the formulation of government policy and fair and expeditious treatment in its administrative tribunals. This right assures consumers representation in forming government policy. To exercise the right to be heard, the consumers should form non-political and non-commercial consumer organizations, which can be given representation in various committees, formed by the Government and other bodies in matters relating to consumers.

Right to seek Redressal

Means right to seek redressal against unfair trade practices or unscrupulous exploitation of consumers. It also includes right to fair settlement of the genuine grievances of the consumer. If the performance and quality be short of expectations, a consumer has right to redress. Consumers must make complaint for their genuine grievances. Many a times their complaint may be of small value but its impact on the society as a whole may be very large. They can also take the help of consumer organizations in seeking redressal of their grievances. In fact, the right to be heard further implies the existence of a mechanism through which other rights can be asserted in particular, by ensuring the right of redressal of legitimate consumer grievances.

Right to Consumer Education

Means right to acquire the knowledge and skill to be an informed consumer throughout life. Ignorance of consumers, particularly of rural consumers, is mainly responsible for their exploitation. They should know their rights and must exercise them. Only then real consumer protection can be achieved with success. Consumer policies should ensure that consumer laws are written in language that is easily understood. Consumers should be informed about their rights and duties/ responsibilities.

As Consumer Protection Act also provides some duties/ responsibilities to consumer which are discussed as under:

Solidarity

The responsibility to organize the consumers and to develop the strength and influence to promote and protect common interest. Developing consumer organization or forum where problems related to consumers are discussed and they can take some actions as per requirements. These forums or organizations are developed to reduce exploitation of consumers in the market.

These organizations or forums can be established by government and non-government for the welfare of the consumers and society.

Critical Awareness

The responsibility to be more alert and questioning about the price and quality of goods and services he uses. Before purchasing any product from the market consumer needs to collect information related to product, mode of payment, services after sale, guarantee/warranty period, etc. Instead of blindly trusted on advertisement or marketing schemes launched by the traders in the market consumer needs to validate information provided in advertisements or in marketing schemes.

Action

Action means the responsibility to assert him and act to ensure that he gets a fair deal. As long as he remains passive consumer, he shall continue to be exploited. After inquiring about product he needs to finalize deal. At the time of finalizing deal, he needs to take bills, receipts, guarantee cards, etc. and keep them safely and maintain them as records. They are the proof of purchase and help in getting redressal in case of genuine grievance.

Social Concern

Social concern means the responsibility to be aware of the impact of his consumption on other citizens, especially disadvantaged or powerless groups whether in local, national or international community. If more consumption of goods and services made by some group of society then the cost of those goods and services increase and due to those goods and services are not available or available at very high price to other group of the society. And it is right of all citizens of nation and globe to get goods and services. So, it is required to make optimum utilization of products and services and reduce waste or misuse of goods and services.

Environmental Awareness

The responsibility to understand the environmental consequences of own consumption. He should recognize own as individual and social responsibility to conserve natural resources and protect the earth for future generations. We have limited resources and that need to be available to all present and future members of the county or globe. Need to show concern for society by making optimum utilization of goods and services. Do not waste any product. Make an effort to conserve resources so that they can last longer.

As these all rights and duties are available to the consumer but still exploitation of consumers are going on at local and global level. For the exploitation of consumers in India is more compared to other countries in the world.

Exploitation of Consumer in India

Today's market is a complex system because it is flooded with products. The new developments and innovations in science and technology have brought about changes in the life style and standards of consumers and they are becoming confused at to what they should buy? In India, consumers are not much aware about consumers' rights and duties/responsibilities. So the consumers are exploited more in India. Some ways of exploitation of consumers are discussed as under:

- *Selling defective goods*: In the market varieties of goods and services are available. Many branded companies are proving their products in the market for consumers but sometimes traders to save own profit sale defective product to the consumer. Even to win competition in the market, companies promise to have high quality or capacity products but actually products are not according to prescribed as per package. In the market many electric items like irons, water heaters, refrigerators, washing machines and many other such appliances carrying potential danger in its usage. Sometimes iron does not get heated according to marked temperature, or refrigerator or washing machine gives shock while touched and the like.

- *Not providing fully or partially services after sales*: At the time of purchase service after sales are promised by the traders and the companies. But sometimes after sale services are not provided. At the time of purchase consumers are attracted by such kind of after sales service schemes free of cost. But sometimes, those services are not provided fully or partially. Sometimes, those are provided then some cost is asked for rendering services.
- *Not providing bills or receipts on purchase*: Most of the time trader tries to sale goods or services without bills or receipts. Seller lures to consumer to purchase goods or services without bills or receipts than the reduced cost of goods or services. Due to most of the time, consumer purchases goods or services without bills or receipts because he feels it is benefited to him.
- *Selling duplicated goods*: In the market with branded name duplicated products are available. Trader is selling duplicated goods to consumer at same cost or sometimes at low cost and consumer is purchasing such goods without knowledge. Even due to low cost of duplicate goods consumer purchases without thinking about its impact on ownself and on nation or globe. Different types of duplicate goods are available in the market including medical drugs.
- *Faulty advertisements about goods and services*: Advertisements are done for marking goods and services. By the advertisements consumers are attracted towards goods and services and they purchase goods and services. But sometimes goods and services are not according to advertised. It misleads consumers. Consumers are not trained for product evaluation and

are not able to distinguish between good quality and poor quality of goods.

These all above ways of exploitation of consumer suggest that there is need to educate consumer about their rights and duties/responsibilities as consumer. In consumer rights, consumers have right to get Consumer Education.

Meaning of Consumer Education

Consumer Education is "the process of gaining the knowledge and skills needed in managing consumer resources and taking actions to influence the factors which affect consumer decisions." It is training for gaining skills to take appropriate decision regarding purchase of goods and services and making appropriate use of goods and services. In other words, Consumer Education means to educate the consumers as to why, what, where, when, how and how much to buy and how to use whatever they have bought. Consumer Education is not only to create awareness about rights and responsibilities of consumers but also to train them to use their rights and responsibilities at appropriate time. Consumer Education is provided by keeping in mind some objectives. These objectives are broadly classified to develop all required skills development in consumers.

Objectives of Consumer Education

The major objectives of Consumer Education are to help the people to manage their money wisely by making wise choice in the market place. Some of the specific purposes are:

1. To understand process of economy functions.
2. To become aware of consumer rights and responsibilities.
3. To become aware of redressal mechanism.
4. To gain skills to make wise purchase in the market.
5. To gain skills to safeguard against

(a) Sales tactics,
(b) Advertising, and
(c) Dishonest selling practice.

Consumer Education has been described as addressing four general areas. These are:

- *Consumer Decision making*: It covers critical thinking skills related to consumers' goals, needs, wants, and the effects of attitudes, advertising, information and opportunity costs on consumer behaviours.
- *Economics*: It means examines the allocation of scarce resources among competing wants. Explores the principles of supply and demand and how prices are determined, growth and productivity, global interdependence and the interrelated roles of consumers, producers, and government in an economic system.
- *Personal Finance*: It includes budgeting, record keeping, income and net worth statements, credit, saving and investing, retirement and estate planning, insurance, and taxes.
- *Rights and Responsibilities*: It includes responsible citizenship concerning consumer protection laws and regulations, and redress mechanisms. Also addresses topics such as the environment, safety, health care and affordable goods and services.

These are covered all the functional aspect of consumer in the market. The education is important and it needs to be provided to the consumer at all the level of life by the education system.

Need for Consumer Education in Non-Formal Education

As aspects covered in Consumer Education are such broader which make it possible to use interdisciplinary approach by design. As a result, consumer concepts may be found throughout the school curriculum. Subjects that may include consumer concepts are economics, civics, mathematics, biology, chemistry, language arts, business education and home economics. Consumer Education offers more than knowledge and skills; it promotes critical thinking, problem solving and action. Consumer Education is not separate subject in school curriculum. And at the time of teaching any subject teacher is mostly focused on subject content rather than include Consumer Education and even teacher is teaching concepts of Consumer Education theoretically. The objectives of Consumer Education is to develop skills in the students but the way teachers are teaching Consumer Education only awareness related to some contents of Consumer Education are created.

In India, the rural consumer remains disadvantaged as their right to information, choice, redress, education and the right to be heard are not sufficiently fulfilled. They are exploited in many ways due to poor knowledge about their rights. The rural consumer who depends largely on weekly market especially in the remote areas, to purchase essential things is often cheated in price, weight and measurement (Misra, 2008). In India, majority dropout from the schools found in rural areas where they have secondary choice is to gain education due to their personal, social and economical problems. It is right of all individual born in India to gain education but still we are struggling due to rigidity of our formal education system and socio-economic problems. To overcome limitation of formal education system new type of education system is established where some flexibility are provided according to the needs of the students and that kind of education is known as non-formal education. In non-formal education there is no age limit for enrolling in any course. In non-formal education system mostly those students apply who are not able to gain education from formal education systems, i.e. dropout students from formal education, who want to earn with gaining education (part-time).

Mostly they are mature students compared to formal education system. The research found that rural people are mostly misled by the advertisements, they do not think much and not verify the information provided in the advertisements and consume the goods and services. The research also said that the people should not to be misled by the advertisements, especially in the electronic media. Those presenting these advertisements falsely highlight the qualities of the products as they are highly paid for it (Misra, 2008). So, it is necessary to provide Consumer Education and the disadvantaged group of the society mostly access to non-formal education to gain education. So, it is advisable to include Consumer Education in non-formal education with formal education. By including Consumer Education in non-formal education affords made to provide Consumer Education to all citizen of the nation. The main aim of Consumer Education is to make them alert about wrong practices in the markets and making them capable to take action to stop those wrong practices in the markets.

Consumer Education can be included as two ways in non-formal education system. One way, introduce Consumer Education by integrating concepts of Consumer Education with other subjects and another way to teach Consumer Education as separate subject. In the case of integrated approach to Consumer Education is such where Consumer Education is integrated with other subjects like languages, science, mathematics, business education, economics, civics, etc. and in the case of separate subject Consumer Education is taught as specific subject like Science, Mathematics, History, English.

Consumer Education in Non-Formal Education

Consumer Education can be introduced as separate subject in non-formal education. The objectives are same as in formal education as integrated with other subjects but approach need to be different from the formal education system. Because students in non-formal education are more mature compared to the formal education. Students of non-formal education have some experience related to day-to-day consumer activities, so they may know little bit about exploitation/wrong practices carried out in the markets.

The approach is not to teach direct the concepts of consumers' rights and duties but need to provide opportunities to the students to understand how exploitation of consumers are going on in the market and what they need to do as consumers to stop their exploitation in the markets, as consumers how and how much they need to consume goods and services for their own satisfaction and for the welfare of present and future the society. It means instead of teaching with the help of lecture method, teaching needs to be carried out with the help of some students centred methods. Students centred methods like assignment method, project method, discussion method, at higher level seminar method and some action research can be used where students get on hand experience they carry out some work and learn the concept.

At lower level of education, concepts related to awareness about consumers rights and duties can be taught to the students and at higher level of education, how to make appropriate use of consumer rights and duties need to be taught to the students with practices. Creating awareness about consumers' rights and duties is not only objective of Consumer Education but it also includes development of skills for making appropriate and optimum utilization of goods and services.

For example, concept is "standardized product need to be purchased." For teaching such kind of concept by using students centred methods then assignment work may be given to collect information regarding standards to check quality of products, which kinds of standards are used to qualified products as standardized products. Even project works may be given to students where they check which kinds of standards are available in the market to check quality of products, why need to purchase products having standardized mark on products, etc. Even action research can be carried out regarding what could be impact of using products which do not have standardized marks on consumers and/or society. After adopting such methods like assignment method, project method or assigning research work teacher can conduct discussion in the small where they can share their experience and even discuss the problem they face to complete task. By discussion they not only gain knowledge related to the concept of Consumer Education but they also develop concern for the society and try to become better consumers of the society.

Sometimes students feel they know all the aspects of Consumer Education because media like television and radio. These media are providing more knowledge about consumer rights and duties but when students carry out such kind of work then they get clarity regarding why these media are providing such kind of knowledge to the society.

Providing practices to students for making use of consumer rights and duties is important because by the practices they can develop confidence regarding use of consumers' rights and develops insides for their duties. They understand the importance of their duties for nation's social and economical development. Consumer Education in non-formal education is not only beneficiary to students but it is also beneficiary to the society and traders.

Benefits of Consumer Education

If the Consumer Education is provided properly with reference to its objectives then it is really benefited by all in the society. It provides benefits to students, society, traders. These benefits are discussed as under:

To Students

Students are real gainer of the Consumer Education. The objectives of Consumer Education are such which brings positive change in students. The benefits the students gain from Consumer Education are as follows:

Gain Knowledge Regarding Consumer Education

Students gain the knowledge regarding Consumer Education which is helpful to them when they carry out some transaction in the market. They gain full knowledge of consumers' rights and duties and they understand their importance in their life. Even they can provide such knowledge to other members of the society.

Become Better Consumer

When they gain the knowledge about Consumer Education then they are able to apply their knowledge in their life. Whenever they do some transactions then they also remember their rights and duties and accordingly they behave. Now they do not allow others to make their exploitation and try to reduce wrong practice in the market.

Develop Higher Level of Thinking

Consumer Education is provided by adopting principle of 'learning by doing'. Due to this principle almost all the knowledge related to consumers' rights and duties is gained with on hand experience and such kind of experiences develop higher level of thinking. As consumer, individual needs to think about why, what, when, where, how and how much he needs to purchase. And by such kind of education higher level of thinking is developed in the students. This education also contributes to individual personality development.

Become Social Responsible Person

By gaining knowledge of consumers' rights and duties, students become aware that it is rights of all citizens to make consumption of goods and services available in the society. In the society some groups are disadvantaged group (having low economical status) and due to more consumption of goods and services by one group of the society give impact to others. Disadvantaged group may not consume goods and services as per their requirements. So, students behave socially responsible person by making optimum utilization of goods and services and reduce wastage of goods and services. They show concern and sensitivity towards society.

Become Ecological Responsible

By gaining Consumer Education, student becomes responsible person. He becomes responsible for his action. He analyses the impact of his behaviour as consumer on present and future society. He knows that natural resources are limited and its rights of all present and future citizens to gain benefits of those resources. He consumes goods and services as much his requirements. He reduces wasting goods and services and making optimum utilization of goods and services.

Ready to take action for unethical/wrong practice in the market

By Consumer Education, students have the knowledge about consumers' rights and duties. So, whenever they find any wrong/unfair/unethical practice going on with them or some body else then they take action again those unethical/ wrong practices. Now, they think it is necessary to take action to stop unethical/wrong practice in the market for their own benefits and the society.

To Society

The society is also gaining benefits of Consumer Education as students are the members of the society. The benefits to the society are discussed as under:

Gain Better Consumer

As students gain knowledge of Consumer Education then they are aware about their duties and rights. And whenever required they practice their duties and rights as consumers. So, society gain better consumer who understand and practice their rights and duties in the market.

Reduce Unethical/Wrong Activities in the Society

As students know about consumers' rights and duties, they can apply their knowledge when they carry out some transactions in the market. When they find any unethical/wrong practice carried out by the trader they raise their voice and not allow trader to carry out unethical/wrong practice with them and any other members of the society. Due to this reason such kind of unethical activities are reduced in the society.

Develop Social Concern in all the Citizens

By gaining Consumer Education, students understand their duties/responsibilities towards the society. They behave like good citizen by showing their concern for the society. They show concern for the society by reducing wastage of goods and services and making optimum utilization of goods and services.

Available Better Qualities of Products

As the students behave like good consumers in the market, The poor quality of goods and services are not available in the market. Traders of duplicated or low quality of goods and services are reduced because they raise their voice by utilizing their consumer rights. So, better quality of goods and services are provided by the seller in the market.

To Traders

Get Healthy Competition in the Market

As the students are raising their voice in the market for low/bad quality of goods and services then traders need to provide good quality of goods and services to the consumers. And due to duplicate and low quality of goods are not available and to remain in the market they need to provide better quality of goods and services to the consumers. This will create healthy competition in the market.

Gain Good Goodwill in the Market

Due to Consumer Education students become aware about their rights and duties and they raise their voice against any unethical/wrong practice done by the trader. They are aware so they select good quality of goods and services and the trader who are providing better quality of goods and services have high goodwill in the market. With the increase in the goodwill of the business it increases their reputation in the market with their business.

These all are the benefits of Consumer Education and when it is provided by both types of education system these benefits are easily available to the students and society as large.

Conclusion

Mahatma Gandhi, the Father of the Nation, described the consumer as: "A customer is the most important visitor in our premises. He is not dependent on us, we are dependent on him. He is not an interruption in our work, he is the purpose of it. He is not an outsider to our business, he is part of it. We are not doing him a favour by serving him, he is doing us a favour by giving us an opportunity to do so."

It means consumer is most important part of the economy. In other words, economy functions with the help of consumer. Consumer and economic actions lies at the heart of modern life. Without existence of consumer economy cannot exist. So it is necessary to treat consumer properly in the market. But to earn high profit trader forget importance of consumer and exploit consumers. To stop exploitation of consumers in the market government has taken many steps but till today exploitation is going on in the market. Consumers are not aware about their rights and duties mentioned in Consumer Act. And consumers are complaining that government is not doing anything for them. Consumers should not ask what the government do for them but first what they can do for themselves.

One way to create awareness and develop skills in consumers is to educate them. Consumer Education, like the general education curriculum, is part of that foundation on which students may begin to build their personal lives, and on which we must begin to build a more responsive and human world. In non-formal education consumer education need to be provided by adopting students centred methods where they gain on hand experience. By such kind of approach objectives of consumer education can be easily achieved. If consumer education is provided then it is not only benefited to students (consumers) but is benefited to society at large. By this way every member of the society becomes socially responsible person and acts for the benefit of the society.

References

1. _______ (2008). *Consumer Rights.* www.business.gov.in/consumer_rights
2. ________ (2008). *Consumer Education: Definition and Concepts.* In www.ue-varna.bg
3. Consumer Protection Council. (2008). *Meaning of Consumer Education.* In www.consumereducation.in/faq.htm
4. Gandotra, V. and Divatia, A. (2005). *Consumer Education.* New Delhi: Dominant Publishers and Distributors.
5. Government of India (2005). *Consumer Protection Act, 2005.* In www.consumerprotectionact.gov
6. Talesra, H., Ruhela, S., Kothari, I. (2001). *Agenda for Education.* New Delhi: Kanishka Publishers.
7. Vyas, A.K. (2006). *Consumer protection and welfare — Role of educational institutions in Manipur.* In www.fullstop.com

12 Education for Sustainable Livelihoods in Rural Areas

M.C. Reddeppa Reddy

It is a fact that about 390 million people are employed in the unorganized sector and about 28 million people are involved in the organized or formal sector. Many of the people engaged in unorganized sector do not have secured livelihoods. They have to struggle hard to find the livelihoods. Most of the workers are out of school or marginal to the educational system. According to estimates of the Planning Commission, more than 12 million additional people in India in the decade 1990-2000 were sought work every year. According to some recent estimates with the modernization of protection systems under liberalization, more than 10 million workers were made redundant in the last five years. The rural livelihoods have been influenced by external as well as the internal developments. Various changes in the rural livelihood occupations are taking place due to many factors such as environment, technological, economic, demographic, social and institutional etc. Education is also playing a major role in bringing changes in the livelihood patterns of the rural people. The literate people are moving from primary (unorganized) occupation to secondary and tertiary (organized) occupations. Sharma (1974) has established that the literacy rate is lowest in the primary sector and it is exceedingly higher in the other two sectors notably in the tertiary sector. Such higher literacy rates are expectedly owing to the nature of the occupations, which essentially require minimum educational background and/or technical skills.

Definition of Livelihoods

The term 'Livelihoods' has become extremely popular in development over the past 10 years. Sankar Datta *et al.* (2001) defined the term Livelihoods, as ways of keeping oneself meaningfully occupied, by using one's endowments (human and material), to generate adequate resources, to meet the requirements of the household in a sustainable manner. Livelihoods, therefore, go far beyond in generating income. A livelihood is also much more than employment. Dictionary definition limits it to being 'a living' or 'a means for subsistence'; others see it only as those particular economic activities that provide income.

The livelihood approach conceives of a livelihood much more broadly. The generally agreed definition of 'a livelihood' in the development context is that it: 'comprise the capabilities, assets (including both material and social resources) and activities required for a means of living'. Thus, a livelihood as defined by Chambers and Conway (1992) is sustainable when it can cope with and recover from stresses and shocks and maintain or enhance its capabilities and assets both now and in the future, while not undermining the natural resource base. The emphasis is thus on what the poor have to make a living and what limits or boosts that potential.

Livelihood Interventions

Livelihood interventions are conscious efforts by an organization to promote and support livelihood opportunities for a large number of people (other than those directly or indirectly employed by them). Livelihood interventions can be in many forms and go far beyond running an income generation programme. Various interventions can influence the livelihoods of many people. Reddy (2006) pointed out that the livelihood interventions include water-shed development, the promotion of irrigation, agriculture, value addition to produce derived from land based activities, proclaiming or asserting the rights of the people, supporting animal husbandry, promoting non-farm activities.

Sustainable Livelihoods

Sustainable livelihoods are a valuable means to ensure human security with the potential to address several dimensions of vulnerability. Emphasis is laid on mobilization of the community, in particular women, and expanding women's livelihoods. For a livelihood to be sustainable, it must be adaptive and able to withstand stress. It should also safeguard rather than damage the natural environment. Sustainable livelihoods put people first and are based on the belief that local struggles against poverty will lead us to development strategies that work. They can be understood as both a goal and an approach. The concept of livelihoods security complements that of human development by ensuring that the benefits of development reach the most vulnerable groups and that the downside risks of development and impact of conflict are addressed to ensure security to the lives and livelihoods of individuals and communities. Defining livelihood security as the removal or reduction of vulnerability to economic, environmental, social and cultural threats that undermine progressive development of communities, the approach is to increase human security for the sustainable livelihoods of vulnerable communities particularly in rural areas.

The Livelihood Principles

The principles governed by the livelihoods are termed by Sing and Gilman (2000) as follows:

- It is people-centred. It puts people at the centre of development. It involves them at all stages, from design to implement and to assess the progress.
- It is holistic, identifying the opportunities and constraints for people to improve their situation.
- It is dynamic. It recognizes that poor people have diverse livelihood strategies and expectations, based on a range of different activities. These will evolve overtime, so support must also move on.

- It links policy to community activities and *vice versa.* This is vital for achieving lasting benefits for the poor. For example, secure access to land by the poor, requires action at community level but may also require changes in policies, legislation and in the institutions responsible. The lessons drawn from the local level must be integrated into development policy, ensuring that policies reflect the priorities of the poor rather than reinforcing the position of the elite.
- It requires the public and private sectors to work together. Poor people require access to the services and goods on which they depend for their living, these needs to be provided by both the public and private sectors depending who is best placed to provide them.
- It takes long-term approach to ensure that improvements are sustainable.
- It aims to achieve practical results. Although a livelihood analysis is holistic, action is focused on a limited number of activities, which will make a practical difference to the well-being of poor people.
- It is not possible to do everything at once. The priority is to identify how rapid improvements in livelihoods can be achieved and to begin by concentrating on these interventions.

Status of Livelihoods/Employment Opportunities

Livelihood/Employment opportunities are being provided in organized as well as unorganized sectors:

- Organized Sector/ Formal Sector
  - The entire workforce in the formal sector would have had education beyond VIII class
  - About 208 million people are employed in the formal sector
  - Reduction in the growth of employment in this sector

- Accelerate or the growth of jobs in private sector after 1994
- Stagnation and declining trend in the organized labour

- Unorganized Sector/Informal Sector
  - About 384 million people are employed in the unorganized sector
  - Unorganized sector includes the occupations such as Agriculture, Weaving, Artisans, Animal Husbandry, and Service Providers etc.
  - Most of the workers are out of or marginal to the educational system
  - Non-literates are remain linked to land as agricultural labour, or who go back to it after a few years of schooling
  - Livelihood means a struggle in some of the unorganized labour and most of them have insecure livelihoods
  - Labour in this sector has increased from around 355 million to 390 million.

Chief Problems in Unorganized Sector

People in rural areas particularly in unorganised sector are continuously confronted with survival problems of food, clothing and shelter. The basic amenities of sanitation, health, education and other social welfare services are at best marginal and at worst almost non-existent. In many villages and backward areas, even drinking water is not available. Animals and human beings using the same pond for drinking, bathing and washing clothes is a common sight in the villages. Destruction of the natural resource base including land, water and forests is seriously threatening the livelihood security of the people. Due to imperfect adaptation to local environments, insufficient provision of nutrients and water, and incomplete control of pests, diseases and weeds, the present average yield of major farming systems in India is just 40 per cent. Oscar Letelier (1994) found that the rural occupational groups are facing multiplicity of problems that frequently involve complex situations. They include:

- Low product price on the domestic market.
- Unfavourable systems of commercialization. The excessive number of middlemen involved in bringing products from the producer to the consumer, a situation aggravated by free-market policies to the disadvantage of peasant agriculture which cannot complete with other forms of agriculture that are subsidized or able to produce at a substantially less cost.
- Progressive decline in the productive capacity of land.
- Increased indebtedness.
- Progressive depletion of fragile and largely exhausted resources.
- Deterioration in the quality of life.
- Loss of land ownership.
- Concentration of property, and change in land use pattern.
- Weakening of the food security base.

APSDP (1984) has identified the following problems:

- The conditions in rural areas are unsatisfactory.
- Land is becoming scarce due to population growth.
- Infrastructure (roads, schools, health centres, communication systems) is not able to cope up with ever-increasing demands.
- Un-employment and under-employment are rampant.
- Increase of unorganized labour.

Determinants of Sustainable Livelihoods

Sustainable Livelihoods would depend on the natural resource base, the geographical/physical location, the local economy/ market infrastructure, linkages available for marketing/credit and the like. Livelihoods may also depend heavily on human capital such as skills and knowledge, as in the case in many developed economies or from a combination of natural, physical and financial capital as in the case in intensive agriculture. The lives and livelihoods of the poorest and most vulnerable groups in rural and remote areas are directly dependent on the natural resource base. Destruction of the natural resource base including land, water and forest is seriously threatening human security. The move towards decentralized, participating, local management of natural resources in the past couple of decades has highlighted the important role of the community as a unit for natural resource management. It also depends on the quality and type of education that the rural communities receive for such resource management.

(a) *Human Capital:* Many of the rural poor also have livelihoods that are heavily dependent on human capital – in this case their manual labour. The poor people are usually landless and have poor access to other natural resources. Thus they mostly work as agricultural labourers, though off – farm, including migration to work as construction workers.

(b) *Ill Health:* The ability to perform manual work is critical to the livelihoods of the poor. Ill-health as their largest livelihood risk. For the poor, dependence on labouring 'good health', 'the livelihood stability and security' are a closely linked chain. ITDA (2002) found that the Health risks, particularly fevers and stomach complaints, represent over 50 per cent of all risks experienced. Ill-health has a double impact on the poorest, it reduces their ability to labour, and thus to earn, and it requires them to make expenditure on medicines and care. The heads of family most frequently borrow money to pay for medical treatment.

(c) *Landless Poor:* Lack of natural capital is a barrier to the sustainable livelihoods of the rural poor. Possessing land and sustainable livelihoods are two closely related conditions. The poor very frequently cite having land as their route of livelihood. It is better to connect the poor to a base of productive natural capital, i.e. land.

(d) *Education:* Education is an investment in human capital that delivers its returns in the future. It is a route of poverty and a means of not perpetuating it. The analysis of livelihood indicators also shows that the education level in most households has increased markedly from a low base of 15 years ago.

(e) *Access to Financial Resources:* Access to financial resources determines the sustainable livelihoods to the poor. The poor are not access to financial resources; but whilst the poor may be able to get some formal credit, the poorest of the poor find obtaining credit is very difficult. The poor have very few formal loans and have to depend on informal institutions such as moneylenders, pawn brokers etc. The inability to get formal credit, because they lack any form of collateral, limits the livelihood options of the poor. Without access to credit, they find it very different to diversify their livelihoods beyond agricultural labouring. Thus, they face all the insecurities that it brings.

(f) *Food Security:* The poor do not have food security. The institutions and programmes such as Public Distribution System (PDS), Annapurna, Antyodaya and Employment Guarantee Scheme (EGS) provide food security. If the poor do not have safety nets, their livelihoods become very insecure.

Strategies to Address Livelihood Problems

The following strategies are suggestive to address the livelihood problems of rural people:

1. Protecting, maintaining and building the critical assets of poor;
2. Empowering the poor so they can use these assets productively with less restriction; and

3. Provide the poor with more and better opportunities for using their assets.

The above strategies resonate well with the World Bank's (2001) three strategies for attacking poverty.

- Three types of assets are important
  - Human: health, skills, education
  - Financial: access to credit
  - Natural: land, land quality, water, forests
- These three are generally required to create more sustainable rural livelihoods.
- The landless need better terms of exchange for their labour. This can occur if they increase the value of that labour by becoming semi-skilled and skilled workers. This protects their stock of productive assets in the short term.
- There is a need to build their stock of human capital that will deliver a stream of livelihood benefits into the long term. This can be achieved through education including getting out of school children into school, and skill building activities.
- All the poor need access to credit in order to use the natural resources productively and effectively.
- Three types of natural resource interventions are required:
  - There is a need for land either through purchase or leasing;
  - Those who have some land or access to it, there is a need to improve its productivity; and
  - There is a need to develop non-land resources, particularly livestock and forest products.

Need of Education for Sustainable Livelihoods

A recent review of education and training programmes for adult women (DFID, literacy and livelihood website) highlights the dominant perception that such interventions have little impact. One reason could be the poor design of the education/training programmes, mostly a mechanic/didactic exercise. Most significant, however, is the prevailing disconnect between the real needs of rural people and the education/training that is on offer. People are also sceptical about 'literacy' – learning to sign one's name or read a few sign-boards may help a woman out of the stigma of illiteracy, but does not (in any substantial way) change anything else. Education has become increasingly alienated from the livelihood and survival needs of people. There is a woeful absence of continuing education opportunities that link literacy and education to self-development and skill training, leading to greater bargaining power and self-esteem. Hence, the following are suggestive for making education relevant to life needs of the people:

- The stagnation and declining trend in the organized labour and the increase of unorganized labour would suggest that corresponding changes in the education system and also reflect the absorptive nature of the latter sector;
- Now, focus on the importing of skills and knowledge to increase the productivity and human quality in the unorganized sector;
- Absent of current content, process and institutional framework of education has become irrelevant for the livelihoods of people;
- Equipping the workers in the unorganized sector to comprehend the changing social and work environment and exercise informed choices about livelihoods and life;
- A skilled workforce is needed not just for the formal sector but in agriculture, handloom weaving, animal husbandry, forestry, dairying, the growing sector of retail and so on;
- We need nurses and laboratory assistants, technicians, electricians, masons etc.;

- We need to cerate support mechanisms for the self-employed – crafts persons and artisans – for skill up-gradation, learning to deal with changed market conditions and so on;
- Learning and livelihood are inextricably interlinked. The question is not whether the two go together, but how they can be woven together; and
- Skills for survival or skills for living a life with dignity.

Reforms Needed in Educational Programmes for Sustainable Livelihoods

Accessing education and improving skills can bring positive changes in the livelihoods of the people and help in sustaining the livelihoods. The skills can be improved through formal, non-formal training or education. The following reforms are needed in educational programmes to create sustainable livelihoods for poor in rural areas:

1. Accessing education to all children, adults including women by starting primary schools, adult and non-formal education centres, farmers training centre, Krishi Vigyan Kendra's (KVKs), Jan Shikshana Sansthans (JSS) in their localities.
2. Linking education with occupations include carpentry, pottery, *agarabatti* making, electric motor winding, scooter repair, garment manufacturing, toys making, etc.
3. Training programmes should be organized and skills to be imparted on the modern methods of farming and use of new technologies/tools in their respective occupations.
4. Strengthening and expanding the Farmers Training Centres to cater to the training needs of farmers and farmwomen. In order to cover all the farmers, the staff of Farmers Training Centres has to form into two batches and organize training programmes.

5. Entrusting certain training programmes to Krishi Vigyan Kendras (KVKs)/Asst. Directors of Agriculture (R) and NGOs.
6. Organizing Farmers Exchange programmes launched by Government of India to the agriculture fields in other states for information and exchange of views. Apart from the above, farmers of one command area have to be taken to another command area for exchange of views within the district under APERP.
7. Arranging interaction programmes between scientists and farmers to enable scientists to get direct feedback, as well as farmers to obtain solutions to their field problems from scientists. FTCs are expected to organize the interaction programmes with the scientists with the help of agriculture department at district level.
8. Organizing the agricultural exhibitions in the districts in consultation with the Joint Directors of Agriculture.
9. Bringing all schemes of agriculture and allied departments under one umbrella along with technology transfer issues to the farmers at their doorstep and assist them in all the farm and non-farm operations as pointed out by Poonam and Devi Prasad (2005).
10. Furnishing/Disseminating new messages/ information to print media, AIR and Electronic media from time to time. The programmes initiated by the Agriculture University, viz., Annadatha, Rythumithra, Gramdarshani, Interactive CDs on different crops, etc.
11. Organizing Field days, Kisan gosthies (Charcha mandal), Kisan melas at block level.
12. Establishing Kisan Call Centres which provide opportunity to the farmer to talk directly and get answers to the queries on packages of practices and impact of weather on all crops grown in the state. The

service runs on a four-digit Toll Free number 1100 that is accessible from all the districts of A.P.

13. For effective transfer of technology to the doorsteps of the farmers through appropriate crop interventions to reduce the yield gaps, reduce the cost of cultivation, optimum use of the resources and ultimately increase the farm income, a naval programme 'Scientists in the fields of farmers' was launched in Andhra Pradesh.
14. To create awareness and educate farmers on latest farm technologies and developments. Kisan Melas are organized at various Research Stations and Colleges throughout the state with an aim to provide an opportunity to see the latest technologies under live demonstrations, agriculture exhibitions, and interaction with scientists and input agencies and get the habit of visiting Research Stations frequently for timely advice.
15. To educate the farmers on reducing cost of cultivation by 15 per cent and increase productivity by 15 per cent on at least three major crops growing in the market area.
16. To create a training environment at farmer doorsteps that will bring productivity gains and efficiencies to agriculture and allied sectors is the aim of Rythu Chaitanya Yatra – Farmers empowerment programme as noted by Poonam and Devi Prasad (2005).

Conclusion

The definition of livelihoods, livelihood interventions and sustainable livelihoods and the livelihood principles are explained. The Status of livelihood opportunities, the problems in un-organized sector and the determinants of sustainable livelihoods are presented in detail. The strategies to address the livelihood problems and the need of educational programmes for sustainable livelihoods, and the reforms needed in educational programmes for sustainable livelihoods are also discussed.

References

1. Sarma, P.V. (1974). Regional integration in Andhra Pradesh. Artha Vijnana, Vol. 16 (3), pp. 298-313.
2. Sankar Datta, Thomas Fisher, U. Mamata Krishna with Gitali Thakur (2001). A Resource Book for Livelihood Promotion, Indian Grameena Series (BASIX) and the New Economic Foundation, London.
3. Chambers, R. and Conway, G. (1992). Sustainable rural livelihoods: Practical concepts for the 21st Century. IDS discussion paper No. 296, IDS, Brighton.
4. Reddy, MCR (2006). Emerging Rural Occupations. Dept. of Adult and Continuing Education, SV University, Tirupati.
5. Singh, N. and Gilman, J. (2000). Employment and Natural Resources Management: A Livelihood approach to poverty reduction, SEPED Conference paper series No. 5, UNDP, New York.
6. Oscar Latelier (1994). Sustainable Peasant Agriculture, Hoja a Hoja, agosto de, 1994, pp. 5-11.
7. APSDP (1984). Rural Vocational Training in Bangladesh, Indonesia, Korea, Malayasia, The Philippines and Thailand. Report of a sub-regional Seminar, Dhaka, Bangaldesh, 5-11 May, 1984.
8. ITDA (2002). Andhra Pradesh Rural Poverty Reduction Project: Livelihood Assessment Report (LAR). Prepared for the Society for Elimination of Rural Poverty by ITDA Ltd., West Sussex, U.K.
9. World Bank (2001). World Bank Report 2000-2001. Attacking Rural Poverty, World Bank, Washington D.C.
10. Poonam Malkondaiah & Devi Prasad, D. (2005). Rythu Chaitanya Yatra (Farmers Empowerment Programme): Issues, Experiences and Ways forward: An innovative approach to extension services delivery, Dept. of Agriculture, Govt. of Andhra Pradesh, Hyderabad.
11. Poonam Malkondaiah & Devi Prasad, D. (2006). Rythu Chaitanya Yatra 2006: Reengineering Extension Approaches in Andhra Pradesh, Govt. of Andhra Pradesh, Hyderabad.

13 Sustainable Development

Rekha Talmaki

Environment has become a major cause of concern of man. This is particularly because of increasing rate of population; urbanization and industrialization in developed and developing world. As a result more and more natural resources are being exploited. Many of earth's minerals, forest, and fuel resources are showing sign of exhaustion. The potable/drinking water is becoming a tanning factory.

There is an urgent need to sustain mankind at reasonably comfort levels and at the same time the environment must be conserved without any further damage. Hence there must be conservation for sustainable development. There have been many definitions. Sustainable development is a pattern of resource use that aims to meet human needs while preserving the environment so that there needs can be met not only in the present, but also for future generations. The term was used by the Brundtland Commission which coined what has become the most often quoted definition of sustainable development as development that meets the needs of the present without compromising the ability of future generations to meet their own needs. This definition creates some questions. What is development? What are needs?

Sustainable development ties together concern for the carrying capacity of natural systems with the social challenges facing humanity. As early as the 1970s 'Sustainability' was employed to describe an economy in equilibrium with basic ecological support systems. Ecologists have pointed the alternative of a 'steady state economy in order to address environmental concerns.

Despite or wide acceptance of the concept of sustainable development no single definition is yet available which everybody accepts. Most of the definitions are built upon the view expressed by the Brundtland Commission which we have already seen above.

The Brundtland Commission definition contains three concepts that require explanation. They are: need, development and future generation. Development is often confused with growth. Growth is an expression for quantitative expansion of the economic system. Development on the other hand is a quantitative concept incorporating notions of improvement and progress and including cultural, social and economic dimensions.

The use of the concept 'needs' in the definition, is linked to the distribution of resources. According to Brundtland Commission report, sustainability is meeting the basic needs of all and extending to all, the opportunity to satisfy their aspirations for a better life. Economic growth has converted luxuries to need for some people while for the poor even the basic necessities are not affordable. Meeting the needs of all, therefore, involves heavy environmental costs.

Edward Barbier defines sustainable development as one which is directly concerned with increasing the material standard of living of the poor at the grassroots level which could be quantitatively measured in terms of increased food, mean income, educational services, health care, sanitation, water supply etc. In more specific terms sustainable development aims at reducing the absolute poverty of the world's poor by providing lasting and secure livelihoods that minimize resource depletion, environmental degradation, cultural disruption and social instability. Sustainable development is in this sense a development that meets the basic need of all, particularly the poor majority, for employment, food, energy, water and housing and ensures growth of agriculture, manufacture, power and service to meet these needs.

Other Definitions

The UNEP/WWF definition (1991): "Improving the quality of human life while living within the carrying capacity of the supporting mechanism."

Principle of the Rio Declaration on Environment and Development (1992): "Human beings are at the centre of concerns for sustainable development. They are entitled to a healthy and productive life in harmony with nature."

The Galdwin/Freeman definition (1994): "Bio Spherically compatible and socially equitable improvement in the quality of life."

According to UNDP (1992): "Sustainable development is a process in which economic, fiscal, energy, agriculture and industrial policies are all designed to bring about a development that is economically, socially and ecologically sustainable."

Sustainable development ensures a future of improved quality of life through economic development, giving full protection to the local environment.

The best convenient definition of sustainable development is "Durable change for better human condition while protecting the earth we inherit" or more simply "Increasing the earth as if we intended to stay".

It means meeting four objectives at the same time:

(a) Social protection, fulfilling the need of everyone.
(b) Effective protection of environment.
(c) Optimum and careful use of natural resources.
(d) Stability in the levels of economic growth.

The growing concern about sustainable development comes at a time when natural resources are depleting fast, more so in the Third World Countries like India. What are the factors have been responsible for increasing need of sustainable development in such countries? The factors are discussed below:

(a) Man is a part of the environment. Man needs many things from the environment for his development. But unfortunately man is unable to keep sustainable balance between man and environment. That is because of rapid growth of human population. World's population is increasing at a very high growth rate (90 million a year) and the growth rate is very high in Less Developed Countries or Third World countries.

(b) Rapid industrialization is taking place in less developed countries. In order to become self-reliant government provides all incentives and facilities to the industries; but again unfortunately laws regarding pollution and waste generation are not strict in less developed countries. Many pollution control methods are beyond the reach of less developed countries and hence they avoid these in order to reduce the cost of production. Industries in less developed countries are also responsible for polluting the environment.

(c) Less developed countries and more developed countries are commonly facing the problem of consumerism. It means that the per capita use of natural resources is increasing. Due to this gross consumption of the world is rising faster than the world population. Due to attractive advertisements and tempting schemes consumers buy more products which is actually not essential.

(d) The biggest problem of all is the rising output of waste. Whereas consumption levels are high, the amount of waste material generation is also high. The total population of more developed countries are comparatively less but their standard of living and consumption level is high hence more developed countries pollute the environment on a larger scale.

Sustainable development is a process in which development can be sustained for generations. It is development which affords to the future generations the same if not more capacity to prosper as the present generation has.

Hence it focuses on inter-generational fairness in the exploitation of development opportunities.

Components of Sustainability

The field of sustainable development can be conceptually broken into three constituent parts: Environmental sustainability, Economic sustainability, and socio-political sustainability.

These three components are interdependent. The objective of sustainable development, according to Edward Barbier is to maximize the goals in the three systems balancing the trade and setting priorities among various goals.

1. *Environmental Sustainability:* This dimension focused on the carrying capacity of nature, preservation and maintenance of the eco-systems.
2. *Economic Sustainability:* Based on equity and security of livelihood, less energy and material oriented development.
3. Social Dimension i.e. equity or development in accordance with the culture and with people participation :
   (a) Environment component requires sustainable resource use, function and maintenance of stock of natural capital, i.e. the environment should be able to perform its three functions effectively and uninterrupted so that ecological stability and resilience are not affected.
   (b) The economic component of sustainability requires that societies pressure growth paths that generate optimal flow of income while maintaining their basic stock of man-made capital, human capital and natural capital. Economic sustainability also requires internalizing all cost including the environmental costs associated with production and consumption. These are three basic goals of an economic system :

(i) Increasing production of goods and services.
(ii) Satisfying basic needs or reducing poverty.
(iii) Improving equity.

The three goals should be pursued in a sustainable way following the requirements explained above.

(c) The social dimension of sustainable development is built on the twin principles of justice and equity. For a development path to be sustainable over long period of time, wealth, resources and opportunity should be equitable shared. All citizens should have access to minimum standards of security, human rights and social benefits such as food, health, education, shelter and opportunities of self-development social equity implies equal opportunities to all for education and for making productive contribution to society. These have to be ensured to achieve the social goals of (a) Cultural diversity, (b) Social Justice, (c) Gender equality, and (d) Public participation.

Indicators of Sustainable Development

What are the indicators of sustainability? It is very clear that that sustainability refers to both ecological and economic attributes. So, the corresponding sustainability indicators will also have to account for both of them. It is quite complicated and difficult to define development indicators within the framework of economic development. Not a single indicator is able to give a perfect and complete picture about the Welfare of the State. Can per capita income GDP and NDP be a reasonable indicates of development? The answer is neither yes nor no. If we look, at the average overall average rate of 'well being' then it is yes. But what about income inequality? Where income is unequally distributed among the people? Or what about the large number of people staying below the poverty line ? If large number of people in the society are illiterate? Or if infant mortality rate is very high? It also includes many other aspects of life, such as quality of life, dignity, status, capability, empowerment of women. These are the aspects required to get a better understanding of economic and real development.

The ecological dimensions invite several new indicators for discussion. Very few of the ecological attributes are quantifiable. In order to capture different aspects of ecological and environmental changes, three types of indicators can be suggested, i.e. (i) Pressure indicators, (ii) Impact indicators, and (iii) sustainable indicators :

1. Pressure indicators refer to flow variables. They show the development over time of amounts or levels of emissions, discharges, depositions, extractions and interventions originating from a set of economic activities. Thus indicators express the burden placed on stocks of environmental goods and resources.
2. The environmental pressure originating from economic activities in a specific region does not necessarily have to affect the same region. Emissions may be imported and exported by the direction of the wind. Timber extractions may take place within the region while the produce of these extractions is used outside the region impact indicators therefore reflect the impact of this environmental pressure on the receptors.
3. Both pressure and impact indicator can be transformed into so-called sustainability indicators by relating pressure or impact with predetermined reference value. These references try to indicate what is considered to be sustainable level of extractions or a sustainable quality level of an environmental good.

Sustainable Accounting

What is sustainable accounting? In essence, associated with all production processes, is a stream of income generation attributable to the use of factors of production. That is what one studies in conventional national income accounting in terms of wages earned by the labour force, rental earned on land, profits earned on man-made capital and so on. But the natural resources are left out. One would like to see an accounting of income to be developed accommodating all the resources, including the use and abuse of renewable and non-renewable resources. That is all about sustainable accounting. While talking of sustainable accounting two different aspects which are very important. First is, non-imputation of the values of environmental goods and services used in production processes and second, absence of any allowance for depreciation, degradation and depletion of natural resources.

Economic Accounting

What is economic accounting? The conventional system of national accounts (SNA) was first started in United States of America in 1942. The starting point for such accounting is an identity. All valued in market prices.

Aggregate Demand = Aggregate Supply.

OR

Domestic Production Imports = Intermediate use in production process + Private consumption expenditure + Public consumption expenditure + Gross investment + Exports.

Using the input-output transactions framework, the gross domestic product (GDP) is defined as:

GDP = Domestic production – Intermediate use consumption.

= Private consumption + Gross Investment + Export – Imports

An added element to system of national accounts (SNA) is the statement on the man-made capital stocks in the economy. The accounting identity for this is:

Closing Stock = Initial stock + Investment during the accounting period – Capital depreciation.

Sustainable Development and Environmental Accounting

Environmentalists have coined the term "sustainability" to classify the desired balance between economic growth on the one hand and environmental preservation on the other. To achieve this end, an increasing number of countries are seeking to establish programmes for sustainable development that is a pattern of development that does not reduce production but changes its quality so as to satisfy the needs of the present generation without compromising the ability of future generations to meet their own needs. A development path is sustainable, "of and only if the stock of overall capital assets remains constant or rises over time". Overall capital assets signify not only manufactured capital (machines, factories, roads) but also human capital (knowledge, experience, skills) and environmental capital (forests, soil, quality, air water purity). It implies that future growth and overall quality of life critically depend on the quality of the environment. The natural resource base of a country and the quality of its air, water and land represents a common heritage for all generation which must be preserved and protected as its destruction and decay penalizes both present and future generations. It is, therefore, imperative that the development planners incorporate environmental accounting in one form or the other into their policy decision if an environmental resource is destroyed or damaged, a resource of equal or greater value be created elsewhere.

Pearce and Warford have attempted environmental accounting as

NNP # = GNP – Dm – Dn

Where NNP # is just sustainable national income, Dm is the depreciation of manufactured capital assets and Dn is depreciation to environmental capital – the monetary value of environmental decay over the course of a year. There is one better measure available, which is more difficult to calculate with present data collection method would be

NNP # = GNP – Dm – Dn – R – A

Here Dm and Dn are as above R is expenditure required to restore environmental capital and A is expenditure required to avert destruction of environmental capital.

Although measures of development performance based on national data do not adequately reflect environmental problems that damage the health and productivity of large number of people in the developing countries, the World Bank pointed out such environmental problems for example inadequate sanitation facilities, safe water problem, unsafe conditions caused by smoke, indoor air pollution (affects women and children's), soil erosion, sanitization etc.

Environmental Laws and Sustainable Development

The concept of sustainable development emerged as we have discussed above an important theme in 1987. The Brundtland Commission on the Environment and Development in its report "Our Common Future" called for the application of sustainability as a criterion for all development initiatives. "In order for development to be sustainable, it must meet the needs of the present without compromising the ability of future generations to meet their own needs", said the Commission.

Sustainable development has to be a long-term process, and one may say it to be a continuing process. Similarly, equity and justice are equally important for sustainable development, which can be looked at from a variety of perspectives, such as environmental, economic, social, political, cultural and technological. In this part the light has been thrown on various laws protecting the environment that has been discussed. Despite all these laws, the environmental situation in India and globally is not better. Today it is late, but tomorrow it will be too late. Therefore, it is hoped that there is a need of the strict enforcement of laws along with the people's participation.

It is very important to see whether environmental laws can bring sustainable development.

Article 14 in the Constitution of India clearly provides for equality before law and equal protection of the law, which is one of the concepts of the Rule of laws as propounded by Sir A.V. Dicey. Hence it may be safely said that if we adhere to the law, we can protect to environment and achieve the goal of sustainable development.

What is the Role of Activists in Sustainable Development?

The laws have not stopped pollution. Even the country's forests present a bleak picture. Poverty and commercialization are responsible for the rapid depletion of the rich ecological resources of India. Specialists and environmental activists have played a useful role in generating public awareness by attracting the government's attention to the ignorant poor and the destruction of the environment because of commercial interests.

Taking into consideration, the above legal provisions, it seems that the Indian Government is well aware of the extent of environmental degradation. However, there are many loopholes in its implementation of the law. There is a lack of awareness of law both among the educated as well as the uneducated people of our country. Some of the following examples show that the laws still remain on paper and not in practice. Some examples are :

- The Bombay Municipal Corporation in its over 108 years existence, has never drawn up a comprehensive waste management plan.
- About 50 per cent of the sewage generated in Ahmedabad city drains into the Sabarmati River without any treatment.
- The case study of Gujarat's "Golden corridor", the 450 km. stretch from Vapi to Mehasana which houses 190 big industrial units, including 100 chemical units in an illustration of the manner in which environmental laws remain on paper.
- The sanitary conditions in Bhopal city are still worse, except for newly developed areas like the Bhopal Development Authority. Only one non-Government

organization has made some efforts to improve the sanitary conditions in Bhopal.

It can be said that the pollution is an evil but unfortunately it is not seen as the responsibility of any authority. Neither law nor the Judiciary can bring sustainable development; unless a well-mobilised public opinion is created against environmental pollution by making people aware of its benefits.

Critique of the Concept of Sustainable Development

The concept of 'Sustainable Development' raises several critiques at different levels.

Critique Regarding Purpose

Maria Sophia A. Quire: "Sustainable development is a policy approach that has gained quite a lot of popularity in recent years, especially in international circles. By attaching a specific interpretation to sustainability population control policies have become the overriding approach to development, thus becoming the primary tool used to 'promote' economic development in developing countries and to protect the environment."

Mary Anderson: "The real purpose of sustainable development is to contain and limit economic development in developing countries, and in doing so control population growth."

Jaon Veon, a businesswoman and international reporter: "Sustainable development has continued to evolve as that of protecting the world's resources while its true agenda is to control the world's resources."

Critique Regarding Consequences

John Baden: The improvement of environment quality depends on the market economy and existence of legitimate and protected properly rights. Some criticised sustainable development because of its vagueness. For example, Jan Marc Jancovici or the Philosopher Luc Ferry expressed this view. The latter writes about sustainable development: "I know that this term is obligatory but it is also absurd, or rather to argue that it says nothing."

References

1. Ramakrishnan, P.S. (2008). *Ecology and Sustainable Development, working with knowledge systems,* National Book Trust, India New Delhi.
2. Subramanian, V. (2002). *A Textbook in Environment Science,* Navosa Publishing House, New Delhi.
3. Trivedi, T. V. and Rena Janata (1995). *Impact of Environment,* Rupa Book Pvt. Ltd., Jaipur.
4. Somashekar, N. (2005). *Development and Environmental Economics,* New Age International, New Delhi. http:/en.wikipedia.org/wiki/sustainable-development.

14 Role of Universities in Imparting Adult Education

Rameshwari Pandya

A wide range of concepts is invoked when we use the term 'adult'. The word can refer to a stage in the life cycle of the individual; he or she is first a child, then a youth, then an adult. It can refer to status, an acceptance by society that the person concerned has completed and is now incorporated fully into the community. It can refer to a social sub-set: adults as distinct from children. Or it can include a set of ideals and values: adulthood.

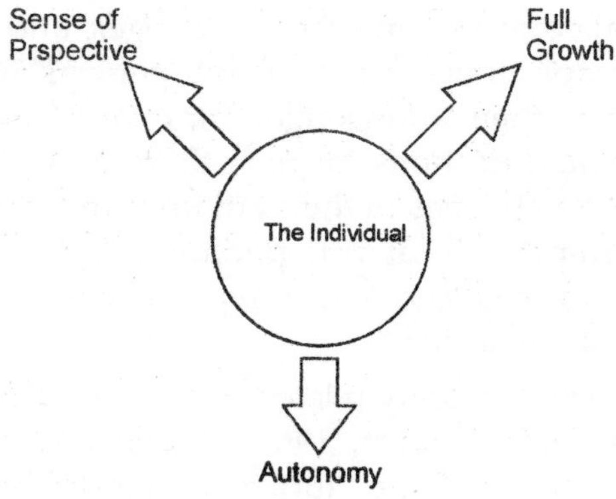

Three main clusters of ideas lie within any view of adulthood. First, the term is used in the sense of being fully grown. An overriding concept behind the word 'adult' is that of maturity. A greater sense of perspective is being shown, a perspective that will lead to sounder judgements about themselves and about others. Adulthood implies some measure of autonomy, responsible decision-making, voluntariness rather than involuntariness.

Concept of Adult Education

The multidisciplinary nature of the field and its practitioners creates many problems in international communication. It is only recently that the concept of adult education as a discrete sector of education has been recognized in many countries; even today some societies view the education and training of their citizens from the perspective of the function such training performs or the class to which participants belong; for example, trade union education or working class education. With the emergence of mass communication and computer technology, information sharing among professionals engaged in the education of adults has multiplied rapidly forcing some rationalization in the technical language of the field. The term, "adult education", denotes the entire body of organized educational process, whatever the content, level, and method, whether formal or otherwise, or whether they prolong or replace initial education in schools, colleges, and universities, as well as an apprenticeship, whereby persons' improve their abilities, enrich their knowledge, improve their technical or professional qualifications, or turn them in a new direction and bring about changes in their attitudes or behaviour in the two-fold perspective of full personal development and participation in balanced and independent social, economic, and cultural development.

Many concepts closely related to adult education, used in the literature since the early 1960s, continue to the subject to controversy. These include "formal", "non-formal", "lifelong learning", "lifelong education", "continuing education" and "recent education". In some countries the term "non-formal education" has been used, as "social education" formerly was used, as a synonym for adult education, but this is not a fully acceptable practice since the term can and should be applied equally to children and youth.

Types of Adult Education can be classified as follows:

1. Education for vocational, technical, and professional competence. (Such education may aim at preparing an adult for a first job or it may aim at keeping him up-to-date on new developments in his occupation or profession.)
2. Education for health, welfare, and family living. (Such education includes all kinds of education in health, family relations, consumer buying, Planned Parenthood, hygiene, child care, and the like.)
3. Education for civic, political, and community competence. (Such education includes all kinds of education relating to government, community development, public and international affairs, voting and political participation, and so forth.)
4. Education for "self-fulfilment". (Such education embraces all kinds of liberal education programmes: education in music, the arts, dances, theatre, literature, arts and crafts, whether brief or long term. These programmes aim primarily at learning for the sake of learning rather than at achieving the aims include in the other categories.)

The term "adult education" has come into general use within the last half century to identify two different but related phenomena – field of social activity and an emerging discipline in social science. Although they are different, these phenomena are interdependent. The disciple finds its subject of study in the field, which is, in turn, dependent upon the discipline for its development. It may be mentioned that in India adult education has travelled a long way, at least in programme implementation. In the early fifties it was known as the 'Social Education' programme. Then came a change in the areas of emphasis and contents of the programme were given a slant. The changed programme came to be known as 'Fundamental Education', as citizenship education in a nascent democracy became of prime importance. Still future down the line in the time perspective, in the mid-sixties it underwent a metamorphosis to become 'Fundamental Literacy'. Still further, it assumed the nomenclature of Non-formal (Adult) Education to ultimately revert back to Adult Education. The nature of adult education is quite confusing in the sense that adult education denotes two levels of activity: one, educating the adults, and two, educating the adult educators. While at the first level it is the practice of adult education, at the second level it is theory and understanding of the basic concepts of adult learning. In other words it can be called/labelled as 'adult education as practice' and 'adult education as a discipline'.

The concept of Adult Education approved by National Adult Educational Programme (NAEP) in India consists of three components:

(a) Literacy and numeracy of a sufficient level to enable the learners to continue self-reliant learning,
(b) Functionality aiming at improvement in the learner's skills and capabilities in the discharge of his function as a wage earner, as a member of the family and as a citizen.
(c) Awareness seeking to arouse a sense of social obligation and consciousness about the manner in which the poor are deprived of the benefits accruing from the various laws, policies and facilities meant to protect and promote their interest.

Salamthllah and Satya Deo Bareth dealing with concepts of adult education in chapter II of their study titled "Adult Education Research in India—A Study" conclude their discussion of the concept of adult education with the following observations: "A critique of the changing concept of adult education reveals that although literacy is basic to the concept embodying reading, writing and numeracy of a level of a Learner's becoming self-reliant and self-learning, the other aspect need to be emphasized in a comprehensive way. The broader concept of adult education considers learning as a life-long and continuous process aiming at improving the quality of life in a substantive way."

Adult education is to help adults learn to do better the desirable things they will do anyway. Another duty of adult education is to help adults discover higher activities and the desire to achieve them. It embraces all forms of educative experiences needed by men and women according to their varying interests and requirements. It denotes the entire body of organized educational processes, whereby adults develops their abilities, enrich their knowledge, improve their technical or professional qualifications and bring about changes in their attitudes and behaviour. Adult education is more functional and closely related to economic and social development then the education given in our schools and colleges.

Definition of Adult Education

In everyday life, however, the expression, "adult education", is often used in another sense, as a collective term covering the institutions and procedures by which adults are enabled and encouraged to experience the process. For many people, this mechanism is adult education. Adult education can be defined as the organized provision of facilities to enable men and women to enlarge and interpret their experience as adults. Adult Education is the action of an external educational agent is purposefully ordering behaviour into planned systematic experiences that can result in learning for those whom such activity is supplemental to their primary role in society, and which involves some continuity in an exchange relationship between the agent and the learners so that the educational process is under constant supervision and direction. Bertelsen has simplified the definition of adult education as "any learning experience designed for adults irrespective of content, level and methods used." Liveright and Hagood define that "adult education is the process whereby persons who no longer attend school on a regular and full-time basis undertake sequential and organized activities within a conscious intention about changes in information, knowledge understanding or skills, appreciation and attitudes, or for the purpose of identifying and solving personal or community problems."

According to UNESCO, "the term 'adult education' denotes the entire body of organised educational process, whether they prolong or replace initial education in schools, colleges and universities as well as in apprenticeship, whereby persons regarded as adult by the society to which they belong to develop their abilities, enrich their knowledge, improve their technical or professional qualifications and bring about changes in their attitude or behaviour in the two fold perspective of full personnel development and participation in balanced and independent social, economic and cultural development. Adult education embraces all forms of educative experiences needed by men and women according to their varying interests and requirements, at their differing levels of comprehension and ability and in their changing roles and responsibilities throughout life."

Need and Importance of Adult Education

Adult education is a powerful auxiliary and an essential incentive to primary education. Adult education is very much needed to change the various facets of the life of our adults. It is essential so that the masses may be trained in various habits to enable them to lead a happier life. Literacy will provide them opportunities of reading and writing and will liberate them from the chains of ignorance. Adult education will bring them in close contact with their community and country's cultural heritage. It will also provide recreational opportunities in rural areas.

Education alone can create the material basis for an improvement in the standard of life of our people. It is also the necessary condition of the training of mind and character which will permit the people to make a creative use of their leisure. The adult education relates learning to living, to the environment, the work, the family, the community. It enables the participants to do more effectively things which they have to do normally in their day-to-day life task relating to their occupation, home and family life, civic and social responsibilities. The educational process is meant to foster in them confidence and competence to acquire and deploy new knowledge and skills for their development. Education is an instrument of social change and development in a society is based on technology and science. It also helps the adult learner to improve his standard of living through participation in various development programmes. Many such programmes have been specially designed to improve the lot of poor and the deprived sections of the society. Due to illiteracy and lack of appropriate skills, they cannot take benefit of these programmes. Education enables individuals to actively participate in the development programmes, so that not only their socio-economic and political conditions are improved but also the national progress and prosperity are enhanced as a whole.

Concept of University

The image of the university is as a closed academic community of scholars and disseminating knowledge. The walls which divide the gown and the town have crumbled and the life of the university and that of the community can be vitally linked for their mutual enrichment. Institution of higher education, usually comprising a liberal arts and science colleges and graduate and professional schools that confer degrees in various fields. A university differs from a college in that it is usually larger, has a broader curriculum, and offers advanced degrees in addition to undergraduate degrees.

A university has several linked components. Professors conduct research and teach theology, canon law, civil law, medicine, and the arts, subjects of grammar, rhetoric, the classics of ancient Rome and Greece, logic, philosophy, mathematics, and astronomy, plus other subjects on occasion, such as medical botany and Hebrew. Written statutes told them which texts and disciplines to teach. A limited formal academic structure provided rules for instruction and student conduct. Students came, lived, studied, and obtained degrees. The university awarded degrees certifying that the recipient had a high level of expertise in a discipline with the approval of a supreme legal authority, such as emperor, pope, or the ruler of the state in which the university existed.

1. A university is an institution of higher education and research, which grants academic degrees at all levels (bachelor, master, and doctorate) in a variety of subjects. A university provides both tertiary and quaternary education. The word 'university' is derived from the Latin universities magistrorum scholarium, roughly meaning "community of teachers and scholars".
2. An institution for higher learning with teaching and research facilities constituting a graduate school and professional schools that award master's degrees and doctorates and an undergraduate division that awards bachelor's degrees, the buildings and grounds of such an institution the body of students and faculty of such an institution testify the practical experiences sprung from the application of theories, allowing students to continue the educational way which starts from the books.

University and Adult Education Programme

None can disagree what S.Y. Shah has said that it cannot be denied "the fact in spite of tremendous expansion of university adult education during the 1980s and hundred per cent financial supports from UGC, they could not make any significant dent in terms of developing innovative models of extension and research." Literacy campaigns require research support for a number of their problems. Only the universities which have experience and are adequately equipped to take up research studies on adult education problems can give proper guidelines to adult education educators, administrators and decision-makers in adult education programmes.

In terms of manpower, infrastructure, and finances they are in an advantageous position and can play a major role in dealing with some of the problems of the society and in contributing to social development and change. In doing so, they would have to go outside the four walls of the campus and address themselves to the needs of local communities and evolve ways and means of redressing their problems. While some of the agriculture universities and Gandhian institutions in India have been trying to actively associate themselves with the problems of local communities for quite some time, the majority of Indian universities have delimited their activities to teaching and research until 1977 when the University Grants Commission recognized extension as the third dimension of the institution of higher education. There has been a continuous debate about the role of universities in developing countries and it is now generally recognized that they should no longer remain confide to discharging the two traditional functions of teaching and research. It is argued that since education is a sub-system of society, the educational institutions cannot remain unconcerned with the problems of society. The universities which have vast resources launching of the National Adult Education Programme in 1978 by the Government of India an opportunity to them to actively involve themselves with the solution of one of the crucial problems of a few universities like Mysore, Poona, Rajasthan, Baroda, Gujarat Vidyapeeth, Madras and Sri Venkateswara, most of universities took up adult education programme only after 1978 and that too mainly in response to UGC policy and persuasion.

At present more than 100 universities and 3000 colleges have got actively involved in various adult education programmes. UGC guidelines on the subject should, however, undergo a substantial change in order to make this participation more purposeful and realistic.

University Administrative Structure

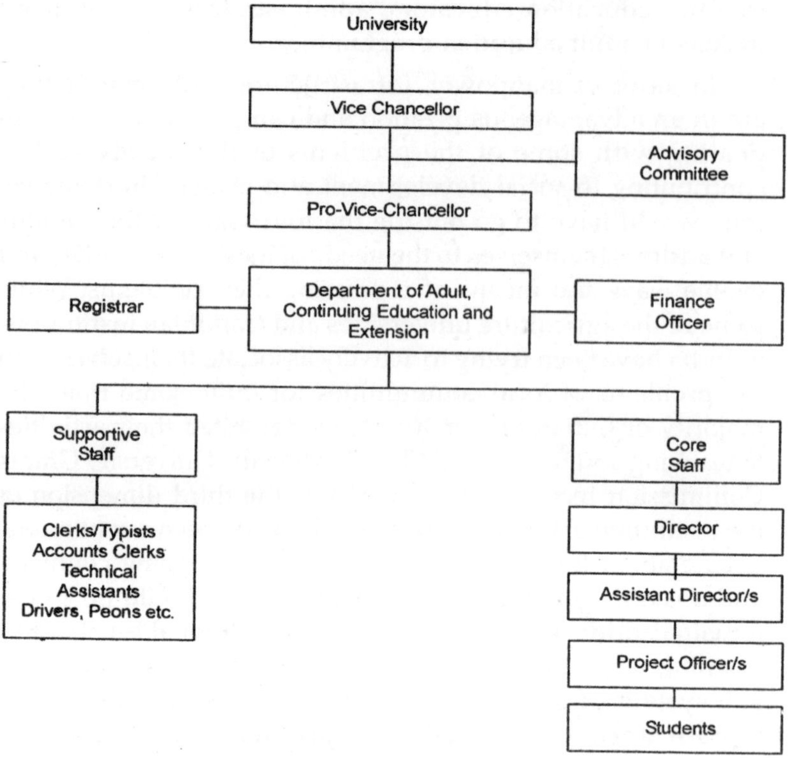

Role of University in Adult Education

- The role of the universities is to help the social, economic, educational and cultural growth of the community which it serves. With its specialized agencies it can create a wholesome impact on certain sensitive areas of economic, social, and cultural life of the people.
- Similarly, universities can effectively undertake a variety of programmes for re-education of the key personnel of the different professions. In this context a special mention of re-education of the teachers is relevant. The need is so urgent and the problem is so vast that the country would naturally look to the

universities for effective leadership for re-educating the teachers and keeping them fully informed of the new teaching practices and methods, new philosophies of education as well as developments in various fields of knowledge with which they are concerned. They can also help in building up healthy attitude of the community towards some of the fundamental national problems, such as public health, sanitation, population control, and building up a national solidarity.

- Organize programmes which will brief the national leadership in civil and political life as well as the people and acquaint them with knowledge and wider experience pertinent to decision making on some of the vital problems challenging national life.
- Motivation is the first step without adequate motivation the adult learners, volunteers, students, teachers, and local elite cannot participate in it. The universities and colleges can design strategies to motivate the public and mobilize the resources for launching adult education programme.
- Material preparation is one of the major roles of universities for adult education. Students and staff can prepare slogans, posters, banners, drama skits, street plays, role plays, pamphlets, articles, newspapers advertisements etc. to develop favourable environment to enthuse the public and the adult learners to join the adult centres. Universities are the right agencies to train the various functionaries for adult education programme.
- Monitoring and evaluation are essential to know whether the programme is making headway, whether learners are attending to their works, whether the programme duration is sufficient, whether there is need for in service training.
- The universities can train the students to work as monitors/*preraks* for post-activities like organizing literacy centres, library, reading room, *charcha mandal,*

sports and recreational activities, and skill development programmes. There is dearth of graded materials for post-activities and the university can develop suitable materials on various topics like income generation, development programmes, immunization, afforestation, mother and child care nutrition, rights and duties, legal knowledge, scientific temper etc.

- The university can provide research support to the total adult education programme as they have expertise in developing research tools, methods and treatment of data through improved statically techniques. The universities can do research through quick appraisal, and short term projects so that results so obtained can be disseminated to the field functionaries to take corrective measures. Documentation of training materials, research report studies etc. is highly warranted for total adult education programme and the universities can undertake this activity for reference and future guidance.

Role of College Principal

The college principal plays a multiple role on the implementation college adult education programme :

1. To help in motivating the staff students and public with a view to mobilize a maximum number of them to participate in adult education based programmes.
2. To help to chalk out plans of action.
3. To develop the skills required for implementing, co-ordinating and evaluating the programme.
4. To encourage and enthuse students and staff with proper incentives and appreciation.
5. To co-ordinate and collaborate with all other agencies concerned.

Thus the college principal acts as a

- Organizer
- Co-ordinator
- Motivator
- Evaluator
- Reporter

Role of Professor-in-Charge

Professor-in-charge is the key person for successful working of the adult education programme and works under the guidance of the college principal. He/She is *interalia* involved in:

1. Formulation of the project proposal.
2. Selection of area of work.
3. Selection of supervisor, motivator, instructor and students.
4. Preparing need based curriculum.
5. Evolving suitable pedagogy according to learners' needs.
6. Procuring teaching-learning materials.
7. Setting up adult education and JSN centres.
8. Organizing adult, continuing, population, education programmes and activities through concerned functionaries and with the help of expert resources persons.
9. Providing necessary guidance to college/field level functionaries for the effective working of the programme.
10. Receiving feedback through meetings and discussions with the functionaries.
11. Monitoring programme.
12. Maintaining and evaluating the programmes.
13. Conducting research.
14. Preparing and consolidating reports.
15. Co-ordinating resources.

16. Undergoing training and attending workshops and seminars.

Role of Students

Majority of the students involved in the programmes perform the following roles and functions :

1. To identify adult learners in the age group 15-35 years.
2. To motivate learners and develop support.
3. To undergo training.
4. To decide regarding place and timings of the classes.
5. To conduct classes for imparting 3Rs.
6. To plan other activities and programmes.
7. To maintain learners' attendance record.
8. To fill-up and dispatch cards and evaluation forms and submit work report.
9. To keep continuous contact with the learners and arrange post-literacy assistance/programmes.

Conclusion

There is no end to the good which the universities can do to the community. It is, however, necessary that each university should measure its own opportunities and plan the best that it can do to be of service to the society which it serves. Further universities should strengthen the extension dimension and develop the extension culture among the students and staff members through flexible approaches. The universities can adopt a few mandals/areas for community outreach fieldwork.

References

1. Agrawal, S.P. (2002), *Development of Adult, Continuing & Non-formal Education in India,* Concept Publishing Company Pvt. Ltd., New Delhi.

2. *Compendium of Instructions on National Learning* (1992), Vol.11, Ministry of Human Resource Development, Department of Education, Government of India, New Delhi.
3. Chopra, R. (1999) *Adult Education*, The Indian Publication, Ambala Cantt., Punjab.
4. Dutta, S. (1985) *From Literacy to Liberation*, Indian Adult Education Association, New Delhi.
5. Jethithor, B. (1996) *Adult Education and Extension*, A.P.H. Publishing Corporation, New Delhi.
6. Mohanty, J. (2005) *Adult and Non Formal Education*, Second Revised and Analyzed Edition, Deep & Deep Publications, New Delhi.
7. Rogers, A. (1989) *Teaching Adults*, Sterling Publications, New Delhi.
8. Singh, M. (2001) *Adult Education in 21st Century*, The Associated Publisher, Ambala Cantt.

15 Problems in Adult Education

Rameshwari Pandya

Illiteracy is a global problem. The magnitude of illiteracy in our country is still very high and constitutes serious handicap in the socio-economic development of the country. After independence of our country, there has been a significant increase in literacy percentage but the number of illiterates has also increased simultaneously due to alarming growth of population. The only solution to this problem is Universalization of primary education and adult literacy in a given frame of time. Adult education is often confused with adult literacy and adult literacy has to accompany adult education; adult education is something more than the teaching of the 3Rs (reading, writing, arithmetic). It is rather teaching the people the values of life. In adult education there has to be more emphasis on teaching the people the art of living rather than the art of deciphering a few alphabets on the printed page.

Adult education should be understood to mean as the education of complete man with a sense of duty, right and citizenship both, as an individual and as member of the community that is Lifelong Education. Hence, adult education is not an alternative, it is a necessity. Adult education is based on assumptions that :

(a) Illiteracy is a serious handicap to an individual's growth and to the country's socio-economic progress;

(b) Education is not confined with schooling but takes place in most work and life situations;

(c) Learning, working and living are inseparable and each acquires a meaning only when correlated with others;

(d) The means by which people are involved in the process of development are at least as important as the ends;

(e) The illiterate and the poor can rise to their own liberation through literacy dialogue and action.

The all inclusive purpose of education in democratic setup like ours is to assist in the continuous growth and development of every individual the fulfilment of his maximum potentiality in directions considered desirable by society. It denotes the entire body of organized educational process whereby adults develop their abilities, enrich their knowledge, improve their technical or professional qualifications and bring about changes in their attitude and behaviour.

Adult education is increasingly being seen in its totality. Liveright and Hagood proposed that "adult education is the process whereby persons who no longer attend school on a regular and full-time basis undertake sequential and organized activities within a conscious intention about changes in information, knowledge understanding or skills, appreciation and attitudes or for the purpose of identifying and solving personal or community problems". According to UNESCO, the term adult education denotes the entire body of organized educational processes, whatever content, level and method, whether formal or otherwise, whether they prolong or replace initial education in schools, colleges and universities as well as in apprenticeship whereby persons regarded as adult by the society to which they belong develop their abilities, enrich their knowledge, improve their technical or professional qualifications and bring about changes in their attitude or behaviour in the two fold perspective of full personnel development. The purpose of adult education is to help people to make choices to help them to define their "world" to help them to write their history, and to work with them to become involved in meaningful and relevant action and learning. Concluding adult education is more functional and closely related to economic and social development than the education given in our schools and colleges.

Need of Adult Education

Adult education is needed on account of the following reasons:

(i) Adult education is a powerful auxiliary and an essential incentive to primary education. No programme of compulsory education for children can succeed without the active support and co-operation of adults.

(ii) India has chosen the path of democracy and the right of vote has been extended to all adults over 18 years. But the success of democracy rests on the quality of the citizens of the state. Because of illiteracy, our democracy is bound to suffer. It is really very difficult to achieve anything remarkable by way of progress—social, economic or political, unless we give full attention to the education of adults.

(iii) The concept of adult education has brought a new hope for adults who could not get opportunity of receiving education during their school years. Through various programmes and techniques of social education, the illiterate farmers in the fields, labourers in the factories and others can be made acquainted with the latest development.

(iv) Adult education is very much needed to change the various facets of the life of our adults. It is essential so that the masses may be trained in various habits to enable them to lead a happier life. Literacy will provide them opportunities of reading and writing and will liberate them from the chains of ignorance.

(v) The greatest good that adult education programmes can do to our adults in various fields is the training in co-operative living. Adult education can inculcate the spirit of co-operation which at present is lacking among our masses.

Aims and Objectives

The aims and objectives of adult education are to transform the society. The most important aim is to improve the social, moral, cultural and economic life of the people and to convey the idea of self-help and self-reliance. According to the general conference of UNESCO 1976, generally speaking, the aims of adult education should be to contribute to :

- Promoting work for peace, international understanding and co-operation.
- Creating an understanding of and respect for the diversity of customs and cultures, on both the national and international plans.
- Developing the ability to grasp adequately the problems involved in the upbringing of children.
- Developing the aptitudes for making creative use of leisure and for acquiring any necessary or desired knowledge.
- Developing the aptitude for learning to learn.
- Developing a critical understanding of major contemporary problems and social changes and the ability to play an active part in the progress.

In some countries the objectives are expressed in a manner indicating the role of adult education in the political context of the country. The aims and objectives of adult education in India can be explained from 2 points of view—From the point of view of the individual and from the point of view of the society.

From the point of view of the individual, it has the following purposes:

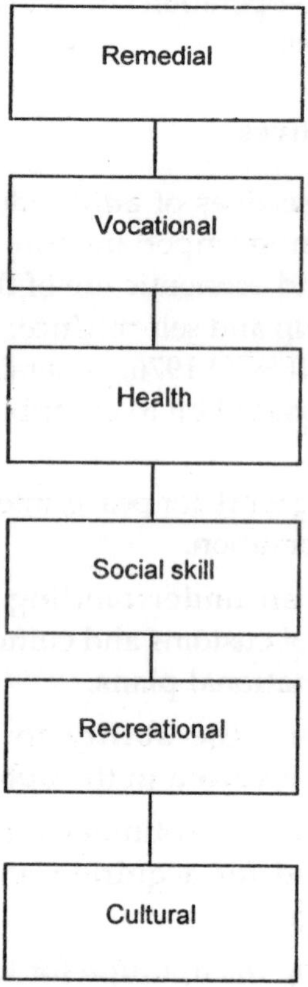

- *Remedial*: It means to make good the lack of formal schooling which the children of more fortunate parents had received. In other words, the adults must remedy their earlier weakness or limitations and manage to find a new opportunity to complete their essential part of education which is to equip them to live in the society as happy and satisfying individuals.
- *Vocational*: Apart from imparting 3Rs for the adults a good programme of adult education should include the provision of commercial or technical education in urban areas and education for agriculture and cottage industries in rural areas.
- *Health*: It applies education pertaining to the principles

of health and hygiene and helps in prevention and eradication of diseases.

- *Social Skill*: The adult desires to get on with his fellows, to advance in life, to make family living effective and to know his rights and duties in the complex world and modern times.
- *Recreational*: It implies knowledge of various ways of recreation for the best use of leisure time and preservation of mental health.
- *Cultural*: It implies cultural achievement and building up a philosophy of life.

From the point of view of the society

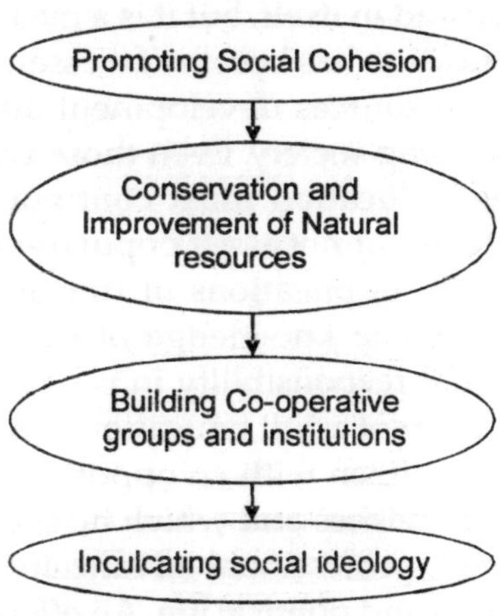

- *Promoting Social Cohesion*: In the clash of interests which is a characteristic of modern society. We need to create common bonds between people. This is necessary not only to remove prejudices amongst groups, but also to check the growing aloofness among individuals and groups which are so characteristic of urbanized and even rural society.
- *Conservation and Improvement of Natural Resources*: Adult education teaches the people to view the gift of India's geography and human stock as resources from which

to build up a worthy standard of life for all the people in this land.

- *Building Co-operative Groups and Institutions*: Adult education has to lead on to teach men the skill which are necessary for building up group qualified and willing to use these resources for the good of all.
- *Inculcating Social Ideology*: One of the most important functions of adult education is to prepare the people to subordinate their private welfare to the welfare of their group, their community and their country and to do this joyfully.

Scope of Adult Education

Education is not an end in itself, but it is a means to the lifelong process. Adult education has become an essential aspect of the strategy of human resources development and of the goal of creation of a developing society. Even those who have had the most sophisticated education must continue to learn. Mere persuasion or coercion cannot assist population growth. People must understand the implications of unchecked increase in population acquire some knowledge of the laws of life and appreciate individual responsibility in programmes of family planning. The function of adult education in a democracy is to provide every adult citizen with an opportunity for education of the type which he wishes and which he should have for his personal enrichment, professional advancement and effective participation in social and political life. An effective programme of adult education in the Indian context should envisage the liquidation of illiteracy—continuing education - corresponding courses - libraries - role of universities in adult education and organization and administration of adult education.

Problems of Adult Education

Adult education is need-based education. The basic needs of people are food, shelter and clothing. The basic needs do not include education. Only when man is able to meet his basic needs than other needs like the social and psychological needs, are considered by the individual, so education becomes a secondary need for a poor man. If he confines himself to basic needs alone then the need for adult education may not arise at all. But human needs do not end with basic needs of food, shelter and clothing. According to the classification of Maslow the hierarchies of human needs are :

- Food
- Shelter and Safety
- Love of Belongingness
- Esteem
- Self-actualisation

Man has, therefore, to acquire knowledge and skills to satisfy all his needs. This means education is an inevitable necessity for every individual. Adult education has problem if the need does not exist in the individual. The individual, the instructor and the community, are actively involved in the process. If any of them lacks motivation, these programmes of adult education may fail. Adult education can fail at any stage if people change their needs or even shift their priorities and the adult education fails to take notice of their changing needs. Looking from the point of view of the organizers adult education also fails due to several organizational lacunae and other limitations. Because the organizers have not been able to recognize the learners' needs they could not have planned an adult education programme responsive to the learners. There can also be faulty planning, improper utilization of resources, including human resources behind the failure. Another contributory factor for the failure of adult education can be found with the sponsoring agencies, or the community or the political set-up. One or all of them may have vested interests which can be detrimental to adult education programmes. In fact in India schemes like the National Adult Education Programme literacy campaigns, community development programmes and many such schemes have not been able to make the hope for impact, mostly because vested interests and lack of drive have taken precedence over national objectives. Each of these factors, which could be responsible for the failure of adult education will be discussed in detail.

Reasons

Adult education attempts to improve the quality of life of the learner. But there are many problems beyond its scope. The learners often face conditions which compel them to dropout of the adult education stream. Some of them are discussed below:

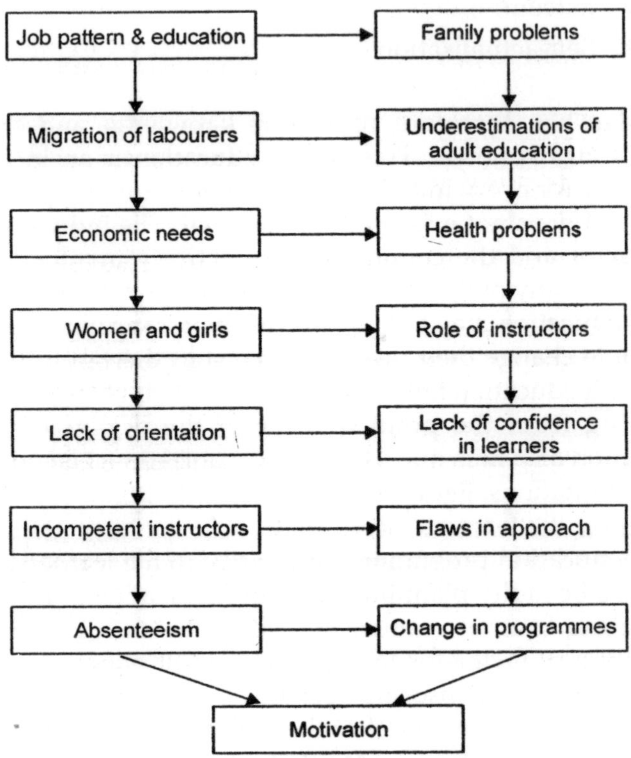

Job Pattern and Education

- Education and the job pattern of the individual may not coincide.
- If the individual has to make a choice, he chooses the job and drops out of education.
- If there is a clash obviously the job comes first and education is dropped.
- Even in the adult education timings are made convenient the individual may get physically and mentally tired from the job and may prefer rest.
- The need to retain a job influences the motivation of learners in a negative way.
- The enthusiasm of the co-workers and their complacency also demotivates the adult learners.
- Sometimes an increment or a short-term benefit may divert the attention of the adult learners from education.
- For instance over time allowances a supplementary or a suitable job can discourage the learners from attending his classes.
- The poor the not-so-poor and at times even the well-to-do may find the attraction of monetary gain too tempting to resist.
- Since all the adult learners are employed their employment issues are the most common factors in determining their availing of adult education.
- An overtime allowance or a supplementary job which gives additional income may divert the individual.
- Since all or almost all learners are employed their employment conditions are responsible for their continuance or drop-out from adult education.

Family Problems

- In some cases, on account of socio-economic conditions the learners may not see the need for adult education.

- Even when the organizers try to reach them they find way to escape.
- The sheer ignorance of the deprived makes them impervious to the benefits of any form of education.
- Ignorance deprives them of the benefits of education.
- Such persons who suffer from ignorance and poverty, even if they join adult education courses by compulsion are under pressure and they soon drop-out.

Migration and Labourers

- Learners mostly of lower socio-economic status migrate in search of jobs or are less stable in their occupation.
- Migration of labour in all sectors, particularly in rural agriculture is very common.
- They move in search of stable job.
- While working they change their residence, in fact their life gets so disrupted that they do not have any time for adult education programme.
- They change residences.
- They need to put in more time in learning, which again is in conflict with their shifting life.
- The easiest way for them is to dropout of the adult education stream or just to keep away.

Economic Need

- The adult learners are more vulnerable to criticism and failure.
- Although the organizers and the instructors do not point out the lack of progress in the learners, the learners themselves are quick to perceive their shortcomings and "solve" them by simply dropping out of the programme.
- Adult education target group are mostly drawn from youth and adults who are wage earners and supporters of their families.

- Many adult learners are in need of developing employable or saleable skills as fast as they can.
- They do not view literacy and general self-development programmes as necessary or useful for them.
- Such programmes in fact are considered to be useless and a waste of time.
- Hence, the economic needs should be met first.
- Any extra time spent on a job or work will boost their income and that too immediately.
- The learners do not consider literacy and general self-development programmes as necessary as they do not generate immediate financial gains.
- The programmes may fail if they do not cater to raising the economic status of the learners.

Health Problems

- The poor who form the majority of adult learners suffer most from illnesses and ailments including the evil of too many children, which affects the health of the mother and also the care of her children.
- Adult learners mostly belong to poorer sections of the society. Illness and ailment are common with poor.
- There is no mother or child care.
- Among the poor families anaemia, enteric disease, chest and lung infestations due to their poor nutritional status it is quite common and they fall sick often.
- Poor housing, unhygienic toilet facilities, unsafe drinking water and an unhealthy environment, make it still worse.
- The learners from slum and overcrowded tenements always seem to be famished and ill-fed as if they are born and bred not to possess physical stamina, or motivation to sustain them through a meaningful training for work.

- It is the impracticality of even the slightest advancement in the adult education programme that keeps these learners away. So at the slightest discomfort or ailment they dropout of adult education programmes.

Women and Girls

- Women and girls are major clientele for any adult education programme. The superiority of men and the secondary status given to women keep many women and girls away from education.
- As for adult education for girls and women the vested interests of their men folk is the principal factor working for its failure.
- Men by and large do not approve of women going out to attend classes to educate themselves because house keeping and child rearing will be neglected or will have to be shared.
- These women must still drudge at home.
- Adult education thus, is always in danger of failing because it does not have the support of the men as far as women's education is concerned.
- Any impoverished women would not keep away from adult education aimed at generating income if her husband, or other male relations encourage her by offering to share the household chores.
- The customs traditions and superstitions add to the dropout rate. Indian women, for long have accepted their place at home and play a subdued role.
- The male relations of the woman adult learners are instrumental in trying to make a failure of adult education specially of adult education for women.

Role of Instructors

- The role played by the instructor is also important. The instructor can contribute either to the success or failure of the adult education programmes.

- Adult education is planned with a variety of objectives.
- The objective differs from one group of learners as their needs also differ.
- It is the unitary and exclusive organizing of adult education programmes errors may be unintentional unforeseen and unavoidable many are not.
- The instructor however competent he may be cannot cover different groups and deliver goods.
- He is likely to make mistakes.

Lack of Orientation

- The term "orientation" is used deliberate against "preparation". This may be one of the reasons for errors on the part of instructors.
- India requires such a vast network of adult education that long, professional training of teachers may not be feasible.
- An orientation means of adult education its magnitude and significance can be given to each adult instructor.
- If orientation to adult education is not given to the teacher he or she is most likely to remain less resourceful, less imaginative and less helpful.
- Adult instructors are vast in number and so it may not be possible to give training for long periods.
- In the absence of orientation the teachers of adult education may prove to be less resourceful, less helpful or less imaginative.
- The failure of the programme then could be due to the instructor's lack of instructional and psychological skills.
- The instructor may not be able to teach and guide or to sustain the interest of the adult education learners.

Lack of Confidence in Learners

- There is general feeling among instructors that the

student of adult education are of an inferior type compared to students of formal education.

- The teacher's perception of the learners can have a positive influence on the learners but some teachers find it hard to convince themselves of the fruitfulness of the progress and the ability of the learners.
- Such negative attitude will contribute to the failure or at least to a lesser degree of success of the programme.
- The teacher if he has a correct perception or opinion of his students will have confidence in the student's progress and ability. A negative attitude will contribute to the failure of the programmes. If the teacher have positive attitude towards his students it will result in the success of the programmes.

Incompetent Instructors

- A teacher may not be trained.
- An untrained teacher with competence and effort can do a good job. But an incompetent one can do only harm and will not be of any help.
- The instructor does not have the adequate knowledge of the subject or the problems, and works superficially.
- The contents of teaching textbooks, without being made known to the learners.
- The second characteristic is that the incompetent teacher cannot motivate the students to a reasonable level.
- The teaching style and the personality of the instructor fail to sustain the interest of the learners.
- Such qualities no doubt are needed in a teacher but their lack of real knowledge which cannot truly enlighten a learner, nor motivate him cannot be ignored. Surely such "success" is illusory and not real.
- He cannot sustain their interest. Such teachers contribute only to the failure of the programme.

Flaws in Approach

- Adult education programmes are planned for voluntary learners mostly adults and aged.
- The instructor may be tempted to employ the teaching strategies of formal education which assume a captive audience and an authoritarian atmosphere in the class.
- It is possible that the objectives of adult education are relevant but the methods of instruction or learning activities may not be.
- The earnest adult learners would want to do things by themselves in order to learn.
- They involve themselves in learning by doing rather than only being observers or passive spectators.
- An exception could be made for those learners who have come at the persuasion of others and are not personally keen to learn, or when the learning activity is not what they seek.
- In such cases the adult learners may not become active participants in the adult education programme of a particular type.
- They desire more flexibility and not rigidity.
- Courses are self-directed and result-oriented and not formal.
- It cannot be a routine drill. This is more necessary in the case of female learners.
- If topics suitable for the temperament of learners are not selected, then the programmes can fail. If the learners may not become active participants.

Absenteeism

- Absenteeism may be on the part of learners and on the part of the instructor.
- If the absenteeism is on the part of the instructors, it will be disastrous.

- An irregular teacher can inhibit or at least dilute the desire for learning.
- It results in loss of seriousness and waste of time.
- Absenteeism raises doubt about the seriousness of the instructors and the learners come to regard adult education classes as a waste of time.
- Absenteeism on the part of learners will result in a negative impact on the programme.

Change in Programmes

- There shall be a plan for the programme and continuity in learning.
- Too many changes and alterations will disturb the continuity of the programme which can only lead to the failure of adult education.
- If there are many programmes with no continuity, the alterations and changes can only result in failures of the programmes.

Motivation

- Motivation is an important factor lack of motivation leads to the failure of the programme.
- If instructors and the learners are not motivated to learn the programme is not going to be successful.

The various problems faced by the adult educators concerning staff, activities of adult education profusion of agencies, finance and diffusion of professional effort have left them little time to engage in research and publication. The attitude of adult educators to borrow and preserve should be shifted to modification development and progress so that it can face the challenges of future.

Guideline for Success of Adult Education Programmes

To decide the guidelines to run the programme successfully it is necessary to know the aims of the programmes and its characteristics :

(i) Adult education yield immediate results as compared to formal education which is a slow process.

(ii) It integrates both education and development.

(iii) It involves the people and the community intimately with its activities.

(iv) It is a social process.

(v) It tends to uplift the poor and the oppressed groups of the society and checks exploitation of all types—social, economic and political.

(vi) It aims at building leadership qualities.

(vii) The time place and curriculum of adult education should be convenient and relevant to the needs and conditions and interests of the learners.

(viii) Inter- and intra-departmental cooperation and coordination should be utilized to the maximum in planning and organizing centres.

(ix) Voluntary and private agencies should be encouraged to share the responsibility in promoting adult education centres.

(x) Local communities and professional bodies should be made established and nobody should have any difficulty in switching from one to the other.

(xi) Suitable learning materials needs to be developed for various groups, in accordance with the needs and interests of the learners.

(xii) Methods and media suitable for the learners of different age groups and the various socio-cultural background should be adopted and utilized for the teaching-learning process.

(xiii) Proper evaluation procedures should be developed and practised for ascertaining the progress, placement and certification of learners.

- It can bring education to the door-steps of million of children and adults who are excluded from the normal stream of education.
- It can help economizing the resources—physical, financial as well as academic.
- It can prove an effective mode of democratizing education and the life style of the people.
- The curricula, content, teaching methods, learning media and materials of Non-Formal Education can be made more relevant and meaningful of the learners.
- In this system, different social, cultural, and voluntary organizations are involved effectively making education accessible to all.

Universities should Give the Leadership

The Universities in India have a major role to play especially in the task of conducting research activities so as to improve upon the machinery and policy-planning of adult education programmes. The University Centres for Adult and Continuing Education have to gear teaching in adult education to development-oriented research inputs and to institute suitable incentive systems for the adult learners. Universities can undertake projects that shall exhibit innovation regarding continuing adult education with productive activities and common cost-benefit or cost-effectiveness logic. At present very little systematic and sustained effort has been made to study the various aspects and problems of adult education in our country. Concerning research there has been *ad hoc* attempts that have hardly resulted in significant contribution to the theory and practice of adult education. Listed below are some of the important research fundamental, applied and action. The universities and apex of the educational leader can undertake more fundamental and applied researches rather than action-research. There are policy planning, economic of adult education indicators for determining adult literacy and adult learning effectiveness of adult education programme development of appropriate materials and methodologies and evaluation. The sub-themes under these broad areas can be taken as under:

- Policy planning,
- Economic of adult education,
- Factor related to adult literacy and adult learning,
- Indicators for determing the effectiveness of adult education programme,
- Development of appropriate materials and methodologies, and
- Monitoring and Evaluation.

References

1. Agrawal, S.P., Gupta, Mithilesh, Sherawani, M.W.K. (2002) ismani Meena, Development of Adult, Continuing, and Non-formal Education in India, Concept Publishing Company Pvt. Ltd., New Delhi.
2. Ansari, N.A. (1984) *Adult Education in India,* S. Chand & Company, Delhi.
3. Grover, R.P., Chopra, Rita (1998) *Adult Education,* The Indian Publications, Ambala.
4. Kundu, C.L. (1987) *Adult Education,* Sterling Publishers Private Limited, New Delhi.
5. Mohanty, Jaganath (1991). *Adult and Non-formal Education,* Deep & Deep Publication Distributors, New Delhi.
6. Sharma, S.N., Prakash, Ravi (1996) Kanishaka Publishers, Distributors, New Delhi.
7. Singh, J.K., Sudarshan, K.N. (1996) *Adult Education,* Discovery Publishing House, New Delhi.

WOMEN AND NON-FORMAL EDUCATION

16 The Roots and Fruits of Women Education

K. Muralidaran
D. Preetha

Education

"Education is the manifestation of divine perfection already existing in man", said Swami Vivekananda. "Education is something which makes a man self-reliant and self-less", implied in Rig Veda (Meenakshisundaram, A., 2007). The aims and objectives of education, when traced in a historical context convey that they were formed by the community needs, social structure and historical compulsion. The development in the present day educational system, reflected in its structure and process, is an evolutionary process stage by stage.

The main purpose of education can be identified as realization of one's self; better understanding and adaptation to one's social environment; learning for earning and living; developing intellectual pursuits and skills and to discover lasting values. Thc development of a nation cannot be measured only through the technological and materialistic advances but only through the quality of life the people live. "Education is the most valuable and imperishable wealth to a person; other things are not wealth", Thiruvalluvar (Meenakshisundaram, A., 2007). Emphasising on education in general leads to the need of Women Education in specific. Pandit Jawarharlal Nehru stated "The status of women indicates the character of a country" (Rajkumar, 2000).

Women Education

Giving equal amenities and chances to women to learn on par with men is said to be women education. Women could be categorised on the basis of their socio-economic status, i.e., those women who have stable economic status, those who belong to middle class economic status, and those who are below poverty line. Among these categories the main concentration should be on second and third class people. Therefore, it is important to focus on expanding the educational opportunities to women as they contribute to their economical development and for the progress of the state (Nagarajan, K., 2007).

Need for Women Education

"Women should receive education at par with men; if necessary provide them specialized education".—Mahatma Gandhi. It is also said that our country constitutes roughly 50 per cent of women and it is futile to think of achieving Universal Literacy without providing educational opportunities. Women constitute half of the total population in the world and they perform an estimated 60 per cent of the world's work but own only one per cent of the world's land and earn just 10 per cent of the world's income. Further, they are denied with the right to education, intellectual obscurantism in the patriarchal society. Even though they are contributing for the national development, their work is unrecognized and uncounted. As a result of this, they lagged behind in all spheres of life and suffering from chronic malnutrition. Recognizing their potentialities and to convert them as active human resources, the Government of India has formulated and implemented education and welfare programmes. In spite of these efforts, their position has not been altered significantly. Looking at the present scenario, participation of women in jobs has been consistently low and working women are engaged in manual labour. Women could not go for higher education because of high rate of illiteracy among them and only a negligible proportion of them are engaged in higher positions. Therefore, need rises for women education for her development which leads to the development of her family and resulting in Nations' prosperity. Thus all are interlinked as Kothari commented "For full development of our human resources, the improvement of homes and for moulding the character of children during the most impressionable years of infancy, the education of women is of even greater importance than that of men."

If a nation has to grow and develop, its women must rise to the occasion. But if they have been socialised in such a fashion that submission, lack of initiative, dependency, reliance on others, self-negation and effacement are the traits engendered, then one can have little hope of active participation and contribution from this half of the population. Providing equal opportunities for learning devoid of gender is said to be Women Education. The term "Women Education" itself gains the importance as it is the Powerful Tool of changing the status of women in the society. By educating women it brings about reduction in inequalities; augment in status in her family as well as in society. In order to encourage education of women at all levels number of schools, college and even universities have been established exclusively for them.

Speaking about women education it is mandatory for a family to thrive, for the cognitive development of her wards, to eliminate illiteracy in the society, to support her family by earning, to actively participate in community development programmes like family planning; child nutrition; health awareness; income generation etc. The social reflection of a woman in the present day is that of an invader in man's world of employment, a woman is a monetary asset in the family. Women are playing the idyllic role by combining home making and career. As a result of Education, they desire to benefit from the sense of economic freedom and to buy certain things of their own without depending on others. These are all some reasons for women to get employed in any organisation which depends upon their education.

The progress and development of any developed country cannot be measured only through the scientific and worldly advances but only through the quality of life the people live. The growth of a Nation lies in its competence to bump up the lot of the weaker section of its society and it is accredited to the role played by the women and hence it is rightly said that "The hand that rocks the cradle, rules the world". Thus women education is supposed to be of great importance in any society.

Importance of Women Education in India

The Indian society still remains at the cross ends, the uniqueness of women are yet to be realised. The education that was imparted to them made them alert that they were one of the two wheels of the life-cart and that they were also key persons in the family. They began to understand that an all-round development of them, equal to men necessary for the growth and prosperity of a Nation.

It is indispensable to identify the female consciousness and her socialization if we have to think in stipulations of enlargement and development. For this we have to understand various development crises that the female undergoes right from the time of birth. Women strive to be economically, psychologically independent and attain their own status, leading to harmonious family existence. The historical development about the progressive status of the Indian women is presented elsewhere in this chapter. Moreover, it is almost certain that it is impossible to study the present without reference to the past. The Indian women have traversed through various stages to reach the present status. Many scholars have precisely emphasized that women education has to be properly planned, developed and looked for community or country to accomplish prominence (Nagarajan, K., 2007).

Hence it can be shortlisted that

- Women's education plays a vital role in the overall development of our country,
- It helps in the development of the human life in improving the quality of life at home and outside,

- Educated women not only have a propensity to promote education of her children, but also provide better parameter for the development of her children, and
- Educated women can also help in the reduction of toddler transience rate and growth of the healthy population.

The importance of women education gained its height slowly from the history which underwent various and serious changes.

Women in Ancient Period

I. Pre-Aryan Period

The status of women during the Pre-Aryan is not known much as review of literature is inadequate. Matriarchal family system, prevalent in Kerala indicates the likelihood of survival of the same system during the period. Idols of 'Mother Goddess' and the seals obtained after excavations in the Indus Valley also exhibits the higher status of women in that period, as expressed by Mukerjee, Radhakamal (1959). It seems that the women in Pre-Vedic period were fairly doting of decorating and making up their outer appearances. They were interested in the art of dancing and participated on equal terms with males, in the social functions and other activities (Kundra, D.N., 1970). The condition of women in the contemporary south India was also high. This establishes the matured culture of the Pre-Aryan period because the more a society is civilized and cultured, higher the status of women.

II. Vedic Period

The indistinct depiction of the early Aryan Society has been depicted in Rig Veda (1500 BC). Hence this interlude is framed as Golden Age because the rank of Indian women reached a splendid phase throughout this time (Sharma, P.D., 1981; Arora Poonam, 2003). From the study of Vedic literature, it is understood that even though patriarchal family system prevailed, still daughters were given all the facilities equal to sons (Kapadia, K.M., 1947). At the time preceding to the epoch of Vedas, girls underwent the thread, a formal procedure meant for the refinement of the body and soul of a person. Among the writers of rhymes of Rig Veda, there were about 20 women contributors.

Rao and Rao (1985) stated that there were learned women philosophers of that period. In that era one section of women called were involved in studies throughout their life. The women were cherished and enjoyed very high status inside as well as outside domicile. Generally, one man used to marry only one woman at a time, though in the case of kings and warriors, this tradition was not being followed austerely (Altekar, A.S., 1962).

During the Vedic period (Mukerjee, 1959), the unmarried girls were not constrained in the mobility and also on the interaction with male members. As marriages were arranged by their parents, even the brides enjoyed the privilege of choosing their own bridegroom. There was no *purdah* system and widows were permitted to marry again. In Atharva Veda, their life after marriage has been called *'Punarbhu'*, means rebirth. In order to get a son, *'Niyog'* that is, the temporary relationship with a man, was also possible. In the case of polygamy, all the wives were kept in an equal prominence of tribute (Mukerjee,1983).

Yaskacharya has long-established the right of a brotherless daughter in the property of her father. According to *'Purva-Memansa'*, husband and wife, both used to be the joint owner of property. According to Rig Veda wife makes home and according to *'Mahabharata'*, wifeless home is like a forest (Mukerjee, R.K., 1986). It can be said that during the Vedic period, under the patriarchal communal formation, women's courteous position in the civilization was tenable. The above mentioned Vedic traditions, in their novel forms, sustained till the occasion when Buddhism emerged and challenged them (Desai, A.S.,1977).

III. The Age of Revolt

The eminence of women began to mortify incessantly amid the Hindu religion. Even in Buddhist and Jain religion the significance of women was not equal to that of men but better than Brahminism (Desai, A.S., 1977 and Krishna Raj, 1987).

Kautilya's '*Arthasasthra*' and '*Manu Dharma Shastra*' show a thorough frame of the social system alive at that time. Women before marriage were allowed to recite the Vedic hymns. Women were dispossessed the familiarity of Vedas due the absence of thread ceremony. Endowment of nuptials to the bridegroom selected by her father came into endurance. The age of marriage, of the girls was fixed before the appearance of physical maturity (12-13 years). In Manu code, wife's faithfulness to her husband, i.e., '*Pativrata Dharma*' was greatly encouraged (Desai, A.S., 1977) and widow's remarriage was allowed only in certain conditions (Mukerjee, R.N., 1985). Considering the assets Kautilya has mentioned that women will have the right of '*Stri-dhan*' only from brother, mother, father and husband at the time of wedding as hand-outs. Widow has the property right to her husband's property. In case of remarriage she has to pay the basic property along with interest. Divorce is endorsed only on certain permitted issues (Mukerjee, R.N., 1985).

IV. The Puranic Age

In this period the terms obedience and forbearance were believed as the fundamental feature of women. The accomplishment of man by devotional to God, a woman achieved the same goodness by serving to her husband considering him to be her God. For women marriage was considered to be an unavoidable one and widow remarriage was completely deprived of. Widow burning was the practice in 510 A.D. The act of *Sati* was brought in Northern India (Thaper, Romila, 1966).

Women in Medieval Period

The significance of women became worse and pitiable after the invasion of Mughal (Aruna Bharadwaj, 1999). The Brahmins in order to protect the Hindu religion, made more rigid rules relating to chastity of women. Education was not the right of women; *Purdah* was encouraged and the age of girl's were reduced up to four years; widow remarriage was completely stopped; *sati* was at its peak; they were made as slave to serve their husband and the only place of right was their kitchen room.

Bhakthi Movement of this period influenced the status of women. Many saints became famous as religious leaders, namely Meera Bai, Jana Bai and Mukta Bai. The practice of unattractive attire was still in existence as women were imprisoned inside the four walls of the house. This situation slowly faded due to the establishment of the British regime in India.

Women in Modern Period

I. Period of British Rulership

It was during this period the status of women was enhanced and various rigid bonds were loosened. The awareness of women came into the reality of public and many organisations were created to prop up this in 19th century. With this lead in 20th century many women took part in National freedom movement and had gradual growth in education and occupation. In this period remarkable personalities like Raja Ram Mohan Roy, Dayanand Saraswati, Swami Vivekananda and many social reformers started the social reform movement. They mainly concentrated on opposing the aspect of religious rituals, idols worshipping, caste discrimination and the reduced status of women etc. These "Social Movements" established a basic and strong foundation for Women Education. Till 1882 nearly 1,27,000 began to receive education by establishing nearly 2500 educational institutions. During the period Lord William Bentinck and Dalhousie the emergence for women education bloomed. The Christian Missionaries also established many Educational Institutions for women. In the year 1854, some provisions for the education of girls was made in organising more schools and increase in grant-in-aid for them (Nagarajan, K., 2007).

The British government fixed the self-governing society with the principles of impartiality and emancipation and accepted markable social legislations concerning the *'Sati'*, 'Child Marriage', 'Widow remarriage', 'Right to husband's property', etc. (Ghurye, 1947).

Education was given to women and they had the opportunity of earning money. Processes of industrialisation, urbanisation and modernisation changed the familial structure. Joint family system were broken and the nuclear families emerged which gave rise to status of women.

II. After Independence

After independence lot of hard work had been taken to perk up the status of women. With the amendment of Child Marriage Restraint Act, 1929, the girl's age of marriage was raised to 18 years in 1989. Through Hindu Succession Act, 1956, women obtained the property rights as men. Medical Termination of Pregnancy Act, 1971 helped in getting rid of unwanted motherhood. The influence of Western culture, industrialisation, urbanisation, modernisation and progress in the means of transportation and communication, have given great impetus to their campaign regarding status. Thus, after the achievement of freedom, the status of Indian women also has improved sufficiently (Srinivas, M.N., 1978).

With the effective growth of education and resulting in educated women, they got absorbed in hospitals; schools and various offices. In the end of 1947 co-education came into existence. In the post-independent India the gradual process of women education was fastened by Radhakrishnan Commission, The Secondary Commission, The Five-Year Plans and The Kothari Commission.

Some committees were formed to stimulate the constant growth of women education. Some of the recommendations are :

(i) Recommendations of various Commissions and Committees on Women's Education,

(ii) Recommendations of University Grants Commission,
(iii) Recommendations of the National Committee on the Education for Women,
(iv) Recommendations of Bhaktavatsalam Committee,
(v) Recommendations of Kothari Education Commission,
(vi) Recommendations Pertaining to Higher Education,
(vii) Recommendations of Dr. Rajammal, P. Devadoss Committee, and
(viii) Recommendations of National Policy on Education.

With tremendous growth of education under various periods, in the present scenario there are some universities exclusively for women –

(i) SNDT Women University in Mumbai,
(ii) Mother Theresa University,
(iii) Sri Padmavathy Mahila Vishwa Vidhyalaya at Tirupathy, and
(iv) Avinashilingam Deemed University at Coimbatore.

The role of educated women is not limited management of house, shaping her wards and the development of human resources alone, the role of women goes beyond it. As she shares equality with man and handles the responsibility for the development of the society certain objectives for women education become imperative.

Women Education: Objectives

As the sky is the limit, Women Education has to expand with certain objectives to attain its greater height (Nagarajan, K., 2007):

1. *Familial Management* : Earlier it was in practice that managing the daily domestic chores, family affairs and performing rituals were considered to be of women's

routine work. But with various developments in the society the responsibility is now being managed rather balanced without any gender bias. Today the whole family share various domestic functions as per expediency and availability of time.

2. *Work-life Balance:* It is essential to be dealt as women have to handle the responsibility of home as well as exhibit their talent in work place they have the problem of balance. This kind of knowledge-*cum*-awareness is counted as an important objective.
3. *Equal Opportunity and Equal Commitment:* With the advancement in education without any gender bias equal opportunity could be given to learning, working, and participation in community activity. When this kind of atmosphere prevails it is sure that society would have its development and at the same time women development.
4. *Decision Making:* In those days it was the right of the men to take decision for the family or for any communal need. But years have brought changes as education had taught the women to think, how to handle any situation or the problem, and decide what kind of decision might be useful and worthy for the family or for the community. Thus training women to decide is a wise objective.
5. *Sense of Worth:* A dignified life with self-respect of women came into the existence only after the emergence of women education. It has paved way that women are worthy of appreciation because they place themselves in high ranking positions and play the role of a wife, mother, daughter-in-law and many other relations which are sensitive. Thus women could feel themselves to be proud and worth by themselves.
6. *Education and Income Generation:* Educate and develop women in turn the family gets developed in its status and financial level. Educated women either get employed in any organisation or get self-employed,

therefore, it leads to income generation. In the post-independence era the income of women was considered as supplementary in addition to her husband's earning. But in the present time it is considered on par with the earning of men.

7. *Awareness about Legal Rights:* Legal Rights are equal to both the gender. According to Geneva UNO Conference 1984, all are equal before law and have equal human rights. Women education is supposed to highlight this view.
8. *Participation in Public Affairs:* Active participation of women in public affairs is also due to education given to them. Women should come forward to participate in awareness programmes on Child Labour, Health Education, Population Education, Women Education, Equal Rights to Women, etc. which in turn may contribute for women empowerment.
9. *Knowledge Gaining:* Women can always seek for gathering updated information in her area of work or study and also in other fields to amplify her knowledge. As knowledge is wealth seeking the wealth implied in knowledge is an important objective of women education.
10. *Developing Work Motivation:* It is well-known that women are motivated to get employed after their education. Employment for women is not merely for earning but also for employing one's talent in their work which leads to the development of the working organisation and resulting in the development of the Nation.
11. *Developing Achievement Motivation:* Achievement motivation could be rightly sown at the time of learning in the minds of girl students. It is only then they fix-up the goal to be attained by them in the course of time. Achievement in any field could be motivated only through education.

Phenomenal Progress

From post-Independence there is general development in women education. Arduous endeavour has been made consistently. Figures given below show the enhancement of women education with that of men even with immense differences in figures (Meenakshisundaram, 2007).

Percentage of Literacy among Men and Women in India

Year	*Men*	*Women*
1951	27.16	8.86
1961	40.40	15.34
1971	45.95	21.97
1981	56.37	29.75
1991	64.13	39.29
2001	79.56	54.28

Social Reformers' View on Women Education

'As Education is an integrating process of discovering the lasting values' many reformists have initiated the facet and stressed on the growth and development of women education. They believed that only women education would strengthen the development of their family, the society and the nation.

Plato quotes "Education consists of giving to the body and soul all the perfection of which they are susceptible". Vivekananda says "The training by which the current and expression of will are brought under control and become fruitful is called education".

Rousseau's View on Women Education

Rousseau, the modern psychologist says that "Woman is made for the man's delight as such she ought to make herself pleasing in his eyes. Her strength is in her charm. To that end, women must be trained carefully but strictly. The feminine arts like cooking, cleaning, keeping the household accounts, housekeeping should be taught to her. Thus, the curriculum intended for girls should be different from that for boys. She must be devoted to God. Her education should aim at developing chastely in her more by example than by precept." (Meenakshisundaram, A., 2007).

Swami Vivekananda's View on Women Education

Vivekananda says "There is no hope of rise for that family or country where there is no education of women, where they live in sadness. For this reason, they have to be raised first". He had stern and strong faith in women and put forth lives of great Indian women as example such as Ahalya Bai and Mira Bai, Queen of Jhansi etc... He wanted the education to be the mode by which women would be fearless, brave, a character which enables them to face the realities of life (Meenakshisundaram, A., 2007).

Plato's View on Women Education

He encouraged women education and suggested that there should be no separate education for women. He writes "For the patronage of state, men and women are equal but women are, no doubt, weaker in strength." (Meenakshisundaram, A., 2007:67).

Causes of Slow Progress of Women Education

1. Women education fall short of proper societal attitudes in the rural areas for the education of girls,
2. Fiscal backwardness of the rural community,
3. Deficiency of education facilities in rural areas,
4. Lack of suitable curriculum,
5. Lack of proper regulation and assistance for supervision of women personnel by the Inspectorate,
6. Lack of suitable incentive to girl students,

7. Co-educational aspects,
8. Acute shortage of women educator,
9. Lack of social awareness among women to move equally with men in work and sports, and
10. Lack of social education for adult women.

Suggestive Measures

1. Women education fall short of proper societal attitudes in the rural areas for the education of girls. Researches can be conducted by the educational institutions to study the various problems relating to women education so as to accelerate the women education process in the country. Therefore, creating public opinion about women education in extreme rural areas is the need of the day.
2. Fiscal backwardness of the rural community. Helping the girl students to get education by providing free clothing, books, scholarship and mid-day meals to those who attend the classes regularly. By doing so the economical backwardness which hinders the women education could be averted.
3. Deficiency in education facilities in rural areas. Construction of primary school within the surrounding of one kilometre, hostel for girls in middle and high school levels and infrastructure facilities to provide a good environment and atmosphere for their education may enhance girls' participation in education. With all these free education can be provided to them.
4. Lack of suitable curriculum is a problem as suggestions made by Smt. Hansa Mehta Committee (1962) recommended that there should be no differentiation in the curriculum of boys and girls, the education should include the teaching of music, fine arts and courses designed to meet the special needs of girls.
5. Lack of proper regulation and assistance for supervision women personnel by the Inspectorate. The

number of women supervisors in the inspectorate is to be increased to inspect the proper functioning of rural schools, adequate members to carry out the functions in the office and equipments to be provided them.

6. Lack of suitable incentives to girl students. Students should be provided with attendance scholarship which motivates them to attend the school hours regularly. Special scholarships can be awarded to girl students who rank first in academics or in sports.
7. Co-educational aspects. Co-education could be adopted even at the elementary level as a general pattern. Number of educational programmes to be organised to overcome the opposition of co-education. The appointment of women teachers in all educational institutions where girls actually attend needs to be encouraged.
8. Acute shortage of women educator. Number of training institutions has to be established to train the women and thereby recruit them as educators. Free accommodation, transportation allowances, free training and on duty training to the fresher have to be increased. All these facilities should be provided to increase women educators.
9. Lack of social awareness among women to move equally with men in work spot. Awareness programme to be organised by the Government for the public to know the value of education, especially women education. Only by education the inhibition of women to move equal with men could be curtailed. By such education they can understand their strength and weaknesses and can act wisely to show that they too aspire for survival of the fittest with men.
10. Lack of social education for adult women. Number of adult literacy classes is to be given for those who lost their opportunity for education at the earlier years. The class should also teach simple functional skills like sewing, knitting, handicrafts, basic knowledge on health and food habits to them.

Work Life Balance of Working Women

Despite creating a dignified position in this male dominated society; the struggle for each and every woman is far from over. Although it is evident that women have left nothing unaccomplished, the percentage of women achievers to men achievers is comparatively low. Women are subject to prejudice by the dominant patriarchy and are in turn left out from supremacy. A woman seems to be relentlessly engaged in a dual conflict; between her and the entire world. Time and again, she has been redefining what liberation means to her and has been assessing the reaction of the society (men) to it. Working women have a whole new set of role to play resulting from the involvement in family life and professional lives. As they go beyond certain boundaries of their home, they are perceived as if they deviate from traditional values. The unmarried women do not have such problems as they do not have any major responsibility. But in the case of married women they have role conflict, as they have overlapping of responsibilities since they perform as mother, wife and bread winner.

In fact the plight of a married working woman is still more distressing. As most husbands want their wives to work, the woman is expected to perform household chores single handedly whereas the husband does not portray an iota of sensitivity in sharing responsibilities. Not all men are insensitive. There are few others who are supportive and understanding towards their spouse but this percentage is quite low in comparison to the autocratic men. Many working women who are married are involved in multiple, potential and conflicting tasks. They are in the position to serve the expectations of their working environment, superiors and as well as their role in family. This kind of expectations creates inter-role conflict (Katz and Kahn, 1978) and stress if they are simultaneously attending the expectations of work and family life (Loerch *et al.*, 1989).

Once children come into her life, challenges keep mounting as she has to take up additional roles. Rearing her children and shaping them to become good human beings along with looking after the needs of her husband and in-laws as well as working outside forces her to take up too many roles at the same time.

Women Empowerment

Empowerment of women is a multi-layered concept. Women's empowerment is a technique in which women achieve superior position in the allocation of control over possessions—intellectual like knowledge, information, ideas, financial resources like money—access to money, decision-making in the home, community, society, nation, and to gain 'power'. According to the Country Report of Government of India, "Empowerment means moving from a position of enforced powerlessness to one of power".

The Government of India has made Empowerment of Women as one of the principal objectives of the Ninth Five Year Plan (1997-2002) and also declared 2001 as the year of 'Women's Empowerment'. The issues of gender equality are discussed in World Conferences, National and International Conferences very often.

Our Constitution has conferred and guaranteed equality before law, universal adult franchise and equal opportunities for men and women as fundamental rights. The imperative of gender partnership in matters of development has been recognised. In order to give a stimulus to empowerment of women appropriate institutional mechanisms and interventions have been consciously built into the development design.

Women and child development institutions, departments at the Central and State levels, creation of the National Commission for Women and also State Commission for Women in several States are some of the important developments for the betterment and affluence of women.

The launching of Rashtriya Mahila Kosh, Indira Mahila Yojana, Mahila Samridhi Yojana, reserving of one-third of the number of seats in Panchayats and the local bodies are programmes launched with a view to improve and empower women socially, economically and in political frontiers.

An Overview of Women Development

- 1886: Kadambini Ganguly and Anandi Gopal Joshi became the first women from India to be trained in Western medicine.
- 1905: Suzanne RD Tata became the first Indian woman to drive a car.
- 1917: Annie Besant became the first female president of the Indian National Congress.
- 1925: Sarojini Naidu became the first Indian born female president of the Indian National Congress.
- 1927: The All India Women's Conference was founded.
- 1947: On August 15, 1947, following independence, Sarojini Naidu became the Governor of the United Provinces, and in the process became India's first woman Governor.
- 1953: Vijaya Lakshmi Pandit became the first woman (and first Indian) President of the United Nations General Assembly.
- 1963: Sucheta Kriplani became the Chief Minister of Uttar Pradesh, the first woman to hold that position in any Indian state.
- 1966: Captain Durga Banerjee became the first Indian woman pilot of the state airline, Indian Airlines.
- 1966: Indira Gandhi became the first woman Prime Minister of India.
- 1972: Kiran Bedi became the first female recruit to join the Indian Police Service.
- 1979: Mother Teresa won the Nobel Peace Prize, becoming the first Indian female citizen to do so.
- 1984: On May 23, Bachendri Pal became the first Indian woman to climb Mount Everest.

- 1989: Justice M. Fathima Beevi became the first woman judge of the Supreme Court of India.
- 1997: Kalpana Chawla became the first India born woman to go into space.
- 1994: Harita Kaur Deol became the first Indian woman pilot in the Indian Air Force (IAF), on a solo flight.
- 2000: Karnam Malleswari became the first Indian woman to win an Olympic medal (bronze medal in the 2000 Summer Olympics at Sydney).
- 2002: Lakshmi Sahgal became the first Indian woman to get listed for the post of President of India.
- 2004: Punita Arora became the first woman in the Indian Army to don the highest rank of Lieutenant General.
- 2007: Gayatri Chakravorty Spivak became the first Indian woman to be appointed as University Professor at an Ivy League University (Columbia University).
- 2008: Renu Khator became the first India born woman to lead a major American university, the University of Houston.
- 2009: Meira Kumar became the first woman Speaker of Lok Sabha, the lower house of Indian Parliament.

Status of Women in the Present Scenario

Women with stern developments have launched their talent in varied areas and have made an incredible identity for themselves in the society. Some have entered the political arena, some are flying planes and others are entrusted their accountability of running MNCs. They are at par with men in terms of their economic standing and status. Women's status today has undergone a drastic change from what it was in the past.

For decades women have suffered in the hands of men folk, faced extreme levels of exploitation; they have been looked down upon as tedious slaves. But with the help of feminist's and other reformist's revolutionary thought, women have uplifted themselves from shedding their household tags. They have even managed to shake the burly walls of social and economic exploitation. The modern woman of today is learning to break away from the fetters of the past. She is no more the traditional, timid, domesticated woman of yesteryears sacrificing her dreams and ambitions for the sake of her family and society. The emerging new-age woman has the ability to equip herself with education thereby seeking her own identity, confidence and not compromising on her self-respect at any cost. This tremendous change in new era has been accepted by all level of men yet even some women are still in dark side of the life. Modern women with their development in present times have to help those who are still downtrodden. Speaking on the development of women now, it is the time to concentrate on women who are still shy to face the outside world and those who stay at home whose husband or father stick on old rather alien thought as women are meant for household works alone.

Women's Contribution to National Development

Women's contribution to Nation started as teachers. More than hundreds of years ago they took this profession and still today we have number of well talented and established teachers. Gradually with the establishment of hospitals and health centres women with proper educational qualification have taken up the roles of doctor, nurse, health visitors, and mid-wives. With the discovery of law, engineering, agricultural and other professional organisation, women have entered in those fields too. Many American studies have stated that there is association between the educational level and their employment (Ginsberg, E., 1967 and Klein, Viola, 1968).

Women not only hold the position as teachers, doctors, lawyers and engineers but also as political leaders who are responsible of moulding and shaping the nation. Women have the right to choose their profession and dedicate according to their ambition but the society and men are problem to them. They do not require mere legal measures for equal rights but the sympathy and understanding in working place as well as in the family life. As they have equal right to choose and lead their life according to their willingness, the society and men do not accept this right attitude of women. Therefore, it remains to be a problem of human values and relationships. Social legislative measures assuring social justice to the society at length is also required for them. The role of educated women in the National development can be understood from the implications of the following hypothetical statements uttered often:

1. Nation's efficiency increases appreciably as educated women adds to the human resources of the country.
2. Education has increased awareness among educated women, the decision making capacity, their public participation is comparatively high and function professionally when compared to those women who were illiterate and ignorant.
3. Learned women develop the tendency of saving for their livelihood and furnish pertinent acquaintance for the wards.
4. Wards of uneducated women endure from undernourishment and consequently their yield is squat.
5. Wards of educated women hale and healthy life while toddler transience rate is very high among the children of uneducated women.
6. With their empowerment and authoritative ability they rule the nation with focused vision.
7. They play the role of fabricating a well-built nation by humanizing the future citizen as an excellent teacher.

Conclusion

Education and egalitarianism are unified concepts, thus the ultimate righteousness demands that all citizens should have freedom from want, freedom from fear and freedom from ignorance. Freedom from ignorance is achievable only if education is established. The social and economic life of the country has undergone a far-reaching change with the help of women education. As years go by the importance of women education is elevated to attain its height. Therefore, 'Women education' is not for the social impartiality alone but to fuel and trigger social ren ovation in the country.

References

1. Altekar, A.S. (1962). *The Position of Women in Hindu Civilization,* Motilal Banarasidas, Delhi.
2. Arora, Poonam. (2003). *Professional Women—Dual Role and Conflicts,* Manak Publications, New Delhi.
3. Bhardwaj, Aruna (1999). *Women in Uniform—Emergence of Women Police in Delhi,* Regency Publications, New Delhi.
4. Desai and Maithreyi Krishna Raj (1987). *Women and Society in India,* Ajanta Publications, New Delhi.
5. Desai, Neera (1977). *Women in Modern India,* Vohra and Company Publishers Pvt. Ltd., Bombay.
6. Ghurye, G.S. (1947). *Culture and Society*. As cited by Desai (1977) reference book.
7. Ginsberg, E. and Associates (1967). *Life Styles of Educated Women,* New York, Columbia Press.
8. Kapadia, K.M. (1947). *The Hindu Kinship*. As cited by Desai (1977).
9. Katz, D. and Kahn, R. (1978). *The Social Psychology of Organisations.* (2nd Ed). New York: Wiley.
10. Klein, Viola (1968). *The Feminine Character,* London: Routledge and Kegan Paul.
11. Kumar, Raj (2000). *Encyclopaedia of Women and Development* (Vol.1) (ed). (2000) Anmol Publications Private Limited, New Delhi.
12. Kundra, D.N. (1990). *History of India and Contemporary World.* Goyal Brothers Prakashan, New Delhi.
13. Loerch, K., Rusell, J. and Rush, M. (1989). The Relationship Among Family Domain Variables and Work-Family Conflict for Men and Women. *Journal of Vocational Behaviour,* 35, 288-308.

14. Meenakshisundaram, A. (2007). *Educational Challenges in Indian Society*: Dindugal, Kavyamala Publication.
15. Mukerjee, Radhakamal (1959). *The Culture and Art of India.* London: George Allen and Unwin Ltd.
16. Nagarajan, K. (2007). *Educational Challenges in the emerging Indian Society,* Ram Publication.: Chennai.
17. Rao, Prakash, V.V. and Rao, V. Nandhini (1985). *Marriage, the Family and Women in India*: Heritage Publishers, New Delhi.
18. Sharma, P.D. (1981). *Police, Polity and People in India.* Uppal Publishing House, New Delhi.
19. Srinivas, M.N. (1978). *Changing Status of Indian Women.* London: Oxford University Press.
20. Thaper, Romila (1966). *The History of India.* Vol. 1, Harmonds Worth: Penguin.

17 Participation of Women Teacher in Development

Anjali Pattanaik
Snigdha Rani Swain

Women in India are perceived as the second sex and considered the most vulnerable and neglected lot in the development strategy. But constituting a larger section (almost half) of the human resource they cannot be neglected to be wasted assets. Since ages women have been assigned to the stereotyped roles of house keeping, child rearing and preserving the ethical, moral and cultural values. But seeing their emerging influential and participatory roles they are called the change agents in their families as well as in the society. It is felt that a literate woman can only gainfully manage the family, thus, it can be rightly said that if a woman is developed, the whole family is developed. So, development strategies are now being solely directed towards the upliftment of women and for the exploitation of their latent potential. But spectacular results are yet to be achieved in terms of their fuller participation. One of the underlying factors may be lack of awareness regarding the development information. Information acts as a potent force in quickening the pace of development by making one aware of the recent developments at the regional, national and international level. It is capable of cultivating rational ideas, attitudes and behaviour in the general public. It also prepares one to be discerning in one's judgment. It possesses the potential of strengthening the decision-making ability and innovativeness of women by facilitating their access to different services and activities. Thus, it enables them to broaden their range of vision and greater participation in the national affair. Development today is emerged with a new emphasis. It is being increasingly realised that people cannot be developed, they can only develop themselves (Tanwar, 1978). Self-reliance and independence is the key to development. Mass Media has always been considered to play an important role in development especially by conveying informative and persuasive messages directed from the Government to the public in a downward hierarchical way (Tanwar, 1978). Communication is an important vehicle that imparts information in favour of change in attitudes and adoption behaviour (Chawla, 1983) termed it as a two-edged weapon, which works both ways—for reinforcement as well as for change. Information is a vital input in the productive community which is considered as a powerful weapon (Joseph, 1979) for it helps to make friends and influence people and also just the reverse has become an instrument in the battle for winning over the souls of men. Keeping in view the importance of information present study had attempted to assess the level of awareness of women with regard to different information. The objectives formulated for the study pertained to:

1. Study the socio-economic background of the sample groups.
2. Ascertain the level of information awareness with respect to political, economic and social activities of their area.
3. Find out the sources of information for the sample groups.
4. Ascertain the level of relationship between the independent variables (demographic background) and dependent variables (political, economic and social information).
5. Draw a comparative picture of the level of information exposure between the sample groups.

The sample and area of study broadly speaking the study undertaken was based on a survey carried out among school teachers of an Indian state, Orissa. A total of 600 samples were selected from the rural and urban areas of Orissa with 300 samples from each area. The villages of Puri district were chosen under the rural area category. Similarly, under the urban area Bhubaneswar, the capital city of Orissa State of Khordha district was selected. Random sampling method was selected for this purpose.

The Tools

The study had used only primary data elicited from the respondents through a structured interview schedule. The schedule consisted of five major segments. The first segment comprised twelve questions pertaining to the demographic background of the respondents. Other three segments (second, third and fourth) referred to three areas of information, i.e. political, economic and social information.

The political information included awareness regarding minimum age of voting; the reservation procedure for women in the Parliament, State Assembly and in the Panchayat elections; and the fundamental rights provided by the Constitution. Similarly, the economic area covered information about reservation for women in government jobs, constitutional provision regarding the remuneration pattern, laws made to safeguard the interests of working women, entrepreneurship development programmes initiated by the government and non-government organizations and the funding agencies for different enterprises. And, information relating to the social area pertained to awareness of women about different welfare schemes for the development of education and health status of women and children; the existence of various personal and family laws made for women against violence and crimes; rehabilitation programmes for handicapped children; and the provision of various support services. Last segment of the schedule contained questions to seek information regarding the media exposure behaviour of the samples with respect to all the development information.

Pilot Study

The interview schedule was pre-tested through a pilot study on 50 samples and necessary modifications were done as required.

Scoring

For the purpose of quantitative analysis the data were assigned with numerical scores. Trivedi (1963) scale was adopted for scoring of demographic variables. Other variables were scored by assigning one score to each positive response.

Analysis

Statistical analysis of the scored data was done by using percentage, mean, co-efficient of correlation and student's t-test.

The obtained results are interpreted in the following manner.

Results

Demographic Profile of the Respondents

The demographic variables of the respondents are presented in Table 17.1. Observation of the table reveals that majority of the teachers (58% of rural teacher and 64% of urban teachers) were in the age group of 35-40 years. In the age group of 30-35 years more percentage of rural teachers (26%) were found while only 4 per cent of urban teachers were in the same age group. Similarly, 32 per cent of urban teachers were in the age group of 40-45 years whereas only 8 per cent of rural teachers were present in that age group. But only 4 per cent of the rural teachers were found in the age groups of 45-50 years and above 50 years.

Table 17.1: Demographic Profile of the Respondents

Demographic variables	*Age Groups*									
	30-35 Year		*35-40 Year*		*40-45 Years*		*45-50 Year*		*50 and above*	
	RT (%)	*UT (%)*	*RT (%)*	*UT (%)*	*RT (%)*	*UT (%)*	*RT (%)*	*UT (%)*	*RT (%)*	*UT (%)*
Age	26	4	58	64	8	32	4	—	4	—
Education										
Graduate (Trained)	—	2	56	23	3	13	4	—	4	—
Above Graduation	26	2	2	41	—	19	—	—	—	—
	Family Income (Monthly)									
Rs. 10,000–Rs. 20,000	5	—	23	15	2	8	—	—	—	—
Rs. 20,000–Rs. 30,000	19	4	35	49	6	24	—	—	—	—
More than Rs. 30,000	2	—	—	—	—	—	4	—	4	—
	Mean Scores of Education of the Whole Family									
	18.69	22.00	21.31	20.87	26.5	18.78	30.00	—	30.00	—

(RT – Rural Teachers, UT – Urban Teachers)

The picture of education of the respondents as shown in Table 17.1 depicts that 56 per cent of the rural teachers and 23 per cent of urban teachers in the age group of 35-40 years were trained graduates, but 41 per cent of urban teachers and only 2 per cent of rural teachers in the same age group were qualified more than graduation. All the rural teachers (26%) and only 2 per cent of urban teachers in the age group of 30-35 years were having education above graduation. In the age group of 40-45 years only 19 per cent of urban teachers were educated above graduation.

The monthly income of the family of the respondents revealed that more percentage of rural (35%) and urban teachers (49%) in the age group of 35-40 years were having a monthly income within the range of Rs. 20,000 to Rs. 30,000. But only 23 per cent of rural teachers and 15 per cent of urban teachers in that age group belonged to the income range group of Rs.10,000 to 20,000. Similarly, more percentage of rural teachers (19%) and all the urban teachers in the age group of 30-35 years were having a monthly income within the range of Rs.20,000 to 30,000 while only 5 per cent and 2 per cent of rural teachers had an income within the range of Rs.10,000 to 20,000 and above Rs.30,000 respectively. Again more percentage of rural (6%) and urban teachers (24%) in the age group of 40-45 years had a monthly income of Rs. 20,000 to 30,000 while only 2 per cent of rural teachers and 8 per cent of urban teachers in that age group were having an income within the range of Rs. 10,000 to 20,000. But all the rural teachers in the age group of 45-50 years and above 50 years had an income above Rs. 30,000.

The educational status of the whole family as observed from Table 17.1 revealed a higher mean score in case of rural teachers (mean score 21.31 and 26.5) than the urban teachers (mean score 20.87 and 18.78 respectively) in the age group of 35-40 years and 40-45 years. But in the age group of 30-35 years urban teachers had a mean score higher (i.e. 22) than the rural teachers (mean score 18.69).

Level of Awareness

Table 17.2 indicates the mean scores of awareness of political, economic and social information in case of both rural and urban teachers. With regard to political information there was no significant difference between the rural teachers (mean score 10.29) and urban teachers (mean score 10.26). But significant differences were found between the rural and urban teachers so far as the economic (rural teachers 16.58 and urban teachers 16.20) and social information (mean score 48.64 for rural teachers and mean score 49.10 for urban teachers) were concerned.

Table 17.2: Mean Score Difference in the Level of Awareness

Areas of Information	*Mean Level of Awareness*		
	Rural Teachers	*Urban Teachers*	*t-Value*
Political Information	10.29	10.26	0.45NS
Economic Information	16.58	16.20	2.4*****
Social Information	48.64	49.10	3.89*****

Key: Level of Significance

*	– at 0.1 level	****	– at 0.01 level
**	– at 0.05 level	*****	– at 0.001 level
***	– at 0.02 level	NS	– Non-significant

Media Exposure

Table 17.3 indicates the sources of information as disclosed by the respondents. Perusal of the table reveals that almost all (100%) of the rural and urban teachers had utilized electronic media, work place and neighbours as major sources of their information. Print media were used by all (100%) the urban teachers and 50 per cent of the rural teachers. Again, 20 per cent of rural teachers had considered extension personnel as a source whereas that happened only in case of 10 per cent of urban teachers.

Table 17.3: Media Exposure

Sources of Media	*Rural Teachers (%)*	*Urban Teachers (%)*
Electronic media	100	100
Print media	50	100
Work place	100	100
Neighbours	100	100
Extension personnel	20	10

Table 17.4 has attempted to depict the relationship between the socio-economic variables and the level of political, economic and social information. The result indicated positive relationships of all the demographic variables with the level of different information with a deviation in a single case. Age was found to have a negative effect on the level of awareness

of information in case of both the rural and urban teachers, but the coefficient of correlation were found to be positive in all other cases and significant in some of the cases.

Table 17.4: Correlation Between the Demographic Variables and the Level of Information

Demographic Variables	*Rural Teachers*			*Urban Teachers*		
	Political information	*Economic information*	*Social information*	*Political information*	*Economic information*	*Social information*
Age	-0.08NS	-0.05NS	-0.06NS	-0.04NS	-0.16*	- 0.28****
Education of the respondent	0.63*****	0.41*****	0.51*****	0.34*****	0.007NS	0.01NS
Education of the family	0.009NS	0.03NS	0.08NS	0.19*	0.14NS	0.26****
Family income (Monthly)	0.47*****	0.37*****	0.38*****	0.047NS	0.08NS	0.10NS
Media Exposure	0.39*****	0.24***	0.24***	0.22**	0.23**	0.26****

Key: Level of Significance

*	–	at 0.1 level	****	–	at 0.01 level
**	–	at 0.05 level	*****	–	at 0.001 level
***	–	at 0.02 level	NS	–	Non-significant

Discussion

The excerpts of the above tables are discussed below :

It is necessary to have a clear understanding of the demographic background of the respondents as it forms the bedrock on which the personality edifice is built. In the present study the demographic profile of the respondents revealed that a majority of school teachers were in the age group of 35-40 years. Again, most of the rural teachers were only trained graduates while a majority of urban teachers were educated above graduation. An interesting fact revealed in this regard was that more number of younger women had education above graduation, which might be due to better opportunities for higher education and the conducive socio-economic status of their families. So far as the educational status of their family was concerned it was found that the families of rural teachers had a higher score than the urban teachers. The figure of monthly income of the respondents' families showed that most of the rural and urban teachers had an income within the range of Rs. 20,000 to Rs. 30,000. And only a few rural teachers had an income above Rs. 30,000.

The findings of the study regarding the mean score of the level of awareness of the respondents had shown a higher score for rural teachers with regard to the economic information. Similarly, urban teachers were found to be more cosmopolite in their social information gathering behaviour. This fact might be attributed to their more interest in these aspects. But both of them were found to have equal interest in gathering political information.

Media have come a long way to influence people by imparting development support information. So the media exposure behaviour of the people is important from the point of their awareness level. The findings of the study in this regard reveals that electronic media like T.V., radio, tape recorder and others were equally used by both the rural and urban teachers. Studies of Neurath (1960), Majumdar (1961), IIMC (1968), IIPO (1967), Roy (1967), Menefee (1964) and ORG (1971) showed similar findings. Also both of the sample groups had considered workplace and neighbours as good sources of information. This finding is also supported by studies of Sengupta (1969) and ORG (1971). But in case of rural teachers the use of newspapers, magazines, journals and other printed materials were not as high as was used by urban teachers. Studies by IIPO (1967) and ORG (1971) corroborate this finding. The reasons behind this might be inadequate circulation and their reluctance towards this media due to lack of affordability. Moreover, more number of rural teachers resorted to the extension personnel for seeking necessary information (Sengupta, 1969). This might be due to better extension services in the rural area.

At last the study had analysed the existing relationship between the demographic variables and the level of awareness regarding different information. It is because the demographic variables were often found to have a more conditioning influence on other aspects. Thus, as expected the study revealed positive relationships of all those variables to the level of information awareness. This result is corroborated with the result of the study by Sahu (2001). But the exception in case of negative correlation in respect of age and demographic variables might be due to reduced interest in information gathering behaviour with the progress in age.

Conclusion

Information is a vital factor in the process of development. In a developing country like India material backwardness is felt to be the cause of our lagging behind. But it is not a fact. It is our inability to make use of the available resources, which is attributed to our limited information dissemination system. The growth and development of a country is conditioned mainly by the amount of information input. From the present study it was observed that rural women fell short of urban women in the use of print media and similarly urban women failed to have much contact with the extension personnel. Again the study revealed that even though the samples were aware of information that were of reasonable importance, a majority of them were found to be oblivious of a wide range of information. In the ever-changing world while knowledge is expanding in degrees and measures to cope with it the information communication system needs to be strengthened and accessible. Or else the ill-informed ones will be left behind. So, investments in this direction should be considered the most fundamental input in a developing country.

References

1. Chawala, N.L. (1983). 'Change: An Overview', *Media Asia,* Vol.10 (2), 79-83.

2. Gupta, Dr. J.P (1978). 'Community and Communication a diagnostic Study Part- II', *Indian Journal of Communication Arts,* Vol. 5 (4), 5-7 and 21.
3. Hussan, A.M. (1983). 'Mass Media as an agent of Social change in Malaysia', *Media Asia,* Vol.10 (2), 75-78.
4. IIMC (Indian Institute of Mass Communication) (1968, January) New Delhi, 'Agro-information Flow at the Village Level', Report of the Survey of Communication sources in the Adoption process of High yielding varieties of Grains.
5. IIPO (Indian Institute of Public Opinion) (1967, September), New Delhi, 'Radio Listening' Published in Monthly *Public Opinion Surveys,* Vol. XII (11 and 12), 40.
6. Joseph, E.M. (1979). 'Information as Input', *Indian Journal of Communication Arts,* Vol. V and VI, 6-7.
7. Majumdar, S.M. (1961). 'Community Listening in the Country side', Studies in road casting, All India Radio, Summer.
8. Menefee, S.C. and Menefee, A.G. (1964). 'Communication in village India: A Social Experiment', Kalpataru College, Tiptur, India.
9. Mughess-ud-Din (1987). 'Family Welfare Communication in Rural Areas', *Media Asia,* Vol. 9 (1), 54-55.
10. Neurath, Paul (1960). Radio Farm Forum in India', All India Radio.
11. ORG (Operations Research Group) (1971, January and May), Baroda. 'The Family Planning Practices', The First All India Survey Report, 13, 25 and 105.
12. Patel, V.M. (1968, March). 'A Study of the effectiveness of the Radio as a medium of communication', *The Journal of Family Welfare,* Vol. XIV (3).

18 Third Age Women, Their Health and Role of Television

Avani Maniar

The world is experiencing an unprecedented demographic transformation and that by 2050, the number of persons aged 60 years and over will increase from 600 million to almost 2 billion and that the proportion of persons aged 60 years and over is expected to double from 10 to 21 per cent. The increase will be greatest and most rapid in developing countries where the older population is expected to quadruple during the next 50 years. India shows a steady increase in the population of the elderly. It was more marked after the year 1951 (5.43%), which increased to 6.42 per cent, by the year 1981. The estimated projection of the elderly in the year 2006 is 81.81 million (7.48%), which would increase to 112.96 million (9%) by the year 2016 (Das N., Shah U., 2001).

Women and Ageing in India

In describing the demographic characteristics of the elderly population, it is important to take into consideration the changing proportion of females to males. Although more boys than girls are born worldwide, men tend to have higher mortality rates than women at all ages, which accounts for imbalances in sex ratios at older ages. Ageing population implies a greater increase in the number of elderly women as compared to elderly men, a phenomenon experienced by most societies of the world. The ageing societies are increasingly becoming disproportionately female. On examining the data on sex ratios for the elderly in India, the gender differential in life expectancy has also widened. The female population shows a greater increase in the expected life span in all age groups, as compared to the male population. This clearly indicates the trend towards feminization of elderly population.

Table 18.1: Age and Sex Wise Distribution of Population (%)

Years	Female			Males			Total		
	60+	65+	80+	60+	65+	80+	60+	65+	80+
1950	6.1	3.8	0.3	5.2	2.9	0.2	5.6	3.3	0.3
1975	6.3	3.9	0.3	6.1	3.8	0.3	6.2	3.8	0.3
2000	8.2	5.4	0.7	7.1	4.6	0.5	7.6	5.0	0.6
2025	13.2	9.0	1.5	11.7	7.6	1.0	12.5	8.3	1.3
2050	21.8	15.9	3.6	19.5	13.7	2.6	20.6	14.8	3.1

Source: World Population Ageing 1950–2050, Population Division, DESA, United Nations (2002).

The sex ratio shows a similar increase in the number of women over the years. Table 18.2 gives the comparative sex-ratio of elderly population and general population. The sex ratio among elderly people was about 93.0 in 1991, which is expected to increase to 96.3 by the year 2011 and would rise to 96.9 till the year 2016. This projected age-sex structure of the population indicates that gender differential among the elderly may decline with time, whereby women would outnumber men, especially at old age. Similar trend is observed for Gujarat. Gujarat shows a persistent increase in the sex ratio from 107.2 in the year 1991, which is projected to increase to 120.5 in the year 2011.

Table 18.2: Sex Ratio of the Elderly Population, India and Gujarat

Years	*Sex Ratio of Elderly Population age 60+, India*	*Sex Ratio of Elderly Population age 60+, Gujarat*
1991	93.0	107.2
2011	96.3	120.5
2016	96.9	122.6

Source: Modi, L., *Ageing and Human Development,* Rawat Publication, Jaipur (2001).

The factors such as increase in life expectancy, increase in the sex ratio, and the medical advancement, seen in the last few years, led us to believe that the female elderly population is on the rise as compared to the male elderly. Along with these factors one should also keep in mind the fact that the females generally live longer than males. This indicates an increase in numbers of elderly females, which lead to feminization of later life.

Critics have accused feminists of focusing exclusively on younger women and turning a blind to the problems of older women. Since last decade gerontologists are working up to the fact that ageing is becoming increasingly a gender issue. The proportion with the feminization of old age, the issues and problems faced by these women would be vast, related to health, economics and their social status. Women in the developing world experience low social status, poor health, economic dependence and domestic violence over the life cycle, which puts older women in a pathetic condition. It becomes the responsibility of society to look after the women at fag-end of her life. The United Nations Projects that by the year 2025, there will be 604 million women over the age 60 in the world population. Seventy per cent of these will be in the Third World countries. In countries like India, with a predominantly patriarchal ethos, older women face triple jeopardy – that of being female, being old and being poor.

Women and Their Health During Third Age

More older women than older men are blind largely because they live longer but also because of restricted access to treatment—the cost of examinations, surgery, or medicine, little family support for treatment and low self-esteem about herself becomes barriers in receiving eye care treatment. The impact of communicable diseases such as malaria, tuberculosis and leprosy grows increasingly severe with time and ageing. In developed and developing countries, older people are at high risk for contracting influenza and its complications, including death.

Heart disease and stroke are significant causes of death and disability in women and especially among women who are poor. The risk for breast cancer increases with age—especially after 50 and declines after the age of 80. Cervical cancer which kills estimated 2,74,000 women every year is the most common cancer in women and the leading cause of cancer deaths in developing countries. Osteoarthritis and osteoporosis are associated with chronic pain, limited quality of life and disability. Between the ages of 60 and 90 years, the incidence of osteoarthritis rises 20-fold in women as compared to 10-fold in men. Osteoporosis is three times more common in women than in men, partly because women have a lower peak bone mass and partly because of the hormonal changes that occur at menopause and the effect of pregnancy which can alter calcium composition in a woman's body in the absence of appropriate diet and/or administration of calcium supplements.

Women, who has compromised her health, all through her life, has to face various diseases of older years like diabetes, osteoporosis, heart diseases, arthritis, cancer, Alzheimer's etc. Numerous studies in different countries have revealed consistently that malnutrition is widely prevalent among elderly females. Nutritional deficiencies like ariboflavinosis, ascorbic acid deficiency and anaemia are the commonest manifestations. This happens due to the common tendency to avoid a varied diet and opt for liquid or soft gruel, which is easy to prepare, takes little preparation time and based on cheap food. Older women who live alone face difficulty in carrying out food related activities like procuring and purchasing food items, making decisions about menu and problems related to pre and post-preparation of food. Older women are found making compromises with their diet and make a single food item, which may not necessarily be nutritionally balanced. All these factors continue to create a nutritionally imbalanced diet, which might be a compromise for their health.

A study conducted on "Women and Third Age" (2005) in Baroda city reported about various health problems elderly women face. The findings of the study emphasized that as age increases problems increase. All the sensory organs were found to be deteriorating with increase in age. More frequency of headache, bodyache, and overall general weakness was found in women. More than 30 per cent of elderly women had dental problems, and 20 per cent of them faced problem of hypertension. Due to their dental problems intake of food gets affected leading to nutritional deficiencies and poor general health. To improve the nutritional status and general physical and mental health it is necessary to eat right kind of food which would be a balanced food, easy to prepare at home, and easy to digest by the elderly. There is also a need to prepare elderly women regarding the health problems, which they may face during the last stage of their life. If they are mentally prepared to face them, they can accept the changes occurring in their body without much difficulty.

Television and Health of Elderly Women

The key socializing agents in any society includes a family, educational institutions, peers in the society and the mass media. In the twenty first century the mass media has an eminent role to play in view of socializing individual in a society, especially the elderly. Most of the elderly citizens do not work and hence their interaction with the outside world is restricted. The prime source of information for them becomes television. Describing about television Davis and Davis (1985) points that the world of television shows and tell us about life, people, places, power and fate. It lets us know what is good and what is bad, who wins and who loses, what works and what does not work and what it means to be a man or a woman. The television thus is a storyteller telling large number of stories to a large number of people. It constantly emits messages which are geared to shaping, moulding and influencing the behaviour of an individual in some way. It is a potent and critical force in terms of its impact on an individual and his behaviour alternatives.

Vivian (2002) reported that the elderly spend much of their time watching television. They usually watch a telecast or the programmes of a premium cable channel. Children and the older generation watch the television the most and young adults watch it the least. According to Heisel, as cited by Delloff (1987), the television viewing increases consistently from the age of 40 years until one advances into the 80s. Various researches on older people show that television viewing is a favourite leisure time activity among the old. Nielsen's statistic exhibits that among persons over 55, women watch the TV slightly over 37 hours per week and men watch almost for 33 hours per week.

A study conducted by Joshi and Maniar (2005) with elderly women residing in Baroda city opined about their television viewing behaviour, 140 elderly subjects belonging to middle income group were selected from free-living population by snowball technique. The findings of the study revealed that:

Both age groups of young-old and old-old women spent most of their leisure time watching TV.

On a daily basis, TV was watched for 2–3 hours. Women from older group watched TV more than those from the younger group.

Across the respondents, the TV channels preferred most were Star Plus and Sony. Other channels like Aaj Tak, Aastha, Sanskar, Zee TV and regional channels were also watched by them.

The five most preferred programmes were serials, news, religious lectures, film and film based programmes and music.

Respondents Across Age Groups Watched TV Keenly

The findings of the study indicate that television has an important place in the lives of elderly women. They spend a chunk of their leisure time in watching television. If the programmes and channels they watch, start discussing about their health issues, problems and how to tackle them effectively would help elderly lead a healthy life. Television programmes must deal with various diseases which women face during their third age. They must project the healthy and active elderly citizens rather than those who are sick, dependants and fragile. Older persons would benefit a great deal if television programmes instruct how to keep physically fit and healthy after one crosses the age of 60 years. Too often, older persons are unaware of such services that would make a significant difference in their lives, whether it is in the health care area or in housing, legal affairs, nutrition or recreation. This type of electronic outreach is particularly helpful to older persons who for various reasons suffer from restricted mobility or are completely homebound. It brings to them all useful announcements right in their living rooms.

Qualitative and quantitative data collected from elderly citizens through a study by Maniar (2006) on Television and elderly reveal that there was high influence of television viewing on the developmental task – "Adjusting to decreasing physical strength and health". In the FGDs, when elderly participants discussed about influence of television viewing on them they reported that it influenced them on their health and health related decisions.

The prime reason for it can be that, "Health" remains an area that is being given lot of importance at this stage of life. Majority of the researches conducted in the field of gerontology focuses on the issues of "health of aged" rather than on any other aspects of their life. Due emphasis is attached to policies and programmes that relate to health rather than other aspects like housing, economic and social development issues. NGOs and various voluntary organizations working in India for the elderly lay prime focus on health issues. The elderly themselves do have realized the importance of health, in their lives and hence, they do understand as well the importance of health related programmes and issues. It is for such reason that while watching television programmes, they concentrate more on health bulletins and information concerning their health. The television also addresses to this need worth more programmes on health than on other issues related to ageing.

Ageing as a stage of life is defined on the basis of health status of an individual. The person is labelled as "aged" or "old" when he or she shows a sign of deterioration in the health status. The functioning of various body organs gets affected adversely due to ageing. It makes it difficult for aged people lead a normal life. Old age is considered curse as one is affected with diseases like hypertension, and kidney and heart ailments. With increasing health problems, other aspects in life too are affected badly. Since the people are so touchy about health they show much concern for health programmes on television.

Hence, health related awareness, knowledge and readiness of the elderly to accept their deteriorating health conditions with various diseases and ways to treat these diseases have to become prime issues of concern for them. Many elderly citizens responded in their questionnaire, and they also represented at the FGDs that they were watching programmes on yoga, meditation and home-made remedies that saved them from various common diseases. When one learns good things from a programme, he continues watching it for a longer duration. This might be leaving high influence of such programmes on elderly.

The itemwise findings for the development task reveals one curious fact that television programmes influence the elderly largely to eat junk food. Harris and Feinberg (1977) reported similar findings in their research study. The elderly considered television advertisements useful to add popularity of food and health products.

Cosmetics and creams are other fascination for the elderly who wish to look younger. Their deteriorating health causes a feeling of inferiority among them about their physical appearance. The reason may be that majority of the characters that appear on television programmes and advertisements look smart and beautiful and also younger, more dynamic and charming. Thus induces strong desire among the aged to look younger and dashing. Therefore, they consider the characters as ideals and try to copy them with a wish that they too would look beautiful and charming. When elderly watch characters on the television they would naturally curse them for looking so dull and old. They want to regain their youth as they looked earlier. In this process, they perhaps forgot that ageing may be delayed but not avoided. It is inevitable and irreversible process. In this respect the television fails to play a positive role. It has to rather help the elderly to adjust themselves positively with deteriorating physical health conditions. Instead it is playing a negative role to make them more conscious about physical deterioration that occurs to them as natural course of ageing. The role that the television can play is to persuade the aged to be realistic, stop running after the mirage of youthfulness and accept the health conditions or changes of physiology as natural course of life. Such a role would call for good appreciation and value for the mass media.

The type of influence that the television exerts on its viewers, such as encouraging them to look younger, or beautiful, suggests that media sells the dreams that cannot be fulfilled by everyone. It takes the viewers to the fantasy and reality, his delusion gets over. The knowledge may cause frustration, dissatisfaction and a feeling of inferiority among them. Hence, there is dire need for channel owners and programme producers to be aware about such harmful influences of television programmes on viewers. In this light a strict code of conduct has to be formulated and implemented effectively so that the impact on viewers can be modified for positive outcome.

Such an influence of the television on elderly people points out that external beauty, and physical appearance are over projected in television programmes basically to allure youths and younger generations. The motive is that channels and programmes keep on earning huge profit from their viewers. In India, 40 per cent of the population is youth. The programmes focus chiefly on this group. Their needs and interests are taken care of while programmes are made and telecast. In it the needs of other target groups are grossly neglected. Further, these programmes are telecast on channels that are urban based. They focus mostly on lifestyles, issues and problems related to upper income groups. Sometimes, middle class may be granted little projection. But poor, rural and vulnerable sections of the society are grossly neglected. Their issues and problems are not addressed so well in television programmes. So it can be said that television fails to play a developmental role.

It is high time for our mass media to realize their role and duty towards development of the country as well as its people. Mass media and especially television should consider issues related to ageing which can help aged live a happy and healthy life. Media must play a prominent role in achieving this goal of the society.

References

1. Das, N.P. and Shah, U. (2001). *The Social and Health Status of the Elderly in India: Evidence from Recent National Level Data.* Population Research Centre, Department of Statistics, Faculty of Science, The M.S. University of Baroda, Vadodara.
2. Davis, R.H., and Davis, J.A. (1985). *T.V. is image of the Elderly—A Practical Guide for Change*. Lexington Books, Massachusetts/ Toronto.
3. Research Report (2005). *Women and Third Age,* Women's Studies Research Centre, The M.S. University of Baroda, Vadodara.
4. Maniar, A. (2006). 'Elderly and Television Viewing', Ph.D. Dissertation, Department of Home Science Extension and Communication, Faculty of Home Science, The M. S. University of Baroda, Vadodara.
5. Joshi, U. and Maniar, A. (1999). Third Age and Media In: *Report*

on Women and Third Age. Women's Studies Research Centre, The M.S. University of Baroda.

6. Bond, John, Coleman, Peter *et al*. *Ageing in Society: An Introduction to Social Gerontology*; Sage Publication, London.
7. *World Population Ageing, 1950–2050*, Population Division, United Nations.
8. Bagchi K. (1999). *Healthy Ageing and Nutrition, Ageing*, Nutrition and Health, Department of Food and Nutrition.
9. Delloff, L. (1985). *Distorted Images: The Elderly and the Media*, Christian Century, January 7–14, (www.christiancentury.org)
10. Vivian, (2002). *The Media of Mass Communication*, 6th ed. Boston: Allyn & Bacon.
11. *Women, Ageing and Health: A Framework for Action*, World Health Organization and United Nations Population Fund, Geneva, 2007.

EXTENSION EDUCATION

19 Capacity Building of Extension Personnel

Rameshwari Pandya
Babita Shukla

Extension education is the process of teaching rural people how to live better by learning ways that improve their farm, home and community institutions. Since learning and teaching are always the keys to education, extension educators must understand at least the elementary characteristics of the process and be able to apply them in their work with village people. Good extension teaching is the successful creation of opportunities or situations in which people gain the abilities and the stimulation necessary for successfully meeting their needs and interests in such a way as to attain continuous improvement and self-satisfaction. The great task of extension teaching is to help people gain a clear vision of what can and should be done, and then to assist them with the ways and means of attaining this condition. This requires opening the minds of others to the great vistas of knowledge and action requisite to improved levels of living. Extension teaching must broaden a life's pursuit of improved living conditions as a person, a family member, and as a citizen of one's community, state and nation. An effective extension worker is dedicated to the task of helping people learn to put knowledge to work for them to put it to use in ways that result in improvements in their living standards and ways of making a living.

As extension teaching is made more effective, extension work becomes more effective in closing the gap between the discoveries of knowledge through research and putting these findings into practice on the farm, in the home and in the community. To help others improve is the central challenge to extension teachers. Physical and economic accomplishments are sterile without the development of people. They are only a by-product or a result of people's development.

There is now emerging in many countries of the world a great awakening and desire for better living conditions. Extension teaching can and must help people attain these aspirations. This requires faith in the ability of people to help them. It requires people who believe in progress which involves acceptance of change, and the idea that change in specific directions is good, and is attainable. Effective extension teaching is the art of encouraging people to want to improve their whole pattern of living and of helping them develop the necessary skills to do so.

A significant development in recent years in many countries of Asia is the creation of organized programmes to help rural people improve their methods of making a living and of living. These programmes differ somewhat in name, form, emphasis and scope but, in general, their purpose is the same – to help rural people live better. Successful development programmes in democratic societies use the process of Extension Education as the activating force. The teaching-learning process is one of the most delicate, significant and complex of all social processes. This is so because the role of education is to change the way people think and act. And the nature of people's thinking and acting determines the nature of a society. To change the way people think and act so as to be sound socially, effective economically, permanent physically, and enduring educationally requires that community development workers skilfully provide learning experiences that induce village people to make the needed changes in what they think and how they act, changes that give them continuing self-satisfaction. Good extension teaching is the successful creation of opportunities or situations in which people gain the abilities and the stimulation necessary for successfully meeting their needs and interests in such a way as to attain continuous improvement and self-satisfaction. The great task of extension teaching is to help people gain a clear vision of what can and should be done, and then to assist them with the ways and means of attaining this condition. This requires opening the minds of others to the great vistas of knowledge and action requisite to improved levels of living. Extension teaching must broaden the horizon of men and women and youth, and encourage a life's pursuit of improved living conditions as a person, a family member, and as citizen of one's community, state and nation. An effective extension worker is dedicated to the task of helping people learn to put knowledge to work for them—to put it to use in ways that result in improvements in their living standards and ways of making a living.

As extension teaching is made more effective, extension work becomes more effective in closing the gap between the discoveries of knowledge through research and putting these findings into practice on the farm, in the home and in the community. To help others improve is the central challenge to extension personnel. Physical and economic accomplishments are sterile without the development of people. They are only a by-product or a result of people's development.

There is now emerging in many countries of the world a great awakening and desire for better living conditions. Extension teaching can and must help people attain these aspirations. This requires faith in the ability of people to help themselves. It requires people who believe in progress which involves acceptance of change, and the idea that change in specific directions is good, and is attainable. Effective extension teaching is the art of encouraging people to want to improve their whole pattern of living and of helping them develop the necessary skills to do so.

Provide skills and training, an effective learning situation consists of five essential elements:

- An effective instructor of leader.
- Learners who want and need to learn.

- Content or subject-matter that is useful to learners.
- Appropriate instructional equipment and materials.
- An appropriate physical environment.

Role to the extension teacher is to so conduct himself and to manipulate the last four elements that the learners have an effective learning experience.

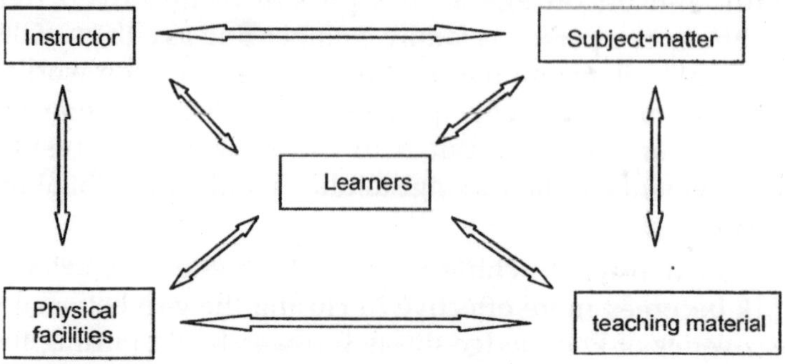

The diagram shows learners as the central element in the learning situations. This is significant, as it should be, since the entire purpose is to cause them to learn. Learning on the part of beneficiaries, therefore, becomes the objective, or end to be attained while the other four elements become the means for achieving this end product. There is always a constant reaction by learners to each of the other four major elements in the learning situations.

There are a number of things an instructor can do that help assure a good learning situation. Some of the important ones are given below:

- Have teaching objective clearly in mind that are significant to the learners that are attainable through the educational process within the mental, economic, physical and time limitations of the learners, and make these clear to them.
- Have a thorough knowledge of significant subject-matter related to the learner's needs.

- Be personable, enthusiastic, and interested in the subject-matter and the welfare of the learners.
- Be able to communicate effectively with the learners.
- Use democratic instructional methods and approaches.
- Encourage learner's participation in the learning situation.
- Be prepared, prompt, and courteous in every teaching-learning session.
- Set a good example of educational leadership and effective teaching.
- Arrange and manage the learning situation so as to prevent or minimize distractions within and outside the learning situation.
- Have suitable teaching equipment and supplies readily available for easy use with a minimum of distraction of the learners' attention from the subject.
- Be skilful in the use of every item of teaching material and equipment—chalk-board, visual equipment, reading materials, etc.
- Always prepare and use a carefully developed teaching plan.

The foregoing discussions are only a small number of the numerous important considerations that enable an instructor to create and manage learning situations that provide effective learning experiences for the participants. Indeed, this task calls for the total professional resources of the extension educator. To become a proficient extension instructor, one must constantly work at the tasks of analyzing his teaching problems, knowing his audience, gaining new technology to extends, gaining further understanding of the teaching-learning process, and developing greater skill in selecting, combining and using the methods of Extension Education.

Guides to Effective Extension Teaching

The only aim of extension teaching is to promote learning that results in desirable behavioural changes in people. For every change in human behaviour there is usually some influence that causes the change. Organized extension teaching is one of these outside stimuli. To apply them effectively requires design, not drift; it requires a plan, not trial and error. Good teaching, therefore, results from carefully planned content, procedures and techniques. Designing good teaching plans is highly professional job, and that when well done pays off handsomely in achievement. A number of conditions must be met and actions taken to make extension teaching and methods effective. Some major conditions necessary for success are listed below :

- Extension teaching requires specific and clearly defined teaching objectives.
- Extension teaching must accomplish certain kinds of educational changes in relation to the subject-matter, content with which the behaviour is to deal.
- Extension teaching requires learning situations that include five major elements. The five elements necessary to constitute an effective learning situation and some important points about each are as follows :
    - Leader or Instructor
    - Learners
    - Subject-matter or Content
    - Physical Situation
    - Instructional Equipment and Supplies
- Extension teaching requires that learners have effective learning experiences.
- Extension teaching usually requires a combination of teaching methods.
- Extension teaching requires careful evaluation of results.

Exposure to Different Areas

Multiple Roles

There are different approaches of teaching. They are based on four different conceptions of what it means to be a extension personnel. Here is a translated summary of descriptions:

1. *The sculptor :* The sculptor takes full responsibility for the presentation of all relevant material. He controls the schedule and the curriculum and controls the work of the students. He does not bother much about motivation, and considers it to be the students' responsibility to learn what he tells them. He devotes some time to help the weakest of the students, because this is part of his task. The dialogue in the classroom aims mainly at clarifying the presentation of the textbook and correcting students' work.
2. *The entertainer:* The entertainer thinks that a teacher is much like an actor. She feels that it is her responsibility to arouse the interest and make it easy to grasp the central issues of her subject. She works with background and perspectives. She tries to establish an active dialogue with at least some of the students, in which she will be able to present and accentuate her view. She is genuinely interested in the subject and in doing a good job, mainly during the classroom performance.
3. *The coach:* The coach believes that results depend on the work done by each of his students, and sees himself as catalyst for this work. He wants to know the background, conditions and capacities of each student, and to create an environment where they can achieve as much as possible. He informs them about the goals and the best methods, and discusses the programme with them. He is clear about evaluation criteria, gives feedback and helps them in tackling all kinds of problems. What counts for him are the results of the students in relation to their individual's capacity.
4. *The manager:* The manager looks at the classroom as a working place, and her task is to manage the joint

efforts effectively towards the best possible result. Everybody should know how to learn, and she delegates tasks and responsibilities. She also varies working methods. She is aware of individual differences and uses much time in explaining what to do and why. She is a democratic leader and discusses strategies with her students, but she also knows that structure and management is necessary.

These examples not only indicate different conceptions of the teacher's role, but also different understandings of how learning comes about.

Selection and Use of Extension Methods

If one could really know the cause and effect relationships involved in changing human behaviour, extension teaching could be made more systematic and less mysterious. As a result the choice of extension methods could be made in such a way that would speed up the educational progress immeasurably. Social scientist in general and psychologist in particular have dealt with this phenomenon with increasing insight and success since the beginning of the science of psychology nearly 100 years ago. But the human mind still presents mysteries unfathomed by man with the best of his insight and devices. Hence, the selection and uses of the means for teaching in any situation are in part of problem of predicating the relationship between selected means and ends. Somethings about teaching, however, are pretty well-known. When these are applied properly significant impacts on learners can be anticipated.

General Guides

The goal of extension teaching for community development is to attain desirable action on the part of many people. The effort is to induce all those for whom a recommendation is appropriate to take the necessary action. Before this can happen or action is obtained, however, the people concerned must become interested and must develop a desire to make the change obtain the skill necessary for doing so, and then take action which results in satisfaction to the teacher. To state the problem differently, all actions are in response to a stimulation provided by an appropriate situation. Often people do not feel they have a problem or that certain action will help them. In short, people often are not interested in change. But, until interest is aroused and people learn how to make the needed changes successfully, no action will result. All of this implies that extension teaching methods must be used to build a background of ideas and suggestion of facts, and above all, to develop in people an interest and a desire for change they need to make. This requires far more than mere telling people what they should do. To tell a person to do something one does not have to know how to do it oneself. But to teach how to do things one must be able to do them oneself. To get individuals to see the need for change, to help them want to make useful changes and to develop in them the skills necessary for success with the action suggested calls for the highest type of teaching.

Learning is habit-forming process. People break old habits and learn new ones only one at a time. In other words, people learn one thing at a time. In extension teaching, therefore, it is usually unwise to present too many ideas at one time. Teaching one step at a time, presenting one idea at a time, is likely to be more successful. Knowing this fact, extension workers should be aware that ideas must be carefully selected and put forcibly before people. It has been said that life is like a stream. In some people this stream may be sluggish and few ideas may enter or be carried forward, but in most individuals the stream of modern life is a torrent in which many ideas are moving along. These may be first on top, then under, then whirled aside and later thrust out. Extension workers try to put still more ideas into this stream. To get them into the stream and keep them there requires careful planning and teaching. Ideas must be big and good enough, that they can be launched in this stream and hold their course. No weak, poorly presented lecture or unplanned village meeting, badly conducted demonstration or unattractive exhibit will force the ideal afloat in the torrent of life. The currents, cross currents and undertow in village life are much too fierce. Not only recommendation must be good, but they must also avoid a lot of other things including too many ands, its and buts. Furthermore, ideas must be reinforced, constantly nourished, and stimulated by the right suggestions if they are to stay afloat and have their effect in changing people's behaviour. This means, for example, that each news article, poster, meeting, demonstration, exhibit and tour must be chosen and used for the special part it can best play in the task of promoting desirable action among people. All these methods, when used skilfully, help to hold before people the main goal, and the action necessary to achieve it. It is necessary that suggested changes be basically sound. They must fit a real need as the people see it. They must be in line with the people's felt needs. People must be successful with the practices when they try them. They must get the results anticipated. Changes they make must ultimately give satisfaction. Success with one action leads people to a desire for learning about and taking other actions. In true form this is the result of extension education in action.

Specific Guides

It has been pointed out that rural people learn primarily by seeing, hearing, or doing the things to be learned. Extension teaching then consists basically of arranging situations for the learner to see, to hear or to do that which is to be learned. These opportunities are provided through the skilful use of extension teaching methods. To obtain action – to cause people to make desired changes and to ensure success and satisfaction—extension teaching effort usually must be planned to develop the six phases in the attainment of successful change in people's behaviour. These are :

- Have the idea call attention.
- Become interested in taking the action suggested.
- Develop desire or want to make the change suggested.

- Have an opportunity to make the desired change and take action.
- Develop some confidence in the ability to make the change.
- Obtain satisfaction from the action taken.

These basic phases of the process of promoting change in people's behaviour do not appear as distinct and easily identified units but in an overlapping and evolving manner. They emerge from the process of logical thought and reasoned wonderment. Hence, they are not a product of the answer but of the learning necessary to arrive at the answer. Accumulated experience and research findings support the suggestions that certain extension methods, when properly used, contribute effectively to the attainment of each of the fundamental steps in people's behaviour required in the process of change.

Trained as Training Personnel

A component of the Co-operative Extension system is a leader in youth development education that:

- works with all eligible youth to provide effective, enjoyable learning experiences.
- develops unity in all types of family structures.
- utilizes a quality applied curriculum in classroom and community-based settings.
- reflects and values cultural and human diversity.
- employs competent, educated, self-motivated staff who are valued assets of the Land Grant University system and are recognized as youth development experts.
- utilizes creative staffing patterns and contemporary working environments.
- Delivers programmes through co-operative efforts of The University of Tennessee, Tennessee State University and public and private sector volunteers.

In order to evaluate different teacher roles and teaching strategies we should be aware of how students generally acquire and build up their knowledge. This is a big subject in itself and there is no time to go deeply into it. I will only put forward a set of relevant basic assumptions, based on fairly well recognized learning theory :

- We know that learners' ability of learning is influenced by what they think learning is about. Many learners think that learning is to pick up pieces and bulks of information, and that the instructors' job is to impart pieces of their subject knowledge to learners. Even some instructors seem to think in this way, or behave as if they did.
- Usually it is difficult to separate knowledge to be learned from the situations in which it is used. Learning is 'situated'. The abstract knowledge has no meaning unless it is used to solve concrete and real problems. Therefore, learning has its base in experience of real or close to real situations. That is why so-called 'problem-based learning' seems to be so effective, particularly in education for professions.
- However, in building knowledge the learner also has to transcend the immediate situation and reflect on the contextual experience in order to construct more general concepts, views of the world and problem-solving methods. Therefore, it is useful to articulate concepts and more general knowledge structures, and to discuss such articulations with other people. In one sense, the construction of knowledge is individual. But also social negotiation of meaning is necessary.

Based on a similar view on student learning, there are identified five aspects of the learning process that should be addressed by learners in order to succeed, and therefore, also considered in any teaching strategy:

- Apprehend the structure of the discourse – e.g. focus on the signified, relate and distinguish evidence and argument, organise and structure the content into a coherent whole.
- Integrate the sign with the signified – e.g. practise mapping between the two, practise the forms of representation of an idea, represent the discourse as a whole as well as its constituent parts.
- Act on the world and on descriptions of the world – e.g. relating knowledge to experience, relating theory to practice, extending experience of the world, manipulating the various forms of representation of that experience.
- Use feedback – e.g. both intrinsic and extrinsic feedback to adjust actions to fit the task goal, and descriptions to fit the topic goal.
- Reflect on the goal-action-feedback cycle – e.g. relating this to the message of the discourse, the structure of the whole.

Guide for Organizing the Instructional Programme

For the extension worker's purpose, curricula are more valuable when learning experiences relate the basic sciences and technical subjects to farm, homes and community situations they will encounter after employment. It is, therefore, essential that effective use of the syllabus is made in formulating outlines for class-room and field instruction. The following considerations may be kept in view while formulating the instructional programme on the basis of the syllabus :

- The three aspects of the instructional programme, viz., class-room instruction, practical training at campus, and extension work in the field, should be followed in a logical sequence.
- The procedures and methods employed in the training should be so devised as to result in maximum learning.

- The programme of institutional training should be so developed as to take advantage of seasonal activities in the field.
- The institutional training should be supplemented with planned visits to villages for field extension work. In other words, an understanding of the basic knowledge in a subject-matter field should be followed by acquisition of skill needed for the transmission of the knowledge to the people.
- A co-ordinated programme of work of various departments such as agriculture, co-operation, panchayats, animal husbandry, etc., should be taken into consideration while formulating the teaching programme so that the trainees have a clear understanding of the necessity of implementing a co-ordinated and integrated programme in the field.

Keeping the above considerations in view, the following is developmental areas that can be used as a guide for use in organizing the instructional programme. The developmental areas are listed below :

- Agriculture
- Health
- Literacy
- Social education
- Environment
- Income generation
- Politics
- Vocational education.

It need hardly be emphasized that the preparation of an instruction programme so essential for any systematic and effective teaching, requires hard work on the part of the instructor. He has not only to be thorough and up-to-date in his subject-matter field but must also possess a basic understanding of the extension educational processes. His task and purpose is to create situations that produce effective learning experience. It can partly be met by systematizing the instructional programme and following a carefully prepared plan of teaching for capacity building of extension personnel.

References

1. Sharma, R.S. (1998). *Extension Education,* Omsons Publication, New Delhi.
2. Saiyadain, M.S., Murthy, N. and Singh, J.P. (1990). *Challenges in Adult Education,* Rajkamal Electric Press, New Delhi.
2. Supe, S.V. (1997). *An Introduction to Extension Education,* Oxford & IBH Publishing, New Delhi.
4. Jethithor, B. (1996). *Adult Education and Extension,* A.P.H. Publishing Corporation, New Delhi.
5. Mcnergney, R.F. and Herbert, J.M., *Foundations of Education: The Challenge of Professional Practice,* New Delhi.
6. Venkataiah, S., *Teacher Education,* Anmol Publication, New Delhi.

20 Knowledge Attitude and Practice of Reproductive Health among CEC Learners

K. Sudha Rani
K. Srilatha Kishori
T. Ananda

India's population is increasing at a very fast rate. From 683 million in 1981, it increased to 846 million in 1991 and 1027 million in 2001. This rate of increase is shocking to many working in the field of population education and family welfare. Under the pressure of increasing population, most of the countries around the world are confronted with shortage of food, inadequate facilities for education and health. Moreover, due to poor economic standards, other social problems like crime, violence, anti-social activities etc. are becoming serious by the day.

As the control of increasing population is a critical factor to achieve overall development, the need for population education was felt. Since the rate of literacy in the country is high, more publicity through media and other campaigns was inadequate and the need for improving the literacy levels along with a few lessons in population education and incorporating and integrating it with adult education was felt not only by the governments both at the state and centre levels but also by the experts within population control and adult education. Adult and continuing education was launched in 1998 to provide lifelong learning opportunities to all people beyond literacy and primary education. This programme is being targeted at neo-literates, school dropouts, primary school pass outs, pass out of non-formal education etc. Population education dealing with advantage of having small family, reproductive health and knowledge in family planning methods were incorporated in the textbooks that were used in adult and continuing education centres.

Since women contribute to reproduction, sensitizing them towards small family norm, reproductive health and child care is a must. However, they are more constrained by gender inequalities and male domination in decision-making in the families on economic, political and social aspects. It was assumed that by incorporating lessons in family planning methods, population control and reproductive health in adult education books, the women adult learners would acquire some knowledge in these aspects which may lead to attitudinal changes in adoption of family planning methods and reproductive health.

Keeping in view the integration of population education messages in the neo-literate materials, and the key role of women in population stabilization and maintenance of good reproductive health, a study was conducted on the knowledge, attitude and practice of reproductive health among women learners in continuing education centres.

Objectives of the Study

1. To study the knowledge, attitude and practice of reproductive health among CEC (Continuing Education Centre) learners.
2. To find out the influence of socio-economic variables (i.e Religion, Caste, Occupation and annual family income) on the knowledge and practice of reproductive health among CEC learners.
3. To suggest measures to make them to adopt better reproductive health care practices.

Sample of the Study

To study the knowledge, attitude and practice of reproductive health among Continuing Education Centre (CEC) learners, women learners in Chittoor district of Andhra Pradesh were selected. Chittoor district consists of 3 revenue divisions namely, Chittoor, Madanapalli and Tirupati. All the three divisions put together have 66 revenue mandals. A total of 1143 Continuing Education Centres are functioning under the supervision of Zilla Saksharata Samiti (ZSS). From each of the division, 2 mandals (1 rural and 1 urban) were selected at random as a sample in the first stage. A total of 6 mandals from 3 divisions were selected. From each mandal 10 centres were selected. Thus totally 60 centres for the three divisions of Chittoor district were selected. 8 regular women learners from each centre (8 × 60) (based on the attendance register) were selected as the sample for the present study by purposive sampling method. Thus the total sample of the present study was 480 learners. The sample of the study is as follows :

District	—	1
Division	—	3
Mandals	—	6 (3 × 2 = 6)
Centres	—	60 (10 × 6 = 60)
Learners	—	480 (60 × 8 = 480)

While collecting back the questionnaires from the sample 5 questionnaires were not returned by the sample. Finally, 475 learners were taken as the sample for the study.

Questionnaires were constructed to measure the knowledge and practice of reproductive health. Attitude scale was also constructed and split method was used to cross-examine the reliability of the scale and its validity was based on the judgements of the experts. The reproductive health aspects as family planning methods, maternal health, infant mortality, reduction and prevention of STDs including HIV/AIDS, have been considered in relation to knowledge, attitude and practice among the selected adult learners.

Data Collection and Analysis

Before administrating the above tools to each respondent, an effort was made to establish rapport with them and detailed explanation about the objectives of this research study. The above tools were administrated to the women learners by meeting them individually in the continuing education centres. Sufficient time was given to the respondents to fill the questionnaires, which were collected back.

The data thus collected was pooled together and analyzed percentages were calculated and the findings were presented below:

Findings of the Study

Reproductive health is condition in which reproduction is accomplished in a state of complete physical, mental and social well-being and not merely the absence of diseases or disorders of the reproductive process. Reproductive health, therefore, implies that people are able to have a satisfying and safe sex life and those they have the capability to reproduce and freedom to decide, when and how often to do. Traditional population programmes have been focusing too narrowly on reducing population through the provision of family planning services in India, on achieving demographic targets by increasing contraceptive prevalence and notable female sterilization and have, as a result, been unresponsive to other reproductive health needs. In this process, women's needs have been generally overlooked by the programme and the consequences of the neglect, in terms of poor reproductive health, are disturbing. Thus, there is an urgent need for the improvement in the quality of reproductive health care. Keeping this in view, the present study is focused on KAP of reproductive health among women learners in continuing education centres and the findings are presented in Table 20.1.

Table 20.1 shows that 184 learners out of 475 (i.e. 38.73%) have high knowledge levels about reproductive health. The next best percentage of 31.58 is scored by the low knowledge

Table 20.1: Knowledge of Reproductive Health among Adult Learners

Sl. No.	Knowledge Level	Number	Percentage
1.	Low	150	31.58
2.	Moderate	141	29.68
3.	High	184	38.74

category which has 150 learners. The remaining 141 learners (29.68 %) fall in moderate knowledge levels towards reproductive health.

Table 20.2: Attitude of Reproductive Health among Adult Learners

Sl. No.	Attitude Levels	Number	Percentage
1.	Unfavourable	155	32.63
2.	Indifferent	139	29.26
3.	Favourable	1181	38.11

A quick perusal of Table 20.2 clearly shows that 38.11 per cent of the sample (i.e.181) fall in favourable attitude level towards reproductive health. 155 samples with 32.63 per cent fall in unfavourable level. The remaining 29.26 per cent fall in indifferent attitude towards reproductive health.

Table 20.3: Practice of Reproductive Health among Adult Learners

Sl. No.	Knowledge Level	Number	Percentage
1.	Low	137	28.84
2.	Moderate	141175	36.84
3.	High	184163	34.32

The study of Table 20.3 shows that 36.84 per cent (175) of the sample falls in moderate practice levels of reproductive health. 34.32 per cent (163) fall in high practice levels, and the remaining 137 (28.84%) of the total sample fall in low practice levels.

Table 20.4: Knowledge and Practice of Reproductive Health among Adult Learners belonging to Different Religions

Religion	*Knowledge*			*Practice*		
	Low	*Moderate*	*High*	*Low*	*Moderate*	*High*
Muslim (50)	20 (40)	15 (30)	15 (30)	15 (30)	21 (42)	14 (28)
Hindu (425)	130 (30.58)	126 (29.6)	169 (39.76)	122 (28.7)	149 (36.73)	149 (35.05)
Total	150 (31.57)	141 (29.68)	184 (38.73)	137 (28.84)	175 (36.84)	163 (34.31)

When we look at religion and its association on knowledge levels of reproductive health, in spite of the total sample of Muslim women being only 10.53 per cent of the whole sample of 475, we have glimpses of the actual trend 40 per cent of the Muslim women have low knowledge of reproductive health and 30 per cent fall both in moderate and high levels of reproductive health knowledge. But among Hindu women, majority of them fall in high level category which is 39.76 per cent. On careful analysis we find that there is a reversal of trend, i.e. nearly 40 per cent of Hindu women have high knowledge of reproductive health. This increase in the high knowledge of reproductive health in Hindu women may be due to the better literacy skills, and more social interaction. The Muslim women on the other hand are on the receiving end due to lower literacy, little social interaction due to *purdah* system and early marriages.

If we analyze religion and practice of reproductive health, we find that the Muslims have 42 per cent in moderate practice of reproductive health as compared to 36.73 per cent in Hindus. Hindus are better placed in both the low and high practice categories. Thus it is seen that Hindus have a better practice rates towards reproductive health.

A careful study of Table 20.5 analyses association of communities with knowledge levels of reproductive health clearly suggest that all communities have a decent percentage in high knowledge level. It is 40.16 per cent in Scheduled

Table 20.5: Knowledge and Practice of Reproductive Health among Adult Learners Belonging to Different Castes

Caste	*Knowledge*			*Practice*		
	Low	*Moderate*	*High*	*Low*	*Moderate*	*High*
Scheduled Castes (122)	43 (35.25)	30 (24.59)	49 (40.16)	28 (22.95)	41 (33.60)	53 (44.44)
Scheduled Tribes (25)	6 (24)	9 (36)	10 (40)	5 (20)	9 (36)	11 (44)
Backward Castes (148)	47 (31.75)	43 (29.05)	58 (39.18)	47 (31.75)	58 (39.18)	43 (29.05)
Forward Castes (180)	54 (30)	59 (32.78)	67 (37.22)	57 (31.66)	67 (37.22)	56 (31.11)
Total (475)	150 (31.57)	141 (29.68)	184 (38.74)	137 (28.84)	175 (36.84)	163 (34.31)

Castes, 40 per cent in Scheduled Tribes, 39.18 per cent in Backward Castes and 38.74 per cent in Forward Castes. The low knowledge level scores over moderate knowledge level only in the cases of Scheduled Castes and Backward Castes which is 35.25 per cent and 31.75 per cent which is more than 24.59 per cent and 29.05 per cent respectively. The above study does not suggest any clear association between community and knowledge of reproductive health. Coming to the practice of reproductive health and community, Scheduled Castes and Scheduled Tribes have high practice levels of 43.44 and 44 per cent. In moderate practice levels, all the communities are on equal terms between 36 per cent in STs and 39.18 in BCs.

It is evident from Table 20.6 majority of the sample falls in the cultivation category 47.58 per cent followed by agricultural labour 31.79 per cent. The business class, which has better chances of education and access to media has better knowledge and has 25 per cent in low, 29.17 per cent in moderate and 45.83 per cent in high knowledge levels. The agricultural labour class has highest presence in low knowledge level 35.10 per cent, and the lowest in high knowledge 33.11, but has 31.79 per cent in moderate knowledge. The analysis clearly shows that there is no definitive trend that can show difference or

Table 20.6: Knowledge and Practice of Reproductive Health among Adult Learners of Different Occupations

Occupation	*Knowledge*			*Practice*		
	Low	*Moderate*	*High*	*Low*	*Moderate*	*High*
Others (26)	8 (30.77)	8 (30.77)	10 (38.46)	11 (42.30)	6 (23.08)	9 (34.62)
Agricultural Labour (151)	53 (35.10)	48 (31.79)	50 (33.11)	41 (27.15)	59 (39.07)	51 (33.74)
Business Women (72)	18 (25.00)	21 (29.17)	33 (45.83)	18 (25)	26 (36.11)	28 (38.89)
Cultivation (226)	71 (31.41)	64 (28.32)	91 (40.27)	67 (29.65)	84 (37.17)	75 (33.19)
Total (475)	150 (31.58)	141 (29.68)	184 (38.74)	137 (28.84)	175 (36.84)	163 (34.32)

association, when knowledge levels of reproductive health and occupation are tabulated.

By observing association between occupation and practice towards reproductive health, the business class has the best practice towards reproductive health, with lowest percentage 25 per cent in low practice category, and has the best percentage of 38.89 in high practice level. Others have a high percentage of 42.30 in low practice, lowest in moderate practice 23.08 but a better percentage in high practice level. Both the agricultural labour and cultivation occupations have the same trends.

From Table 20.7 it is evident that 42.53 per cent people fall in below Rs. 25,000 annual income, followed by 45.47 per cent in Rs. 25,000 to 35,000 income level. Only 57 people 12 per cent of the total sample fall in the Rs. 36,000 and above income group. It is clear from the total that Rs. 25,000-35,000 group and Rs. 36,000 above group have the same percentages. The Rs. 25,000 of annual family income groups have almost equal percentage of 34.65 and 34.16 in the high knowledge categories, and 31.19 per cent in the moderate knowledge levels. The analysis of the Table 20.7 does not show any clear indication that as the annual family income has any association or difference in knowledge level of reproductive health.

Table 20.7: Knowledge and Practice of Reproductive Health among Adult Learners Belonging to Different Income Levels

Annual Family Income	*Knowledge*			*Practice*		
	Low	*Moderate*	*High*	*Low*	*Moderate*	*High*
Below Rs. 25,000 (202)	70 (34.65)	63 (31.19)	69 (34.16)	60 (29.70)	73 (36.14)	69 (34.16)
Rs. 25,000 to 35,000 (216)	63 (29.17)	62 (28.70)	91 (42.13)	61 (28.24)	80 (37.03)	75 (34.72)
Rs. 36,000 & above (57)	17 (29.82)	16 (28.07)	24 (42.11)	16 (28.07)	22 (38.60)	19 (33.33)
Total (475)	150 (31.58)	141 (29.68)	184 (38.74)	137 (28.84)	175 (36.84)	163 (34.32)

By observing association between annual family income of practice Rs. 36,000 and above annual family income group has the lowest 28.07 per cent in low practice category. Rs. 25,000 to 35,000 income group has the highest (34.72) percentage of high practice category. A careful study of the table does not show any association or difference between annual family income and practice towards reproductive health.

Findings of the Study

- 38.58 per cent of the learners possess with high knowledge of reproductive health followed by 31.58 per cent with low knowledge and 29.68 per cent of the learners with moderate knowledge levels.
- 36.84 per cent of the sample falls in moderate practice levels of reproductive health. 34.32 per cent fall in high practice levels and the remaining 28.84 per cent of the sample fall in low practice levels.
- 38.11 per cent of the sample is of favourable attitude towards reproductive health, 32.63 falls in unfavourable level. The remaining 29.26 per cent fall in indifferent attitude towards reproductive health.
- 36.84 per cent of the sample falls in moderate practice levels of reproductive health. 34.32 per cent fall in high

practice levels and the remaining (28.84%) fall in low practice levels.

- 40 per cent Muslim women have low knowledge and moderate practice of reproductive health. Majority of the Hindus fall in high level knowledge and practice of reproductive health.
- Majority of the learners (above 35 %) of all the castes have high knowledge of reproductive health. Whereas the practice of reproductive health among SCs and STs is higher than the BCs and FCs.
- 45.83 per cent of the learners undertaking business, 40.27 per cent of the cultivation and 33.11 per cent of agricultural labourers fall in high knowledge levels. The business class has the best practice of reproductive health followed by agricultural labourers and cultivators.

Suggestions

- New and simple ways of imparting reproductive health to adult learners have to be found out so that the learners can understand and put them into practice. This problem needs further research.
- The optimum amount of knowledge that is required to be imparted on reproductive health to neo-literates has to be researched upon. Since neo-literate capacity to understand intricate knowledge is limited this aspect requires further research.
- Merely incorporating lessons in primers on population issues does not bring results but what is required is effective communication by the teachers (*preraks*) in the adult education centres. This in turn requires the teachers to acquire knowledge beyond what is given in primers and they should be trained in sample communication methods for effective communication to the adult learners who have just learned only three 'Rs' (Reading, Writing and Arithmetic).

- The adult education teachers should be trained in basics of social science research which will equip them to understand the constraints faced by the adult women learners not only in changing their attitudes but also in putting the acquired knowledge into practice.
- It should be the duty of the *prerak* to identify the learners with low knowledge and educate them and enhance their knowledge on par with the other who has high knowledge.
- As seen in this research study, having high knowledge does not lead to high levels of practice of reproductive health. This may be due to various factors like tradition, preference for son, religion, children being considered as economic assets, fatalism etc. To counter these aspects adult education department along with women welfare and other related non-government organizations need to intensify the awareness programmes among the masses.

21 Life Skill Education : Reengineering of the Human Capital

Lalita Sharma

Education should develop Physical, Social, Emotional and Spiritual abilities among students, so that they can cope with life and living successfully. In the twenty first century there is a need to develop critical thinking, problem solving abilities and decision-making. If so, whatever education we provide, needs to be relevant and sustainable. Mahatma Gandhi has very aptly mentioned that education should help in developing body, mind and spirit of all children. Consequently, the National Policy of Education 1986 has evolved a National System of Education in the spirit of our constitutional needs. New School curricular has been evolved and new textbooks have been developed to achieve this objective of education. The education process is continuously evolving to meet the emergent needs of children and the society.

The World Health Organisation (WHO) has pointed out the 14 per cent of Indian children have emotional problems and need counselling. Similarly, Vidya Sagar Institute of Mental Health and Neurosciences, New Delhi has observed, "In the past decade we have seen an increase in the number of children (between the age of three and seventeen) whose mental functioning gets affected due to external reasons, which results in behavioural problems." Consequently, there is a need to understand the physical, social and emotional problems of school students. During school life they also face personal and social problems during adolescent period. In this context UNICEF has argued for Life Skill Education. Life Skill

Education is related to the Socio-Psychological abilities for adaptive and positive behaviour that enable individuals to deal effectively with the demands and challenges of everyday life. National Curriculum Framework for School Education (2000) has included Life Skills Education as one of the curricular concerns. It has argued for linking education with life skills. It suggests to link content with the living experiences of students. "Education ideally must prepare students to face the challenges of life." Therefore, there is a need to develop general skills like communication skill, decision-making skill, stress coping skill, problem solving skill, social skill etc., related to a wide variety of areas such as health and social needs. It is through these skills that students can fight with social challenges, drug addition violence, health problems and AIDS. It will also help them to understand civic and legal issues related to personal and social problems.

An important characteristic of life skills is that they are temporal and spatial in natures. Hence, they are required to be contextual. There are certain core skills, such as, problem solving, critical thinking, communication, self awareness, coping with stress, interpersonal relations, decision-making, empathy, creative thinking etc. which needs attention of the curriculum planners and teachers so that these skills can be inculcated among school students.

Need of the Study

All of us expect our educational system produce a good generation of competent people. Educationists also desire that the youngsters of today become good citizens of tomorrow, that their behaviour and attitude be modified by education. Therefore, Board of Secondary Education, Rajasthan and Central Board of Secondary Education has started life skill education programme.

Statement of the Problem

A study of Development and Assessment of Life skills among prospective teachers.

Objectives of the Study

1. To develop selected life skills among the prospective teachers.
2. To measure an understanding of life skills.

Hypotheses

1. Female teachers lack general awareness about life skills.
2. There is no correlation between the life skills and academic achievement of the pupil teachers.

Some important life skills used in the project :

1. Self concept/awareness skill
2. Decision making skill
3. Communication skill
4. Stress coping skill
5. Problem solving skill
6. Critical/Creative thinking skill
7. Social adjustment skills

Terms Defined

Life skills are abilities for adaptive and positive behaviour that enable individuals to deal effectively with the demands and challenges of everyday life (WHO). In particular, Life skills are a group of psychosocial competencies and interpersonal skills that help people to make informed decision communicate effectively and develop coping the self-management skills to lead a healthy and productive life. Life skills may be directed towards personal actions or actions towards others as well as towards those actions which change the surrounding environment to make it more conducive to health. National Curriculum Framework for School Education (2000) by linking education with life skills introduced certain core life skills such as problem solving, critical thinking, communication, self-awareness, coping with stress, decision-making, creative thinking and generative thinking, interpersonal relationships and empathy. These are of enormous importance for successful living.

Effective acquisition of skills can influence the way we feel about others and ourselves and will in equal measure influence the way other perceives us. These skills can enhance our productivity, self-efficiency, self-esteem and self-confidence. Life skills can give us, the tools and techniques to improve interpersonal relations. Life skills are the important keys for quality of life and with the help of so many core life skills a man can achieve quality of life. Thus, the life skills are the important point to built our character.

Life Skills

This term refers to a large group of psycho-social and interpersonal skills which can help people make informed decisions, communicate effectively, and develop coping and self-management skills that may help them lead a healthy and productive life. Life skills may be directed towards personal actions and actions towards others, as well as actions to change the surrounding environment to make it conducive to health.

Attitudes

The term "attitudes" is used throughout this is to encompass the broad domain of social norms; ethics, morals, values, rights, culture, tradition, spirituality and religion, and feelings about self and others.

Health

WHO's broad view of health as "the state of complete physical, mental and social well-being" is assumed here. Using this definition, social and economic conditions and the broader environment are considered key determinants of health.

Health Promotion

The process of enabling people to increase control over and to improve their health. Health Promotion not only embraces actions directed at strengthening the skills of individuals, but also action directed towards changing social, environmental and economic conditions so as to alleviate their impact on public and individual health (from WHO Health Promotion Glossary).

Adjustment

Life is a series of change and challenges and people are in the process of changing. They adopt new technicrowded situation. Many environmental Psychologists believe that the relationship between crowding and outcome behaviours such as negative forms of social activity is mediated by psychological stress reactions.

Sample

The present study is based on thirty-nine female pupil teachers of the year 2005-06, H.B.U.C.T.E. Hatundi, Ajmer.

Description of the Tool

The researcher has used a Self Evaluation Test Paper prepared by the Secondary Board of Education, Rajasthan. Test is divided into three parts.

In Unit 1 the questions were related with self-identification and relation with others in the society. All the questions were quantitative in nature.

- The unit covered different dimensions of a person like—self-confidence, emotional maturity, strong determination friendly behaviour, effective communicator warm relations.

  The Unit 2 also contained 6 questions. Question No. 3 demands open and free responses. Unit 2 concerns with the human physiology and health. It consists of following types of questions :

- How much healthy I am?
- How much I am responsible about my health?
- Who is a healthy adolescent?
- Knowledge about H.I.V./AIDS infection?
- How much possibilities that I may to adopt bad habits.
- My views about bad habits.

In Unit 3 there are four questions. Three questions were in qualitative in nature and only fourth question was quantitative. All the first three questions were qualitative in nature demands open and free responses and starts from the views and end at the inferences, related with the professional interest, marriage life and responsible parenthood. This unit is related with our present abilities and future plans.

Methodology/Developmental Process

All student teachers were informed about the subject matter of the research. A long informational session was held in anonymity of participants was assured fact Final data would only be displayed in are aggregate format. Because of the trust and secrecy developed within the group and with the facilitator, 39 pupil teachers volunteered to participate.

Some skills are developed naturally/automatically in particular environment while others are developed by learning and regular practice.

In developmental process many factors help in acquiring certain life skills, such as praxis and role model. In addition to these life skills can be developed through dialogue, effective communication and interaction in classroom and home.

Teacher and parents may solve many problems of their wards. Life skills education is closer to social science education, therefore, a teacher can solve students, social problems very effectively. The researcher has adopted the following procedure for it:

1. The researcher initially warm up the class with "A thought of the day."
2. The researcher then takes up the life skills book prescribed by the Board of Secondary Education, Rajasthan and asked the pupil teachers to learn the related lesson carefully, which would help in the development of the cognitive skills. When pupil teachers are able to understand the cognitive part, the researcher invites their views on the particular skill. Generally, pupil teacher raised various types of social problems.

   Then the researcher and peer group explained how to effectively communicate their problems to their teachers.
3. Teacher carefully listen to the students' problems.
4. The researcher invited the alternative solutions on the particular problem with the help of discussion method.
5. The pupil teachers choose the best solution in the related circumstances. Affective component of the skill is concerning the feelings and attitudes of the pupil teachers, was developed with the help of story/telling technique, examples and narrations of the events.

   The traditional methods of teaching as well as the innovative methods of teaching were used in the classroom by the researcher.

Statistics

Simple Mean and Spearman's Rank difference correlation was used for the data Analysis

$M = \frac{\sum x}{N}$; M = Arithmetic mean

$$= \frac{6\sum D2}{N\left(N2^2 - 1\right)}$$

P = 1.

P = Coefficient of Correlation calculated from Rank Difference Method

$\Sigma D2$ = Sum of the Squares of differences in rank.

N = Number of Pairs

Findings—Qualitative Aspects

1. The best girl of the year (2005-06) Miss Kiran Sharma was also among the students involved in this project.
2. The pupil teachers are more obedient, practical and flexible in their nature. They try to give their best to parents and teachers, when they are satisfied logically. They cannot compromise with their self-respect.
3. As regard profession—Administrative work was their first choice and teaching was the second. Here researcher tries to explain them—teaching also required a good administration and leadership skill.
4. They demand a responsible and economically stable life partner. It show pupil teacher has the clear picture in their brain about successful marriage life. They know that marriage institution needs Management, Sacrifice and Compromise.
5. They show their full competencies if they have favourable environment but they cannot cope up with unfavourable circumstances. Therefore, life skill is subjective in nature. It differs from person to person. They cannot be successful in every sphere of life. They are good in one but not in another.
6. It was found by the researcher that pupil teacher answered honestly.
7. Life Skill Education enables a person to choose best options available in life.

Quantitative Aspects

1. The first three rankers of the year (2005-06) participated in this project regularly.
2. Scoring shows the attitude of pupil teacher was positive. They provided open and free responses towards their life. Only one student complained that her mother scolded her. The researcher personally made contact with her and tried to satisfy her.
3. Unexpectedly and boldly indeed one of the pupil teacher went to the extent of saying that she was fed up with listening to her mother's repeated instructions that she should behave like a girl, and she was prepared to change her behaviour if she stopped doing it.
4. There was a student in the class who did not know the meaning of the word 'Brown Sugar'.
5. A comparison of mean scores obtained in Pre and Post-test given to pupil teachers shows effective results on various dimensions, viz. Increased self-confidence, Emotional maturity, Strong determination, Effective communication and awareness about health and effect of media.
6. Negative Correlation was found in the university examination scores and life skill test scores.
7. The study reveals that life skill education provides good academic results both in schools and colleges. All above findings are based on I and III Part of the Book. But in the second part of the book the researcher faced communication problem and therefore she avoided to teach that part of the content.
8. I think school teachers also face this problem. Specially, in Co-educational schools. This problem could be solved when parents interact with their teenage children directly. Report of the local newspapers also supported the above view.

   Dainik Navjoyti – 12.05.2006
   Rajasthan Patrika – 13.05.2006

9. Now-a-days generation eat ignorance, drink fear, covered by injustice and wear dissatisfaction. For effective life we all should avoid above situations. In the cup of truth, put the logic and stir it with faith and beliefs.

Delimitations

1. Research studies have also shown that sex education based on life skills was more effective in bringing about changes in adolescent contraceptive use, delay in sexual debut, delay in the onset of alcohol and marijuana use and in developing attitudes and behaviour necessary for preventing the spread of HIV/AID. But in our Indian culture it is very difficult to parents and teachers discuss above issues in front of children/pupils.
2. From a practical standpoint this project suffered from a lack of resources like time and labour. Only few practical exercises were done.
3. Present study is conducted only on the 39 Pre-service teachers of the H.B.U.C.T.E. Hatundi, Ajmer (Rajasthan).

Precaution

On the cautionary side, power imbalances, confidentiality and intrusion were issues took on added significance in this type of setting. In this study, the researcher was especially vigilant to any potential for personal harm to any participant or any perception of pressure or coercion. Aside from the life skills philosophy of mutual respect, researcher observed the participants, safety and regards.

Suggestions

1. Life Skills Education should start from class VI up to the class XII continuously.
2. It should be self-evaluated education programme. Parents, teachers, and pupils should participate willingly.

Conclusion

'Learning by doing', 'Learning by living', 'Learning without Tears' are the main characteristics of the modern concept of education.

Education accordingly is seen in terms of 7Rs, i.e., Reading, Writing, Arithmetics, Rights, Responsibilities, Recreation, and Relationship.

The remarks of the Secondary Education Commission: "The school is not merely a place of formal learning whose aim concern is to communicate a certain prescribed quantum of knowledge but rather as a living and organic community which is primarily interested in training its pupils in what we have called the 'gracious art of living'. Knowledge and learning are undoubtedly of value but they must be acquired as a by-product of activity because it is only then that they can become a vital part of the student's mind and personality and influence his behaviour. But the 'Art of living' is much more comprehensive concept than the acquisition of knowledge, however, intelligently planned. It includes training in the habit and graces of social life and the capacity for co-operative group work. It calls for patience, good temper, sincerity, fellow feeling and discipline."

1. Life skills course helps in the development of—
   - Excellence
   - Empowerment
   - Emotional Intelligence in our young teachers.
2. Life skills course helps in the 'Adjustment' towards their environment. Adjustment needs patience which is a qualitative noun.

   It is affected again by 3E
   - Environment (Home + School)
   - Education
   - Experience

3. Life skills course helps to provide TQP—Total quality people to the nation having a pleasing personality.
4. Preparation of young teachers needs = Purpose + Principal + Planning + Practice + Perseverance + Patience + Pride
5. Like birds jet's leave behind what we don't need to carry...................Grudges, Sadness, Pain, Fear and Regrets.

   Life skills help human beings in flying light, because life is beautiful.
6. Life skills course helps in the development of right attitude in students. They start their assigned work with full / complete aptitude. It helps them to fulfil their right ambition and aspiration according to their competencies and in this way they accomplish the work.
7. Life skill is not only a subject-oriented programme but it includes 'whole life experiences' of a person. It is total Art of living.
8. Whatever you do in your life, you should make it clear to others.
9. Life skills are the balanced vital force. It is essential for mental and emotional development.
10. Life skills help in the establishment of biological balance. The personality traits depend upon the biological factors. These traits develop in pupil teachers to provide them effective environment. A human is affected by the family, school and society environment.
11. One should have faith in one's own competencies. From the viewpoint of psychology infinite knowledge, power and joy are inherent in man. Modern science reinforces the same truth. Creating faith is a great achievement.
12. The great historian Toyenbee says that we face two questions concerning faith and breed. Faith without breed and breed without faith prove dangerous. We need both breed and faith.

13. Skill of living is refinement, which has three forms—refinement of outlook, refinement of behaviour and refinement of feeling.
14. The secretions of hormone from our endocrine glands are responsible for our mental attitudes and behaviour. The curriculum of life skills is a stepping-stone in this direction.
15. Effective life skills help us to promote 'Art of living'. Art of living is a technique. Those who know this art in real life are gifted artists. One should identify their potentialities and plan them properly. We should nurture our sensitivity through which we can feel pleasure, which only is the art of living. In the art of living emotions and intellect should not overlap.

    The first step of Art of living is to try to make a complete personality, which is required to survive in this behavioural world and then dissolve this personality into spiritual world. First creation and then sublimation are the stages of development. Art of living should enable us to unfold innumerable mysteries of human life.
16. Life Skill Education is nothing but 'Re-engineering of the human capital'.
17. Pre-test mean score shows that the pupil teachers have life skills and they use it effectively whenever required in their day-to-day life. But after conducting post-test the mean score shows considerable increase, which obviously reveals the utility of the Life skill course.
18. Negative correlation is found in academic achievements and life skill scores. It shows that only bookish knowledge is not enough for the successful living. Successful living needs wisdom.

Index

Absenteeism, 211-12
Adult and Continuing Education, 74
Adult and Non-Formal Education, 96-8, 102-3
Adult Education
  aims and objectives of, 199
  definition of, 185
  failure of, 203-4, 208, 212
  importance of, 186
  scope of, 202
Adult Education Programme (AEP), 69, 72, 74-6, 105, 188-9, 191-3, 198, 203, 206, 208-9, 211-12, 214-15
  guideline for success of, 212
Adult illiteracy, 13
Adult instructors, 209
Adult learning, 184, 215
Adult literacy, 59-60, 66, 69, 82, 87, 196, 214-15
Adult neoliterates, 47
Adult women learners, 292
Adulthood, 5, 181-2
African Model of lifelong learning, 55
Agencies of Lifelong Learning, 9
Ailments, 207-8
Anaemia, 130, 132-3, 257
Anchored instruction, 34, 36, 43
Anganwadi workers, 66
Animal husbandry, 87, 155, 158, 163, 280
Anthropometric measurements, 125, 128
Art of living, 303, 305
Aryan Society, 223
Assistant Project Officers (APOs), 71
Audio and visual aids, 106-7
Awareness programme, 230, 234, 292

B-complex vitamin deficiencies, 131-3
Baroda city, 115, 258-9
Basic literacy, 14, 16, 70
Batter System, 135
Blended learning, 31
Board of Secondary Education, 294, 299
Body mass index, 125-6
Brain drain, 100
Broadband connectivity, 35
Broadcasting, 61-2
Brundtland Commission, 168-9, 177
Business education, 145-6

Capacity Building of Extension Personnel, 267
Capacity development, 105-6
Central Advisory Board of Education (CABE), 66
Charcha Mandals, 18, 25, 61, 165, 191
Child welfare, 93, 95
Citizenship education, 183
Civil society, 55
Classroom learning, 11
Clinical symptoms, 129, 131
Co-educational schools, 301
Communication, 49, 55, 77, 87, 104, 111-18, 120-1, 227, 244, 294-5
  extent of, 115
  gap, 115, 118
  skills, 81, 114, 294-5
  suitable mode of, 118-19
Community development programmes, 203, 221

Community development workers, 268
Community Learning Centre, 30-1
Competitive market, 138
Complex society, 13
Compromising, 118, 168, 176-7, 239
Compulsory education, 28, 198
Conference of State Education Ministers, 60
Conscientization, 68-9
Constitution of India, 28, 177
Consumer Education, 139, 143-50, 152
benefits of, 148
gaining, 149, 151
objectives of, 143, 145, 148
Consumer Protection Act, 136, 139
Consumer rights, 143, 147-8, 151
Consumers exploitation, 139-41, 147
Consumers rights, 137, 147
Continuing Education (CE), 13-18, 20, 22, 26, 53, 58, 74, 77, 81, 163, 182, 202, 214
Continuing Education Centres (CECs), 15, 17, 20-2, 24-6, 81-2
Continuing Education Programme (CEP), 13-17, 19-20, 22-4, 26, 77
Continuing education scheme, 18, 81
Correspondence education, 67
Counselling sessions, 116, 120
Cultivation, 7, 56, 89, 99, 166

Daily intake, 127-8
Data Analysis, 39-40, 299
Dehydrated drumstick leaves (DDL), 108-9
Dental caries, 130-1
Department of Education and Social Welfare, 66
Departments of Adult and Continuing Education, 74
Dev Research Institute, 39-40
Developmental programmes, 67, 90
Dietary inadequacies, 129, 133
Dietary Pattern and Nutritional Deficiencies in Rural Areas, 125
Directorate of Adult Education, 63-4, 66-7
Disadvantaged groups, 146, 149
Distance education, 101
Distance learning, 31
District Adult Education Officer, 71
District literacy committees, 18
Dominated society, male, 235
Drop-out, 29-30, 77, 204-6, 208

Economic accounting, 175
Economic development, 58, 87, 170, 173, 179
Economic growth, 51, 68, 138, 169-70, 176
Economic Sustainability, 172
Education Commission, 60
Education for Sustainable Livelihoods, 162
Education programmes, 82, 193
Educational agenda, 69
Educational leader, 214
Educational leadership, 271
Educational process, 185, 187, 270, 281
Educational system, 30-1, 33, 154, 158, 219, 294
Effective Extension Teaching, 268-9, 271
Effective extension worker, 267, 269
Egalitarian society, 96
Elderly citizens, 258, 260-1
Electronic media, 54, 78, 101-3, 146, 165, 251
Elementary education, 28, 30
Emotional problems, 293
Employment Guarantee Scheme, 161
Employment opportunities, 157
Enrichment learning, 11
Environmental accounting, 176
Environmental capital, 176-7
Environmental goods, 174-5
Environmental laws, 177-8
Environmental pressure, 174
Environmental problems, 177
Environmental Sustainability, 172
Equal Rights to Women, 230
Equivalency Programmes (EPs), 25, 82
Experimental learning, 47

Extension education, 68, 265, 267-8, 271, 276
Extension methods, 274, 277
Extension teaching, 267-9, 271-2, 274-6
Extension workers, 275
External educational agents, 185

Family planning, 91, 93
Farm broadcasting, 61-2
Farmers Training Centres, 164
Farmwomen, 164
Female learners, 211
Feminization, 255-6
First-generation learners, 107
Fiscal backwardness, 232-3
Five Year Plan, 60, 67-8, 74-5
Food consumption, 126-7
Food security, 161
Formal credit, 161
Formal education, 5, 31, 101, 103, 135, 145-6, 210-11, 213
Formal educational centres, 31
Formal learning, 303
Formal mode of education, 46
Functional literacy, 16, 58-62, 64-5, 68, 75, 77, 80-2
Functional perspectives, 59-60
Fundamental Education, 183

Gain skills, 143
General education curriculum, 152
Generation gap, 121
Global society, 29
Globalization, 47, 51, 55, 136

Health centres, 159
Health Education, 230
Health problems, 207, 258, 294
Health promotion, 104, 296-7
Higher education, 10, 29-30, 74, 93, 100, 187, 220, 228, 251
Human capital, 97, 109, 160-2, 172, 176, 293, 305
Human personality, 97, 99
Human Resource Development (HRD), 15, 74-5, 77, 202

Illiteracy eradication, 18
Improved Pace and Content of Learning (IPCL), 78
In-service education, 54
Income Generating Programmes (IGPs), 82
Independent learning, 11
Indian Air Force (IAF), 238
Indian National Congress, 237
Indian Police Service, 237
Individual Interest Promotion Programmes (IIPPs), 82
Industrialisation, 227
Information Centre, 18
Information technology, 29, 36
Informative programmes, 90
Institutional training, 280
Instructional programmes, 279-81
Integrated Child Development Scheme (ICDS), 66, 74, 108
Interaction programmes, 165
International Women's Year, 74
Interpersonal communication, 107, 115-16, 119, 121
Interpersonal relations, 294, 296
Interpersonal skills, 295-6
Intrinsic motivation, 51, 54
Irregular learners, 31

Jan Shikshana Sansthans (JSS), 164
Journalism, 101-2
investigative, 101
yellow, 101

Kisan Melas, 165-6
Kisan Saksharta Yojana, 73
Knowledge acquisition, 46, 49, 53, 303
Knowledge understanding, 186, 197
Knowledgeable personnel, 63
Kothari Education Commission, 228
Krishi Vigyan Kendra's (KVKs), 164-5

Learning Centre, 18, 30
Learning resources, 40-1, 54
Lengrand, Paul, 5
Life expectancy, 255-6

Life Skill Education, 293, 300-1, 305
Lifelong education, 5, 14, 47-51, 182, 196
Lifelong learning, 3-10, 14-15, 17, 46-56, 182
Literacy
  campaigns, 14, 58, 80-1, 188
  centres, 191
  component, 61
  programme, 13, 66, 82
  skills, 14, 18, 61, 73, 81
Literate society, 53
Livelihood problems, 161, 166
Living conditions, 14, 16

Mahatma Phule Education Guaranty Schemes, 31
Malnutrition, 97, 129, 133, 257
Malviya, Pandit Madan Mohan, 98-9
Mass communication, 101, 103, 182
Mass Programme of Functional Literacy (MPFL), 75
Maximum learning, 279
McGill Institute for Learning in Retirement, 6
Mean corpuscular haemoglobin concentration (MCHC), 132
Mid Day Meal Scheme (MDMS), 105-6

Naidu, Sarojini, 237
National Adult Education Programme (NAEP), 69-72, 78, 184, 189, 203
National Board of Adult Education, 66
National Commission for Women, 236
National Literacy Mission (NLM), 9, 13-14, 17-18, 75-8, 80-2
National Policy on Education (NPE), 75-6, 228, 293
National Service Scheme (NSS), 68
National Service Volunteers (NSVs), 74
Need-based education, 202
Nehru Yuvak Kendras (NYK), 74
Neo-learners, 50, 52
New Education Policy, 100
Nodal Centres (NCs), 20
Non-formal education centres, 164
Non-government Organizations (NGOs), 50, 54, 78, 95, 108, 121, 165, 245, 261, 292
Non-permissive society, 49
Nutrition Communication Programme, 107
Nutrition heath education, 105, 108
Nutrition security, 104
Nutritional deficiencies, 104, 125, 131, 257-8

Oliver, Ron, 41
Open universities, 9, 31
Oppression, 76, 96
Osteoarthritis, 257
Osteoporosis, 257
Outsourcing, 39

Packed Cell Volume (PCV), 126, 132
Part-time supervisors, 62-3
Patriarchal society, 220
People careers, 10
People participation, 172
20-point programmes, 72, 74
Population Education, 230
Post Literacy Campaign (PLC), 13-14
Post-Literacy Programme (PLP), 15, 19, 80-1
Poverty alleviation, 56, 58
Pre-Aryan Period, 223
Pre-service teachers, 302
Problem-based learning approaches, 42
Problem solving, 18, 145, 294-5
Programme of Action (PoA), 75-6
Public Distribution System (PDS), 161

Quality of Life Improvement Programmes (QLIPs), 82
Quality of products, 147
Quaternary education, 188

Radio, 9, 35, 42, 87, 89-90, 92-3, 148, 251

Random sampling method, 20-1, 245
RDA, 127-8, 133
Reservation policy, 50
Rig Veda, 219, 223-4
Rousseau, 231
Rural Functional Literacy Project (RFLP), 73

Sanitary conditions, 178-9
Scarlet raw tongue, 130-1
Scheduled Castes, 69, 88-91
School health education, 107
Secondary Board of Education, 297
Secondary Education Commission, 303
Self-governing society, 227
Self-learning, 11, 98, 184
Self-management skills, 295-6
Self-reliant learning, 184
Sex education, 302
Shramik Vidyapeeths, 67
Skill Development (SD), 14, 73, 76, 82, 192
Skill upgradation, 16, 164
Skilled personnel, 53, 55
SNDT Women University in Mumbai, 228
Social awareness, 71, 233-4
Social education programme, 183
Social equality, 48
Social groups, 51-3
Social information, 244-5, 248-9
Social problems, 293-4, 298-9
Socio-economic background, 23, 88, 244
Socio-educational status, 51
SPSS SOFTWARE, 38-9
State Literacy Mission Authority (SLMA), 18
State Resource Centres (SRCs), 70, 76, 78
Stress coping skills, 294-5
Supplementary food (SF), 108
Sustainable livelihoods, 6, 154, 156, 159-62, 164, 166

T-test, 246
Teaching-learning materials, 63
Teaching-learning session, 271
Technical education, 47, 101, 200
Telecommunication tools, 36
Total Literacy Campaign (TLC), 13-15, 18-19, 28, 78-80
Total Literacy Programme (TLP), 15-16
Trade union education, 182

UNESCO, 5, 15, 47, 58, 60, 62, 76, 186, 197, 199
Universalization of primary education, 196
University Grants Commission (UGC), 74, 188-9, 228
Urbanisation, 227

Value-based education, 98
Value education, 98
Vedas, 46, 224-5
Visual aids, 106-7
Vivekananda, 231-2
Vocational education, 66, 82, 280
Vocational skills, 17, 70, 73, 81-2
Voluntary learners, 211
Volunteer Teachers (VTs), 79

Widow remarriage, 225-7
Women Development, 237
Women education, 208, 219-23, 226-34, 241
Workers Education Programme, 67
World Bank, 29-30, 75, 162, 177
World Conference of Ministers of Education, 59
World Conference on Adult Education, 58
World Literacy Programme, 60
Writing skills, 61-2

Youth development education, 277

Zilla Saksharta Samiti (ZSS), 78, 82
Zone of Proximal Development, 32